Harry Potter and the Myth of Millennials

Harry Potter and the Myth of Millennials

Identity, Reception, and Politics

Priscilla Hobbs

LEXINGTON BOOKS
Lanham • Boulder • New York • London

Published by Lexington Books
An imprint of The Rowman & Littlefield Publishing Group, Inc.
4501 Forbes Boulevard, Suite 200, Lanham, Maryland 20706
www.rowman.com

86-90 Paul Street, London EC2A 4NE

British Library Cataloguing in Publication Information Available

Library of Congress Cataloging-in-Publication Data

Names: Hobbs, Priscilla, 1980- author.
Title: Harry Potter and the myth of millennials : identity, reception, and politics /
    Priscilla Hobbs.
Description: Lanham : Lexington Books, [2022] | Includes bibliographical references
    and index.
Identifiers: LCCN 2022011946 (print) | LCCN 2022011947 (ebook) |
    ISBN 9781793620279 (cloth) | ISBN 9781793620293 (paper) | ISBN
    9781793620286 (ebook)
Subjects: LCSH: Rowling, J. K. Harry Potter series. | Rowling, J. K.--Appreciation--
    United States. | Generation Y--United States. | Popular culture and literature--United
    States. | LCGFT: Literary criticism.
Classification: LCC PR6068.O93 Z7327 2022 (print) | LCC PR6068.O93 (ebook) |
    DDC 823/.914--dc23/eng/20220420
LC record available at https://lccn.loc.gov/2022011946
LC ebook record available at https://lccn.loc.gov/2022011947

For Kaitlin,
the Gryffindor who started it all

Contents

Preface

How It Began

This project was a long time coming. I began working on Harry Potter scholarship in 2004. Rather than dwell on what took so long to get here, it is better to instead reflect on what has changed since then. When I first dabbled in the research, *Half-Blood Prince* had not yet been released, so it was challenging to analyze the epic when we did not know if Harry would live or die. We had no idea what a horcrux was, and we were still mourning the death of Cedric Diggory. Also, 2004 seemed like nothing compared to 2016. We were naïve to think that nothing could be worse than the 9/11 attacks that started the 21st century. We were not yet jaded and beaten down by recession, though something about Harry Potter resonated with deep feelings of distrust in the government and cultural leaders, which we pondered while dipping our "freedom fries" in ketchup.

Let's step back a little: I remember the first time I held a *Harry Potter* book in my hands. It was Christmas 1999, and I was helping my sister with gifts for her oldest daughter by wrapping (still one of my favorite holiday pastimes) and hiding them from my niece. One of these gifts was a boxed set of the first three *Harry Potter* books. I called my sister at work to ask about them. My niece, in fourth grade, struggled with dyslexia and reading. I was surprised to see such a heavy (literally) gift in the stack. My sister told me how those books inspired my niece to read. To this day, we credit the series with teaching her how to read.

Inspired by this love of Harry, I preordered *The Goblet of Fire* for her birthday and took her to the book release party at a local bookstore. Kids were running around in black robes, plastic glasses, and lightning bolt tattoos on their foreheads. I decided it was time to give the series a try and later bought myself a copy of the first book.

I would spend a few evenings here and there, reading a chapter of *The Goblet of Fire* to my niece. The writing drew me in, even though I could never settle on a pronunciation of Hermione, later learning that it is pronounced her-MY-oh-nee, not her-MEE-own. By the time the first movie was released, I had read all the books published to that point, sorted myself into Gryffindor (now, I'm a proud Ravenclaw), made t-shirts with a friend, and hosted a Potter-themed party. This was the first real event in what became my fevered fandom that included listening to podcasts and audiobooks, attending fan cons/academic conferences, merchandise consumption, and a master's thesis. My niece joined me at the final book release party at Book People in Austin, Texas, and we stayed up all night reading our copies to avoid the inevitable spoilers that would hit our circles in the coming days.

When the fever of the fandom began to die down, I focused my dissertation research on Disney and took a break on a decade of Potter-induced fever pitch. But then came the 2016 election. How everything unfolded did not sit well with me. It was somehow familiar. I felt compelled to do another, overdue, read-through of the series, and it seemed as though Rowling predicted the questionable politics that have defined the post–Potter United States. The parallels were shocking, especially in the latter half of the series when Harry and his peers grow to distrust political authority and how the Ministry of Magic retaliates. It was equally shocking to watch *Fantastic Beasts: The Crimes of Grindelwald* after the inauguration as well. The compelling charisma of Grindelwald resonates with that of Donald Trump, serving as a kind of cinematic warning. Living through the vitriol and propaganda of the Trump Administration and the divisiveness surrounding it makes *Harry Potter* seem more important now than ever. The lessons the magical children learn in their time at Hogwarts School of Witchcraft and Wizardry are needed as the American zeitgeist becomes more and more fractured.

As someone who entered identity consciousness during the late-1990s/early-2000s, the Bush Administration and *Harry Potter* are symbolically linked in my mind. This project began as a response to contemporary political events that were difficult to process. In fact, the only thing that made sense for the first few years of the 21st century was the slogan, "Republicans for Voldemort," and why it was very important that Harry would question the Ministry. During the Bush years, speaking out about the administration prompted cancellations before "cancel culture" had a name. The country trio The Dixie Chicks (now just The Chicks) criticized Bush at a concert—cancelled. The French criticized Bush—cancelled (hence "freedom fries"). The seemingly logical question was what was the Bush Administration doing that it would prompt such a reaction? And, really, was it the Administration or its constituents? In many ways, these questions were echoed within the Potter fandom—we came together to make sense of our worlds under the shared wisdom of a young adult series.

Cornelius Fudge is a political boob reminiscent, at the time at least, of George W. Bush in a lime green bowler hat. He is corrupt in his own way, but after tasting power, does not want to let it go easily. When we first meet him in the *Sorcerer's Stone*, Hagrid implies that Fudge relies on Dumbledore's advice to know how to lead the government. When Dumbledore begins to caution about the return of Voldemort, Fudge chooses to ignore him, believing that Dumbledore is spinning lies to try to take his place. His response, as with the response to 9/11 by the Bush Administration, is to enact restrictions to keep everyone—hopefully—at bay and prevent any further attacks. The problem, though, with this kind of politics is that the more rights that get taken away, the more the people counterreact. It is one thing to restrict the people who are in the airport at any given time and to increase security measures to prevent more hijackings, but do we really need to take off our shoes?

Fudge's restrictions are most obvious at Hogwarts with the appointment of Dolores Umbridge as a ministry liaison at the school. Her "educational decrees" represent government-sanctioned dictations of the education experience from curriculum to conduct, such as the removal of practical lessons in Defense Against the Dark Arts. The rationale is that children do not need to know about the Dark Arts, which has the potential effect of leaving an entire generation unable to defend itself against the Dark Arts. This has played out in American culture as the sanitized curriculum of the Bush-era No Child Left Behind initiative that increased the emphasis on state aptitude testing for funding while squashing the ability of teachers to teach valuable critical thinking skills, the same skills that influenced the younger votes in the 2016 election. Younger voters have become jaded by the vitriol of the media but lack the skills to see through the propaganda and make informed choices and decisions. However, they do have access to video games that allow the player become a vigilante or militia fighter to battle any threat to society. Without the lessons of love from Potter, this mentality can jump from fantasy to reality. The influence of the media, no matter how conscious or unconscious, can be seen in protests that turn into riots and in the coup attempt of January 6, 2021.

In my opinion, the four years of the Trump Administration were awful. Many of the characteristics of Voldemort's time in power echo events in American culture during this time. The fear of speaking out against Voldemort in the event that one would find themselves a target of the Death Eaters. The slow overtaking of the Ministry by the Death Eaters, ultimately leading to the expulsion of Fudge as the Minister of Magic. And, importantly, the loss of rights for witches and wizards who come from Muggle families. They could not go back to the Muggle world for fear of bringing the conflict to their families, but they were unable to stay either—the ultimate flaw in the ever-popular "If you don't like it, just leave" argument. While prejudice and racially motivated attacks are not unique to Trump's presidency, they did hit a new level at the same time when people were also seeing their access to medical support and social supports slowly eroded. Then the 2020 COVID-19 pandemic escalated frustrations as unemployment surged and death rates climbed exponentially. Those frustrations manifested in protests against BIPOC (Black and Indigenous people of color) deaths and the lack of conviction of the police who murdered them. Right-wingers claimed they had a right to do what they wanted, becoming a viral caricature on social media. It began to seem like the Death Eaters had gained control of the government and were fighting tooth and nail to keep the power in their favor, at the expense of the people. It still seems this way.

I am not suggesting that Voldemort and Trump belong in the same category. It would be too easy to default to that kind of comparison and would not do either character any favors, nor would it solve the problem of a divided country that lies ahead. But the lessons learned from watching Harry battle Voldemort come in handy for figuring out how to battle the Trump machine. Being a "Muggle supporter" becomes a metaphor for supporting the fundamental human rights of any Other, from Black Lives Matter to LGBTQ+ rights to the needs of those who struggle for basic needs in the current economy. COVID-19 could become the metaphor for Voldemort, and the rest of the players are the Death Eaters supporting his mission of annihilation. However, in this metaphor, no one is safe. Even Trump and his family were diagnosed with COVID, in large part due to their blatant ignoring of CDC guidelines for social distancing and mask wearing. Trump would host/stage large rallies of people crowded together and not wearing masks, earning the nickname "anti-maskers," punning off the phrase "anti-vaxxers" (people who are opposed to vaccines).

The lack of critical thinking and information literacy reveals a population for whom the education system has failed: they believe anything they hear on the news and from the president, even if it is counterintuitive to their own health and safety, something even the Slytherins are taught to recognize. This is a perfect reflection of privilege: while other witches and wizards, especially Muggle-borns, are faced with oppression long before these students had to even think about it, the Slytherins only have to confront realities when the battle came into the school and they themselves are under threat. On one hand, for some Americans, that is precisely what COVID awakened for them as they were on the front lines of those who lost their jobs or found their hours cut when it was not safe for a place to be fully staffed. On the other hand, some media claimed that the masking was anti-American and part of a fascist plan to restrict freedoms. Ignorance is born out of lack of critical thinking and empathy for the Other, which is why lack of education and lack of tolerance is a great threat to democracy. Trump was able to get as far as he did politically, because he was speaking the right rhetoric to that audience who felt they had been ignored and Othered. As one meme that made the rounds in the month before the 2020 election notes, "If you've never had your rights challenged in an election, then you have privilege."

The idea of white privilege became a point of narrative during the Obama years, when racist America felt threatened by the election of a black president (twice!). With the death of Trayvon Martin in 2013 and the launch of the Black Lives Matter hashtag, "white privilege" became a buzzphrase to describe the reality that white people are not killed for walking down the street. The media spins these kinds of stories such that both sides of a shooting are made into victims, and people choose to resonate with the part of the story that speaks most closely with their values. Thanks to the media coverage of this and similar stories, the struggles of BIPOC gained a new level of empathy from supporters. These kinds of things happen often and appear throughout American history and can be shared quickly on social media.

It is no accident that a post–Harry Potter 21st century became an era of awareness movements like Occupy and Arab Spring, #metoo, #BlackLivesMatter, cancel culture, and more, as millennials began their political activism. Nor should it be a surprise that post-Potter young adult fiction is epic in scope and dystopian in nature but built on messages of inclusion and diversity as themes worth fighting for. A post-Potter 21st century recognizes that being politically correct is not the same as love and acceptance; it is the by-product of ignored reality.

But *Harry Potter* is not a political text; it just happened to be the right text at the right time to play an influential role during a paradigm change of the sort that accompanies any new decade, century, or millennium (in this case, all three!). The story of The Boy Who Lived is essentially whatever we want it to be, and that is the heart of this book.

So, what you hold in your hands is the result of nearly twenty years of research and the lived experiences of a jaded millennial who happens to be an academic who specializes in American cultural narrative. Many people played a role in shaping my political persona and in influencing my love of Potter. I believe now is a good time to share my exegesis, because Potter and America are both transitioning as the first quarter of this century comes to a close.

Wands up, my friends, and constant vigilance! (And please wear a mask).

—Written September 2021

List of Abbreviations

The Potter books, films, experiences, and common terms are referenced using the following abbreviations:

BOOKS/FILMS:

SS	*Harry Potter and the Sorcerer's Stone*
CoS	*Harry Potter and the Chamber of Secrets*
PoA	*Harry Potter and the Prisoner of Azkaban*
GoF	*Harry Potter and the Goblet of Fire*
OotP	*Harry Potter and the Order of the Phoenix*
HBP	*Harry Potter and the Half-Blood Prince*
DH	*Harry Potter and the Deathly Hallows*
CC	*Harry Potter and the Cursed Child*
FB	*Fantastic Beasts and Where to Find Them*
FB:CoG	*Fantastic Beasts: The Crimes of Grindelwald*
ToBB	*The Tales of Beedle the Bard*

EXPERIENCES:

HP:NY	Harry Potter New York (store)
WWoHP	The Wizarding World of Harry Potter (theme park)

COMMON TERMS:

DA	Dumbledore's Army
DADA	Defense Against the Dark Arts
MoM	Minster of Magic

FOR EASE OF CLARITY

Wizarding World (capitalized) refers to the Harry Potter franchise and accompanying website; wizarding world (lower-case) refers to the magical community within the books.

The Sorcerer's Stone describes the Potter book; the Philosopher's Stone is the alchemical result.

Introduction

Why Harry?

J.K. Rowling's *Harry Potter* series has taken the world *en force*. The series of seven books have found fanatic popularity in all corners of the world driven by a rich story, archetypal symbolism, and a brilliant marketing department. The story is malleable enough to respond to everyone's projection. There are multiple interpretations of the meaning of the series, the meaning of specific symbols, speculation on how the series would end (prior to the release of *Deathly Hallows*); to analysis of the fandom that arose because of the books, including fan fiction, crafts, cosplay (costumed play), Quidditch teams, and more. Every reader, fan, and scholar projects something different into the series, and, therefore, finds a different meaning and significance within the text. For example, fan fiction writers write alternative versions of the events, sometimes imagining themselves as an already established character or creating an avatar in a new character. Wizard Wrock musicians don the guise of a character to write and perform music from that character's perspective, such as Harry and the Potters, Draco and the Malfoys, and the Remus Lupins, to name a few. The readers who interact in some fashion with the books reenact the myth, owning and internalizing the material to experience a figurative heroic transformation in a world that consistently fails to make sense. This fantastic world becomes more real, maybe even hyperreal. The Wizarding World invites us to dive deeply into a world that is accepting, fantastic, and constantly changing.

The hypothesis informing this project is that *Harry Potter*, as a conjoined franchise and fandom, is the foundational millennial mythology. In order to qualify as a mythology, the series has to resonate with the culture of readers in such a way that it becomes part of their social identity. Millennials, the generation born roughly between 1980ish to 1997ish, grew up immersed in popular culture and media, were among the first to have computers as a central part of their education, and were connected to the Internet. Millennials played video games on various consoles, watching the technology evolve from minimalist games like Atari's *Pong* to 8-bit action with Nintendo's *Super Mario Brothers* and *The Legend of Zelda* to enhanced 3D computer graphics creating more realistic worlds for fantasy adventure and first-person shooters. Despite the political climate, millennials were raised with a utopian optimism that made everything in the world seem possible, even while uncles, aunts, and parents were being sent to the Middle East in Operation Desert Storm, or O.J. Simpson was chased down the Los Angeles freeway, or President Bill Clinton was caught with Monica Lewinsky. Millennials watched the adults bicker and debate whether the CDs of their favorite performers needed explicit lyrics stickers or if the record companies should be held accountable for self-censoring lyrics. Meanwhile, reality television like *The Real World* and teen shows like *My So-Called Life* painted an image of America that resonated when shows like *Friends* did not. For millennials, listening to MP3 files and sharing them over Napster was completely normal, as was chatting with strangers all over the world through internet relay chat (IRC) or instant messaging.

The other thing defining the '80s was the surge in themed experiences.[1] Theming was not a new concept going into the '80s, but the decade allowed theming to kick into hyperdrive. With the success of experiences like the Disney theme parks, theming suggests that the *experience* is just as important as the consumption of it. Behind theming is the notion that the place or experience is itself the brand and that everything inside of it must support it.[2] A successfully themed location sets the bar for expectations of both similar-type places and the customer experience, so when those places expand nationally or globally, one expects to have the same basic experience at each location.[3] George Ritzer's case studies focus on McDonald's and attribute this predictable consistency to its global success, which has been further cemented by localization. For instance, in addition to key menu staples, franchises are given leeway for local and regional variation, so those audiences can experience familiarity and travelers can try new things. A win-win for Corporate.

The change-over to the millennium was both exciting and terrifying, experiencing the change of a decade, a century, and a millennium all at once. As the first millennials graduated high school, the millennium marked a life-transition from childhood into young adulthood. But the media shared fears of a Y2K meltdown, when all the computers around the world would stop working because they were not programmed to roll dates over from 19- to 20-. As the new year ticked over and everyone anxiously watched, nothing happened. The year 2000 came, just like any other year.

Millennials also were primed for franchises. Tie-ins to any show or film was normal, and the most popular franchises were entering their next wave.

Millennials already knew that *Star Trek* had a next generation and were meeting new characters on *Voyager* and *Deep Space Nine*. *Star Wars* rereleased the original trilogy and geared up to release the prequel trilogy. Meanwhile, shows like *The X-Files* and films like *The Matrix* offered new views of other realities. The link between the franchises and the tie-ins reinforced millennial consumption; however, the older millennials felt nostalgia for their childhood diet of '80s cartoons and sharing in the joyful experience of their little siblings.

It is in this small piece of a generation's personality that *Harry Potter* filled a niche. The experiences of Harry and his friends are easily recognized by millennials of all ages, who are drawn in by the familiarity of Harry's social and school experiences. All millennials know a Draco or a Hermione, and likely even a (less abusive) Snape. The brilliance of Rowling's world was that it seemed accessible, because it was positioned so close to the Muggle world. Quickly, the relationship between reader and *Harry Potter* transcended logic, and the culture that sprung up around the series justifies the claim that this is a myth for millennials.

CULTURAL CONNECTIONS

To the casual observer, it is apparent that popular culture increasingly serves as a vessel for cultural and social realities in today's fast-paced, disposable consumer society. By "popular culture," I am invoking beyond the delineation of "high culture" versus "popular" (i.e., that of the elite versus the populace).[4] That definition no longer holds merit when the products of "popular culture" situate alongside the Great Works canon. Instead, popular culture here refers to the transcendent elements of culture that connect all aspects of a broader society together, often through creative works. Recent popular culture research embraces an interdisciplinary perspective to look at all aspects of media, including film, television, and digital; the arts, including visual and performing arts, literature, and music; and leisure culture, including experiences, toys, and sports. The very nature of contemporary American culture is one that is closely defined by and identified with popular culture. Indeed, the simulacra of American popular culture eventually winds its way into the cultural reality such that America is essentially locked in a simulated construct, in essence—a hyperreality.[5]

Post–World War II America became increasingly disposable in the abundance of resources, economic and otherwise, that had been withheld during the Great Depression and war-time austerity measures. From TV dinners to plastics, consumptive behaviors freed an entire generation from the slog of responsibilities and fueled leisure culture and the development of the hyper-real experiences that constructed a utopian ideal rooted in the Imaginary.

When combined, leisure culture and simulacra blend together perfectly within popular culture, and it is here that American mythology, the undercurrent cultural narrative that adapts to and reforms the heart of the American psyche—where the logos becomes the mythos—takes center stage. It is in this realm of the imagination that forms the backbone of the American heroic: the image of a rags-to-riches savior who embodies the rugged individualistic cornerstone of the cultural self-concept (i.e., who we *want* to be). The backdrop of this hero is the perception of who America truly is: the lonesome wanderer seeking a community, a sense of belonging, and a purpose. Mid-century media broadly imagined this hero. From the lonely cowboy of Westerns to the superhero of comic books, America's hero myth focuses on the ways that a community could be rescued from a threat, possibly from outside the group but perhaps from within. A Cold War America did not know who to trust. The popularity of Westerns resonated with an American nationalism that needed to return to its roots for comfort. Westward expansion and Manifest Destiny are synonymous with those roots. Overcoming the harsh wilderness of the frontier, and any one they encounter there, give reassurance that Americans are capable of anything.

Reassurance is a central theme within Cold War popular culture. From the *Disneyland* television show to *Star Trek*, American utopianism imagined a country that was familiar and protected, but also curious and progressive. Disneyland became a model for hyperreal utopias demonstrating that it was possible to construct an idyllic place that is safe and essentially out of time. From here, a loose concept of progress continued experimenting with constructed spaces, from suburbs to downtown centers to tourist attractions. Before long, these spaces became normal, even expected, as utopias of consumption and comfort.

Events in popular culture occur because the infrastructure of a hyperreal culture lends itself to unique manifestations of the popular. Most recently, the Internet has proven the tool for creating this space, allowing for the possibility to live a completely second life through one's digital avatar. Sometimes, these manifestations are nothing more than fleeting blips on the imagination of the people, but sometimes they evolve into their own institution.

The secret to the success of any popular culture event is the degree it resonates with its audience and how they build a subculture around its worship and experience. When an artist gives to this hyperreal world, their creativity is in competition with volumes of cultural noise. It seems like effortless luck when something takes off and leaves its mark on the imaginations of fans, especially when critics and academics take note and analyze the popularity and response an event has garnered. This is when words like "phenomenon" get attached to the franchise, for example, "the Harry Potter phenomenon."

Since its publication in 1997, the *Harry Potter* series has earned laurels within the various categories of success: Over "*half a billion* Harry Potter books have now been sold. On average, this means one in fifteen people in the world owns a Harry Potter book."[6] This also includes translation into over eighty languages. The eight films have "earned a total of $7.73 billion global on a combined budget of $1.155 billion," and they occupy spots in the top forty biggest global grossers to date.[7]

The success of the adventures of the Boy Who Lived indicates that these characters and the world Rowling created have tapped into a need within the world's collective psyche, using potent archetypal images that people from many cultures can relate to. This archetypal need, especially among American readers, served as a compass for fan communities, bringing readers who discovered in Potter a mirror of their own desires and experiences into *communitas* with others needing the same connection. It was perhaps serendipity that *Harry Potter* landed at the same time that the Internet entered homes and schools, becoming a central tool for community building, a victory for globalization, and a key component in the development of the millennial identity.

ABOUT THIS BOOK

This book's focus is on the American intersection between *Harry Potter* and society. One might call out American appropriation of a British story, and that would be a fair assessment if this book were merely a cultural literary analysis of the impact of *Harry Potter*. Such a perception also assumes that the magic of the Wizarding World is unable to transcend culture, which is blatantly untrue given the global popularity of the series. Of particular interest is the role *Harry Potter* has played in the awakening of social consciousness for its readers, and the timing of this series could not be more perfect. The primary assumption of this analysis is that *Harry Potter* is a central mythology for millennials. Harry grew up alongside that generation, and his struggles became those of millenials growing up in a post-9/11 America. Through Harry, millennial readers found courage to advocate for the essential infrastructure for a society of equity and inclusion. To love Harry is to love and to spread love across a world marred in hate and death, an ever-growing shadow underneath the cultural psyche twisting and turning the American narrative against itself.

To be sure, America has a deeply rooted shadow that governs treatment and acceptance of the Other, most often characterized by any person who does not align with the white male-dominated self-perception of those in power. The players on the political stage tend to carry the narrative of the American people, and the dual-party system, in particular, concretizes a black-and-white us-versus-them ethos that has justified the Othering of entire swaths of Americans since colonials first landed on the East Coast. America, according to its founding mythos, is a utopia like no other in the world. Any Others in that landscape need to either be subsumed into society as a lower class and/or fully assimilated to eliminate any previous ideologies to guarantee loyalty to the concept of the nation. Or, they need to be removed from consciousness, especially if they resisted the godly efforts of the missionaries sent to "clean up" the frontier and tame its "savage" wild.

Rolling into the new millennium, Harry Potter gave new language that challenges this single-minded hierarchy, and even the very concept of the heroic. While Harry is most often analyzed as the hero, the truth is that the idea of Harry the Hero also carries his friends, Ron and Hermione—a collective hero—a team working in synch with each other to accomplish the journey. This teamwork makes intuitive sense to a generation raised on principles of friendship and inclusion. The media of this era taught children and young adults the moral values surrounding good versus evil as a spectrum rather than a binary, seeing much of their experiences with spectra reflected in narratives: the Autism spectrum, the gender spectrum, the rainbow of skin color. They were taught to see prismatically and to love and respect all people, but they also saw the cracks in the illusion after 9/11. These cracks grew into fissures throughout the first decades of the 21st century. Those readers who absorbed Harry's latent civic engagement recognized a need to rise against the divisive rhetoric that plagues social media, news commentary, and the very seat of American politics undermining any remaining utopian optimism they inherited from the previous generations—even having the courage to speak against their founding hero, Rowling herself.

One key assumption this book is making is that the reader is already familiar with the Potter books, films, fandom, and extended works. As such, spoilers, when someone reveals a key plot point to someone who has yet to reach that point in the story, will abound. Summaries will be used only as essential elements to the analysis rather than provided for context. Additionally, this book is written from an interdisciplinary perspective. The goal is not to contribute to a single field, such as education or literary studies, but to unify various theoretical lenses to explore Potter as an early-century phenomenon with a potency to help form the cultural narrative inherited by future generations.

The chapters in part 1 of this book delve into a literary analysis of the mythic symbolism of the series to establish a baseline for the attractiveness of Harry's adventure. Readers become fans because of the archetypal connections they feel to the series; Harry Potter becomes a part of their narrative, their identity, and their worldview. This first part approaches the *why* behind that love. The three chapters in this section deconstruct the mythological frameworks of *Harry Potter* (chapter 1), the characters and their archetypal significance (chapter 2), and the role of the media in the Potter mythos (chapter 3). These three perspectives are themselves collective, working together to create a three-dimensional understanding of the Potter experience.

The remaining chapters explore the social lessons readers learned from the books and how they are applied to foster change in American culture. Woven throughout these analyses are the events that significantly shaped millennial discourse, with a particular focus on the four years of the Trump Administration, 2016–2020, because this window was the first real opportunity to apply learned Potter skills following the release of the final book and film adaptations. There is unashamedly a liberal bias informing the criticism, because within contemporary American politics, themes of diversity, equity, and inclusion are seen as fundamentally liberal (Democrat), such that the conservative (Republican) media hyperbolically cite these efforts as the reason the country is so divided.

Millennials recognize the social disconnect and discord, because they read it in the pages of *Harry Potter*. They watched Harry and his friends attempt to speak out against governmental repression. The challenge ahead is deconstructing decades of misinformation and ignorance. This is not as easy as changing the language around certain concepts or trying to strip them from curricula. The very core of America's mythology needs to be reconceptualized. Harry and Dumbledore's Army show that it is possible to tackle Big Change and survive.

NOTES

1. c.f. George Ritzer, *Enchanting a Disenchanted World: Revolutionizing the Means of Consumption*, 2nd ed. (Thousand Oaks, CA: Pine Forge Press, 2005).

2. Alan Bryman, in his analysis of Disneyization and its impact on society, outlines five behaviors for successful theming: theming, hybrid consumption, merchandising, performative labor, and control and surveillance. When combined, these behaviors successfully create a homogenous, globalized experience that is predictable and entertaining. Alan Bryman, *The Disneyization of Society* (Los Angeles: Sage Publications, 2004).

3. George Ritzer, *The McDonaldization of Society: Into the Digital Age*, 9th ed. (Los Angeles: Sage Publications, 2019), 4–6.

4. c.f. Herbert J. Gans, *Popular Culture and High Culture: An Analysis and Evaluation of Taste*, rev. ed. (New York: Basic Books, 1999).

5. c.f. Jean Baudrillard, *Simulacra and Simulation*, trans. Sheila Faria Glaser (Ann Arbor: University of Michigan Press, 1994).

6. Pottermore, "500 Million Harry Potter Books Have Now Been Sold Worldwide," February 1, 2018, https://www.wizardingworld.com/news/500-million-harry-potter-books-have-now-been-sold-worldwide. Emphasis original.

7. Scott Mendelson, "Harry Potter Movies Ranked by Worldwide Box Office," Forbes, August 13, 2020, www.forbes.com/sites/scottmendelson/2020/08/13/harry-potter-movies-ranked-box-office-jk-rowling-emma-watson-daniel-radcliffe/?5h=344a4e0952da.

PART I

From Book to Cultural Establishment1

Chapter 1

The Mythology of the Boy Wizard

THE AMERICAN DREAM

The collective utopianism underlying the American mythos is commonly known as the American Dream. Informed by the hopes of a new life in the New World, the Dream tells a story of prosperity that is achievable to everyone. In an early description of the American Dream, James Truslow Adams described the Dream as

> a vision of a better, deeper, richer life for every individual, regardless of the position in society which he or she may occupy by the accident of birth. It has been a dream of a chance to rise in the economic scale, but quite as much, or more than that, of a chance to develop our capacities to the full, unhampered by unjust restrictions of caste or custom. With this has gone the hope of bettering the physical conditions of living, of lessening the toil and anxieties of daily life.[1]

In postwar America, as returning veterans leveraged their G.I. Bill funds, this image included owning a house, being married with a family, having a job, and contributing to progress. Inherent in this perception is also the ability to have leisure: family vacations, lounging in the living room reading the paper, backyard barbecues, all familiar images of television sitcoms.

But there is inevitably a shadow under all dreams, the sort that can turn into nightmares if ignored. The American Dream is homogenous and exclusionary.[2] In the segregated South, black communities were locked in a liminal space that offered some prospects but barred them from the luxuries of the white communities. Motherhood became increasingly clinical, and the sisterhood of women that naturally forms to raise children and support each other was warped into gossip circles rather than communal support. Social stigmas quickly marked anyone who rolled past the status quo.

The children of this postwar America, the baby boomers, found new worlds in television. The ideals of America bounced off the screen, conveying utopian optimism through the captivating stories of a savior hero, there to protect the community and family from any outside threat, from "Redskins" to school bullies. Not shockingly, these kids were the teenagers who rebelled, seemingly, without a cause and celebrated a renewed sense of passionate love that released the tension from the uptight family life of trying to live up to unreasonable social expectations set by a wartime generation. In many ways, while awareness has morphed and awoken, the boomer experience parallels that of the millennials, with whom boomer parents wanted to share the love of their childhood.[3]

The aim of the first part of this book is to delve into a literary analysis of *Harry Potter*, reflective of the volumes of previous research conducted about the franchise. This approach to understanding the series helps to unlock the significance of it, dissecting the layers of symbolism and meaning to get to the core of what appeals to the readers and fans. Primary attention is given to frameworks that frequent Potter scholarship: the hero's journey and the alchemical process. Both of these frameworks are each one language of a larger structure of experience around the essential cores of how humanity forms culture. One of the challenges of these frameworks is that they are limiting, remaining firm within a Western lens. For instance, educators, in the earlier days of the Potter craze, hypothesized that the power of Potter was due to the educational experience as a universal connection. The flaw in this perspective is that it relies on assumptions about what constitutes an education around the world. Literary scholars compared Potter with other popular fantasies, notably those of J.R.R. Tolkien and Orson Scott Card. This, too, is flawed because it relies on applying a known system to what is seen as a new kind of literature. While it is possible to keep analysis of Potter wholly in the realm of established theorists and frameworks, the challenge with this approach is that the outlined structures are not fluid enough to address the changing nature of the myths that are coming out popular culture. Key to understanding Potter, especially within the American millennial experience, is the ability to weave in and out of different frameworks, while acknowledging that this methodology can help explain meaning but not the experience that built and sustains the fandom.

The attractive feature of the Potter experience is not just shared delight in the stories within the fan community, but the extent to which the fan community has built a ritual experience around that enjoyment. Fans in the feverish period when the books were still being released, especially between *GoF* in 2000 and *DH* in 2007, exploded onto the Internet looking for other people and for connection into this fantastic world.[4] Fans were hungry for an experience that went beyond common social experiences, a primeval instinctual need to ritualize the mythology. Maybe it was a Potter Party, or a website or blog, a Wizard Wrock group, Deviant Art™, fanfic, or knitted socks for Dobby or a Weasley sweater for their family. In creating their own experience, fans immersed themselves into a world they desperately wanted to be a part of, because it gave purpose and made more sense than the cultural chaos in the aftermath of 9/11. It seemed that Rowling had tapped into the collective unconscious and spoke directly to the millennial mindset through potent archetypes in a compelling mythos.

A Sense of Meaning

As a utopian construct, the American Dream is essentially an imaginary construct, an idyllic vision. If the American Dream is not attainable, then what is there to look forward to? What, then, is one's purpose? Joseph Campbell remarks the role of art is to give a "sense of existence" as opposed to "an assurance of meaning," such that

> those who require an assurance of meaning, or who feel unsure of themselves and unsettled when they learn that the system of meaning would support them in their living has been shattered, must surely be those who have not yet experienced profoundly, continuously, or convincingly enough, that sense of existence—of spontaneous and willing arising—which is the first and deepest characteristic of being, and which is the province of art to awaken.[5]

Campbell's definition is rooted in an archaic understanding of art and "high culture," but still applies when considering popular culture and media. When the "system of meaning" loses its meaning, people naturally gravitate to the creative realms to rekindle a meaning, and this is especially true for the younger groups. As Marshall McLuhan observed, "The young today live mythically and in depth. [. . .] Many of our institutions suppress all the natural direct experience of youth, who respond with untaught delight to the poetry and the beauty of the new technological environment, the environment of popular culture."[6]

Over time, the American Dream has woven in and out of the civic and community spheres. Samuel notes that as more focus was put on the self and personal matters, it knocked the American Dream out of synch.[7] In ritualizing Harry Potter, the fandom built a new system of meaning around their collective experience of the books. And while Samuel's observation remains true, the Harry Potter fandom shows a natural tendency toward the collective, of going on the journey together, much like Harry and his friends. The renewed sense of meaning is shaped by a collective hero, not a single hero, who works collaboratively and equally with others throughout the journey. This is intuitive for millennial fans.

Harry Potter has earned an established place in American popular culture. The books evolved into films and merchandise, then into theme park attractions, games, and other attempts at immersive experiences that bring the magic into the Muggle world. This trajectory is not unique to Potter but is also not something that is a common accomplishment for other franchises. Two other success stories, *Star Wars* and Marvel, helped pave the way for Potter. In turn, Potter inspired new directions for those franchises (especially under Disney ownership), but also for the construct of media series as a whole. Following *Potter*, serial epics became normal. Publishers increased publication of young adult series to try to find the next Potter. The Hollywood machine also saw an opportunity for serials, especially as new CGI technology made it more affordable to produce high-quality shows. Even films began to have more sequels. Series are risks, because there is no guarantee that it will take off, but they also feed the fans who consume as much of the franchise as possible.

The relationship between fan and franchise is symbiotic. The fan falls in love with a thing and connects to it through play and craft, bringing it out of the pages or off the screen into their physical world. This gets recognized at the corporate level who produces "licensed" play (toys, games) and other tangibles (clothes, home decor, breakfast cereal).[8] The fan buys the things, and eventually those homemade connections are forgotten or replaced with corporate kits for the curious crafter. Buying the products and consuming the brand becomes a part of the fan identity while also providing free marketing for corporate. Added to this is the very strategic marketing device of multi-tiered product schemes that make products accessible to all (most) economic demographics juxtaposed with "collectables." These collectables can be expensive rarities or, in a more recent phenomenon, can be a series of toys in their own right, such as the Funko Pop figurine collection. Funko Pops are cutified and cartoonised figurines of popular culture characters and public figures. They are packaged in boxes that can double as display cases or they can stand on their own. Funkos are not ideal to play with, distinguishing them from action figures or dolls. For widely successful franchises, such as Harry Potter, there are multiple versions of each character representing different costumes or scenes. As of September 2021, there are 147 distinct Harry Potter Funko Pops with an additional twenty-five sold in exclusive multipacks.[9]

This consumption of a franchise is the natural evolution of associating with American mythology in a capitalist, leisure-driven society. Associating with a mythology in the place where storytelling intersects with ritual brings the stories to life. Academic tomes are filled with descriptions of rituals and collections of myths that appear throughout the cultural record to be essential to the human experience. Cave paintings, painted pottery, temples, and statues litter the landscapes of the ancient and modern worlds recording cultures full of myth. Myth helps humanity contextualize the human condition within the natural world. Myths give people meaning and serve as cultural guideposts to keep society organized and structured.

J.K. Rowling wove a web of symbols throughout her narrative, many of which are lifted right out of myth and folklore. Harry encounters creatures like centaurs, mermaids, giants, and goblins, living in pockets around each other but not coexisting due to fears of the other groups, especially witches and wizards with their punitive laws restricting their freedom. Many character names are likewise mythological. Minerva McGonagall is named after the Roman goddess of wisdom (often equated with the Greeks' Athena). Sirius Black, an illegal animagus that can turn into a black dog, is named after Sirius, the dog star, the brightest in the *Canis Majoris* constellation. Hermione's name is derived from Hermes, the Greek trickster god. Numerous companion books attempt to catalog the various instances of mythological or folk references throughout the series. This approach can help skim the surface of meaning for the books, but to better understand the mythology of Potter, one has to dive deeply into the narrative.

Mythological studies emerged as an academic discipline in parallel with the social sciences as anthropologists published their findings about the cultures and stories of foreign (i.e., not European) people. Coupled with a fascination for Greco-Roman myths, writers started to piece together a deeper meaning behind the myths in an attempt to better understand why so many cultures had stories so similar. Otto Rank, for example, a student of psychoanalyst Sigmund Freud, defined a "mythic hero" in his 1909 *The Myth of the Birth of the Hero*. Here, he identifies a number of traits that characterize the hero, especially in regards of their birth. In other words, he was seeking to identify what makes a legend. Anthropologist Sir George Frazer conducted a lengthy comparative study of various myths and religious traditions in *The Golden Bough* (1890). His work analyzes the accounts of anthropologists and missionaries while attempting to write a familiar catalog on par with the Grimm Brothers' fairy tales or Thomas Bulfinch's mythology. Joseph Campbell enters the field in the 1940s. His personal origin story is mythologized describing how, as a young scholar affected by the Great Depression, Campbell hunkered down with as many books as he could read over the course of four years. This allowed him to cover a wide enough array of literature to make informed comparisons about mythic narrative, resulting, notably, in his seminal work *The Hero with a Thousand Faces*. One common thread to these reviews is the types of works considered for their analyses.

Foundational mythological analysts typically ignore popular culture, criticizing instead the deviation away from "traditional" religion as a "death" of myth that needs resurrecting for the health of humanity. Joseph Campbell is often cited throughout the heart of popular culture and literary analyses because he wrote extensively about myth systems and their role in constructing society. At the root of his academic legacy is his theory equating the hero archetype with what he describes as the *monomyth*: the essential formula for all hero myths. His formula became a convenient outline for Hollywood writers to develop a script that structurally should be a solid product of storytelling.

As a mythologist, Campbell is very concerned with the preservation of a society's myth, but not in the same manner as anthropologists, ethnologists, and folklorists who want to preserve a cultural artifact as it is. Campbell, though nostalgic for older myths, is open to the evolution of new myths, recognizing that they are likely to evolve as humans and culture evolve. This evolution is a necessary response to the changes brought about by science and technology. "The propositions of science," he writes, "to which we are referred for our mortality, knowledge, and wisdom, do not pretend to be true in any final sense, do not pretend to be infallible, or even durable, but are merely working hypotheses, here today and gone tomorrow."[10] Science, he is suggesting, can be a gateway to myth, but should be seen as a piece of the image, not the myth itself. In his assessment, this is the success of *Star Wars*, especially given George Lucas's claim to have used *Hero* and the monomyth to craft the plot. Campbell is here less cautionary against science, but more concerned about what happens when myths lose their meaning, which occurs when a system of symbols are actively refuted and no longer inspire connections.[11]

With the rise of the young adult (YA) literary genre comes an attempt to preserve society's myths by combining folk and popular culture with philosophy, psychology, and human interactions. The stories give fundamental "truths" in a way that is entertaining and informative, targeted at younger readers. In doing this, they have created an air of religiosity about them in response to shifting sentiments not globally felt toward the established cultural myths and doctrines. The stories are something new, fresh, and invigorating.

The YA epics not only reflect our deepest cultural and ethical traditions; they also feed the mythic imaginations of the young and help to shape their value systems that will inform later cultural trends. Children's stories provide the valiant models for emulation and the frightful monsters they must learn to overcome. The battles and triumphs of fantasy heroes teach the most esteemed standards of conduct, the grand ideals of heroic souls, and the glories of honorable enterprise. When writing from this perspective, authors have creative leeway to build cultural systems and fantastic worlds that do not have to rely on the familiar rules that restrict the adult imagination.

In his work, *The Flight of the Wild Gander*, Joseph Campbell recites the definitions of myth, legend, folk- and fairy tale that appear throughout his oeuvre. In keeping with the trend of his era, he separates myth from fairy tale as sacred text from profane entertainment, not to diminish the value of fairy tales but to divest their value from myth. Campbell recognizes myths as "religious recitations conceived as symbolic of the play of eternity, in time."[12] In other words, myths are metaphors for the human spirit irrespective of a specific culture at a specific time in a specific place. Fairy tale, used interchangeably with folktale, are, in his assessment, merely pastime and amusement composed of myths that have lost their meaning over time.[13]

In a different perspective, J.R.R. Tolkien, author of *The Lord of the Rings* and popularly identified as the father of modern fantasy, gives as much reverence for fairy tales as Campbell does myths. In his essay, "On Fairy-stories," Tolkien describes the primary distinction between myth and fairy tale is the inclusion in the latter of the realm of the Faërie, understood to be the fantastical realm of magic. Because of the inclusion of the Faërie, fairy tales are often discounted by adults, "regulated to the 'nursery,' as shabby or old-fashioned furniture is relegated to the play-room, primarily because the adults do not want it, and do not mind if it is misused."[14] Tolkien argues that adults need fairy tales as much as Campbell says we need myths: in order to retain a link with the imagination and fantasy. This can be interpreted as being a link to the mythic, only placed within the context of fantasy rather than sacred settings.[15]

Tolkien's works inspired a new understanding of fantasy literature, which has encompassed new categories: the literature of the Faërie, such as *The Lord of the Rings*; stories of characters from our world traveling into the Faërie like they do in C.S. Lewis's *Chronicles of Narnia*; and, more recently, stories in which the non-magical world and the Faërie coexist, as in J.K. Rowling's world of *Harry Potter*. These stories bring fantasy out of Tolkien's nursery and into everyday experiences that stretch beyond the literary and into the realm of role-playing video games, live-action and table-top role-playing games, and, as in the case of the *Harry Potter* fan community, creative interactions that include arts and crafts, music, fanfiction, and lots of costuming. Through these interactions, participants ritualize and concretize the stories with a religious fervor. The experiences are possible because contemporary culture is primed and welcoming of the reality of hyperreality—the lived experiences of the fantasy are no longer confined to the imagination. As such, fantasy and popular culture phenomena cannot be dismissed as mere entertainment.

MYTH AND RITUAL

Religion and myth are often identified together, with the former providing the container to reenact the latter through ritual. Traditionally, this split is seen as that of "sacred" versus "profane," separating the religious experience—the *numinous*—from the every day.[16] The bliss from a ritual tickles a specific region of the human heart that is transcendental. Mythologies throughout time have tried to explain what this experience is, imaged as deities or some unknowable force, and the goal of rituals is to bring that numinosity into the human experience, to embody the archetypal force behind the mythology. The American religious framework is complicated by a country founded on the principles of religious freedom to worship as one chooses. Thus, it is difficult to identify a single religious tradition to inform the American Dream. As such, consumerism has helped fill the void, notably in the development of Santa Claus or the Easter Bunny as unique, agnostic ritual containers to celebrate certain times of year.[17] While these rituals are engaging, they are time-bound. Hungry consumers want gratification more frequently than that, and ultimately find meaning in unexpected places such as media, which is why any exploration of modern myth without media and popular culture ignores the reality of America.

The Potter fandom is a well-documented example of a grassroots effort to build a ritual around a mythology. The consumables around Potter, whether fan or corporate made, mean little to someone outside the fandom, just as religious objects mean little to non-practitioners. An artifact is considered sacred if it is esteemed above all else. In its truest form, a sacred object or belief "will only be recognized as such if it is grasped at its own level, that is to say, if it is studied as something religious."[18] Without that sacred meaning, Potter is just another set of books in a sea of media. But when sacred meaning is applied to these ritualistic objects, these little totems to Potter, it gives them the symbolic significance of pointing to something higher beyond the text and into an allegorical meta-text. Those trinkets and crafts need the experience behind them in order to fully become part of the ritual.

The idea of fan conventions as gathering space can trace their lineage to community fairs and World's Fairs. Here, entire environments are built to celebrate different facets of culture, new inventions, a variety of foods, and, of course, to buy souvenirs. Some fairs, especially those following the 1893 Chicago World's Fair, included some kind of carnival space with midway games and rides. Going to the fair lays a foundation for amusement parks, bringing the carnival into a permanent home with repeatable experiences over the years. Disney's theme park ritualized this space through the intentional immersion into American mythos, with lands designed around different important themes—adventure, frontier, fantasy, and progress—separated from the outside world. With the synergistic approach of sharing the construction of the park on its weekly television show, Disney brought mythic embodiment of popular culture into American consciousness.

Harry Potter conventions are the natural evolution of the sacred space of the fandom to reinforce the bonds of the community. Here, fans can interact with each other, meet their favorite blogger (and sometimes an actor or two), play games, and, of course, buy things. The merchandise at these events range from the corporate products sold by independent sellers, books, artwork, and homemade tributes. For many fans in the earlier years, the conventions (Cons) were the only place where they could buy a complete, good quality school uniform in any house, not just Gryffindor or Slytherin. The energy at the Cons was intoxicating, turning the fandom into a Dionysian ritual where fans could be free to express their avatar in real life. Here was the mythic process in action, when a living mythology unique to the contemporary world transcends into the sacred.

The two theoretical models that have informed numerous analyses of the wizarding world and the magic of Harry Potter are Campbell's hero's journey and alchemy, the latter cited by J.K. Rowling as an intentional symbolic repository referenced throughout the series. When these are overlaid, they form an interchangeable language for interpretation because both are symbolic of transformation enriching Harry's character arc.

THE POWER OF MYTH AND THE HERO'S JOURNEY

"My favorite definition of mythology: other people's religion. My favorite definition of religion: misunderstanding of mythology."

—Joseph Campbell[19]

Core to understanding Joseph Campbell's myth framework, it is important to consider his understanding of myth. He saw myth as a force of the world that translates itself into ritual through religion. It resonates with all people, but only a limited few—artists, poets, priests, and shamans—who are adept at bridging myth and reality serve as translators of the symbolic into cultural reality. In essence, Campbell equates the force of myth with the transcendent rather than the human construct that is the byproduct of artists who deliver myths through their artistic creations. Thus, myth could theoretically continue to exist even if humanity did not. This is a very poetic notion, and it is easy to interpret Campbell's myth as a living organism whose influence is on par with the natural and cultural forces that regularly shape and transform the human condition. To capture the essential connection between myth and culture, Campbell defines four key functions of mythology, used as characteristics as much as purpose.

1. *The Cosmological Function*: the extent to which myths formulate a creation narrative, or the development of a cosmos.
2. *The Religious Function*: the extent to which myths represent the divine and influence belief traditions.
3. *The Sociological Function*: the extent to which myths mirror both their origin society and human/global society to convey values and mores.
4. *The Psychological Function*: the extent to which myths help shape the individual and their connection to the cosmos.[20]

Within a comprehensive mythos, aspects of these functions work in tandem. The two main elements of culture, beliefs and behavior, are then influenced by myth depending on the degree to which myth is included in everyday life. Myth provides the rules for beliefs (religion and cosmology) and behaviors (psychology and sociology), while a culture and its people influence the appearance of myth through symbols and imagery. An example fundamental to this discussion is the character of the hero, who reflects what a culture recognizes as heroic and who morphs across time and culture to suit contemporary values. Many readers, young and old, have no problem identifying the hero. The hero is the character, usually central, of a story or myth. This character begins their journey in ignorance of what lies ahead, even the world of the adventure. The journey brings the hero to a new level of maturity, enabling them to receive the boon associated with all possible changes.

There are three types of hero: the reluctant, the eager, and the curious. The reluctant hero intentionally avoids the call to adventure and tries to avoid the quest at all costs. Once on the quest, this hero can be whiny and difficult to teach, making the quest laborious. They will favor an easier solution whenever possible and are not afraid to use trickery to achieve their ends, often placing themselves and their friends into more danger than if they had just stuck to the seemingly more difficult route. The eager hero will set out on the quest right away. No task is too small for this hero. They will only use trickery if all other options are exhausted. The curious hero is neither eager nor reluctant but is attracted to the quest by something that grabs their attention. Once on the journey, the hero will continue the quest eagerly to learn more about the new world and the people in it. Curiosity will drive the hero at all possible occasions, but without leading the hero in a fatal direction.

Harry reflects aspects of all three heroes, because his circumstances allow each to manifest in the early chapters of *SS*. He is an eager hero because, as

Rowling makes brutally clear, he would love nothing more than to get away from the Dursleys, who are painted as the most abhorrent suburban family possible.[21] Until he is revealed as a wizard, the Dursleys keep Harry in the closet under the stairs, like a forgotten possession in storage rather than as a member of the family. It is his prison, especially when locked in there as punishment. His eagerness is palpable; going to Hogwarts means freedom.

In contrast to his eagerness, Harry's reluctance as a hero is deeply rooted in doubt. Having not been raised in the wizarding world, he is nervous of whether or not he will pass muster, compounded by the unintended pressure of his fame as "The Boy Who Lived." As Hagrid and Hermione both point out, Harry is in the history books and members of the Wizarding community know his story better than he does. When he first walks into The Leaky Cauldron with Hagrid, he is instantly recognized by the patrons who flock to him for a handshake. When rumor spreads that he is on the Hogwarts Express, Draco Malfoy introduces himself as an opportunity to recruit Harry and bask in his celebrity, which backfires when Harry figures out how disingenuous Draco is. His first few weeks at school are spent dodging watchful eyes who are assessing his magical worth. He finds his proof in the first time he rides a broom, finding a natural talent for flight.

And then there is Harry's curiosity. Having grown up under the stairs, Harry's exposure beyond the Dursleys and school is minimal, so the invitation to enter the magical world and take his first trip into Diagon Alley is nothing short of awe-inspiring. Rowling never reveals how other Muggle-born magic people react their first time, leaving us to wonder, along with Harry, at the whimsical world he is entering. From his first day at school, Harry is curious and questioning, stumbling on clues that lead him into puzzles and adventures that were never meant (or were they?) for Harry and his friends.

Campbell's mythic formula outlines the journey this hero must take, regardless of their willingness to take the adventure. There are three key stages to the journey, each with their own unique elements: Separation, Adventure, Return.

Separation
- The Hero receives the call to adventure
- The Hero confronts a threshold guardian
- The Hero crosses the threshold

Adventure
- The Hero gains friends and magical tools
- The Hero is tested
- The Hero faces the Ultimate Test and wins the boon

Return
- The Hero crosses the return threshold
- The Hero is reintegrated into society
- The Hero shares boon/reward[22]

While it is possible to drop the *Potter* plot into this framework, Harry's over-all journey does not follow the formula literally. In every book, he does have a separation, adventure, and return; but each successive school year brings him closer to the point of leaving the Muggle world entirely and remaining in the magical. This gives the series two views of the hero's journey, the complete cycle of each book, and the overarching cycle of the entire series.

Separation and Call to Adventure

In order to begin the quest, the hero must have a cause they are called to do, usually to rescue someone or something or to battle a particularly diaboli-cal enemy. The call to adventure can come in different ways and, for Harry, it is the arrival of his letter. In stories, the call is either eagerly accepted or persistently repeats until it is. Because the Dursleys keep it from him in *SS*, letters fill the Dursleys' home to make sure he gets it. In the event that the call still does not stir the hero, a herald will appear to escort the hero to the threshold. The herald is a messenger for whomever sent the call. For example, Hagrid acts as Dumbledore's herald when he goes to pick up Harry from the Dursleys. The appearance of the herald encourages the hero to undergo the journey, either by choice or by force, and helps the hero to cross the threshold into the realm of adventure.

Before the hero can begin the quest, they must face a threshold guardian. This is a creature or challenge that attempts to prevent the hero from starting, and it may or may not have been laid by the enemy. It is the first difficult challenge the hero will face and should be comparably easy compared to what lies ahead.

Call to Adventure

For the first part of the series, Harry's call to adventure is the annual Hogwarts letter listing school supplies and other notices to prepare for the school year. The Dursleys try to keep him from receiving it in *SS*, because they are convinced that it is the only way that they can snuff the magic out of him, after realizing that keeping him locked under the stairs and otherwise neglected failed to work. In *CoS*, Dobby prevents Harry from receiving his letter in an attempt to try to keep Harry from returning to Hogwarts. He is well-intentioned in his attempt to keep Harry safe from whatever he heard the

Malfoys plan, but ultimately, Harry gets his letter while he is at the Weasleys' house. When it is time for Harry to receive his letter in *PoA*, he is already in Diagon Alley, having run away from the Dursleys after inflating Aunt Marge. After the first letter, it stops being a call to adventure to bring Harry in, but serves as a calendar marker so help Harry count down to the return to school.

While he does receive letters in the remaining books, they serve less of a purpose because the expectation is that Harry will return to Hogwarts without interference. In these cases, Harry receives a different kind of call that brings him into the wizarding world. For *GoF*, he is invited to spend part of the summer with Ron's family to attend the Quidditch World Cup; the invitation is the call, and the event gives Harry new insights into the nuanced culture of the magical world. He is summoned to the Ministry of Magic in *OotP* under allegations of using under-age magic to protect his Muggle cousin from Dementors. The trial is rigged against him, as though intended to make an example of Harry or keep him from Hogwarts. Harry wins the case with Dumbledore's support. In *HBP*, Dumbledore arrives to escort Harry into the magical world, leveraging him to bait Horace Slughorn, a retired teacher, into coming back to Hogwarts for the school year. Slughorn was a vital piece of a carefully devised puzzle Dumbledore tries to solve with Harry, and he knew that Slughorn would capitulate to Harry in memory of his favorite student, Harry's mother Lily.

Where *Harry Potter* diverges from the hero's journey is in *DH*, when Harry leaves the Dursleys for the last time. The magical spell that protected him while at their home ended on his seventeenth birthday when, according to wizarding custom, young wizards came of age. This departure essentially reflects Harry's choice to move into the magical world, presumably leaving the Muggle world permanently.

Threshold Crossing

Each successive year, while Harry roots deeper into the wizarding world, the expectation is that students return to Hogwarts via the Hogwarts Express. The train leaves from King's Cross station in London from Platform 9 3/4 and goes straight to Hogsmeade. First-year students are taken to Hogwarts in boats across the lake in an initiation ritual that culminates with the Sorting. Older students ride in carts pulled by invisible creatures called thestrals that can only be seen by those who have personally seen death. Going into *OotP*, following the death of Cedric Diggory, Harry is now able to see the thestrals.

Harry rides the Hogwarts Express as planned every year, except his second year. In another attempt to keep him from getting to Hogwarts, Dobby blocked the passage through the wall to Platform 9 3/4. Harry and Ron, panicking about missing the train, chose to take the Weasleys' flying car to school instead. From the sky, they found the train and followed it to the school, believing they were being so cool for taking this alternate route. But then they crashed into the Whomping Willow, a violent tree whose branches come down on anyone who gets too close. The boys more or less learned their lesson to wait for their parents rather than taking the journey to school into their own hands.

Again, *DH* is different. Knowing that the protection is coming off the Dursley home and that the Death Eaters were definitely going to come after Harry once it did, the Order of the Phoenix devise a plan to get Harry to the Weasleys' home, the Burrow. In this plan, each one of his friends would take polyjuice potion to turn into Harry, and each Harry would be escorted with an adult member of the Order of the Phoenix. The idea is to deflect the Death Eaters from Harry and split them up. The plan mostly worked, and the crew got to the Burrow more or less intact, but the battle getting there was more than they were expecting, especially once Voldemort figured out which Harry was the real Harry.

In Campbell's model, the threshold crossing is never meant to be easy and as simple as crossing over and arriving in the magical world. Each of Harry's journeys, whether on the train or not, is met with some kind of trial or threshold guardian. In the first two books, the trial is the simple act of getting through the barrier. For the next four books, Harry faces a different guardian, sometimes on the train (Dementors in *PoA*, Malfoy in *HBP*) or in some other area of the magical world (the World Cup in *GoF*, the Ministry trial in *OotP*). Without the friends that he has made in the wizarding world, some of Harry's crossings would have gone sour given his lack of awareness about magical social mores.

Adventure

While on the journey, the hero will encounter two primary types of characters: helpers and testers. The helpers are friends and guides who accompany the hero on the quest. Often these include a wise elder who teaches the hero and provides magical tools to use, and travel companions who provide friendship, company, and support to keep the hero moving ahead. The testers are affiliated with the enemy and will try to stop the hero. Each test strengthens the hero in preparation of the Ultimate Test. Distractions can occur, such as injuries or a temptation[23] to throw the hero off course or delay their progress.

At the heart of the journey, the hero will face the Ultimate Test to either overthrow an evil or retrieve a stolen boon or elixir. This is meant to be the most difficult battle for the hero to accomplish. Campbell likens this character to a dragon, because the dragon symbolizes a creature that can operate in all environments, breathe fire and make magic, and is capable of remarkable strength and power. The hero has the option of confronting the dragon directly or sneaking past it at the risk of the dragon chasing the hero to the threshold.

Helpers

Campbell defines the helpers as ancillary characters who support the hero. Harry's stories rely on a collective hero structure in which all "helper" characters contribute equally to the journey. At the core of a collective hero is the realization that each part of the collective contributes a unique skill to the team. This is not a "safety in numbers" collaboration, because these heroes realize that they are never safe as long as the looming evil shrouds their journey. They do not even pretend. Similarly, by spreading the heroic skills across a team, it humanizes the central hero such that they do not have to rely on supernatural talents or carry the heroic burden alone. This type of hero is not unique to modern times, but its prevalence is new. Because the collective hero is made up of multiple heroes, there are, theoretically, just as many monomyths influencing the narrative; however, those individual journeys are never allowed to supersede the group mission. Part of their journey includes the ups and downs of relationship building (especially for teenagers). Together they learn and grow and come to the realization that together—and only together—can they succeed.

Being able to rely on his friends is one of the largest lessons Harry has to learn. He keeps falling into a trap thinking that he is the only one who can defeat Voldemort, because it is his destiny. Every time he goes into a confrontation with Voldemort, he has friends with him, but it is not until *DH* that Harry truly appreciates their value to his journey. He initially thought he would go horcrux hunting alone, but Ron and Hermione insisted on going along as an expectation. When Ron breaks off from Harry and Hermione over a horcrux-induced spat, Harry realizes how much he misses him. Ron is Harry's more reactive side. He is the voice of the magical world within the trio and provides the emotional stability that helps bond them together. Ron is also the team's strategist. Hermione is Harry's thinking side. As the most brilliant Hogwarts student, she is full of knowledge and helps balance the two boys.

Ultimate Test

In all of the books, Harry is separated from Hogwarts for his Ultimate Test. This added threshold personalizes the test to Harry, which helps establish a framework for understanding the prophecy that prompts Voldemort's fury against Harry. As written, the prophecy implies that the Harry/Voldemort confrontation must be, in the end, a one-on-one dual. The collectivity of the Potter heroic actually turns the Final Battle into a collaborative effort, even while Voldemort remains myopic about Harry as his opponent. All seven of Voldemort's horcruxes are destroyed by a different person (including one by Voldemort), and Harry's closest friends are always nearby protecting his back.

There are two books in which Harry's Ultimate Test does not include Voldemort; instead, he confronts Voldemort's supporters. In *PoA*, Harry is caught in the resolution of the Marauders. Lupin was convinced that he was alone: James was killed by Voldemort, Pettigrew was killed by Sirius, and Sirius was in Azkaban. In the span of a couple hours, Lupin learns that Pettigrew framed Sirius and staged his own death, and that Sirius is innocent. Lupin and Sirius reminisce about their youth, friendship, and the nature of James's death, sharing much of their secrets. Harry learns much about his father from their exchange and feels that he gained family in Lupin and Sirius. While they focus on Pettigrew's betrayal, Pettigrew uses the opportunity to escape. In the opening scenes of *GoF*, Rowling reveals that Pettigrew is a Death Eater and reunites with Voldemort for protection.

In *HBP*, Harry's test seems like it revolves around Snape, chasing after him as he and the Death Eaters escape Hogwarts after killing Dumbledore. They duel, but Harry does not have it in him to commit the revenge he feels in his heart. Instead, Harry's test is realizing the death of Dumbledore and the heavy cost of the horcrux hunt, acting as a springboard for the next year's adventure. Dumbledore was the teacher Harry admired most, to such an extent that it is Dumbledore he sees in his transcendental liminal space at King's Cross in *DH*. Dumbledore's death frees Harry from his ties to the school and launches him on the final adventure.

Return

Before returning home, the hero will come to another threshold between the worlds. At this point in Campbell's model, the hero will have to leave any friends or magical artifacts behind. The hero can return with only memories and the boon and will need to reacclimatize to their home community should they wind up there. After fully recuperating, the hero is then ready the share the boon. The hero will either (a) share the boon with the community to restore it to grandeur and remain, (b) share the boon with the community to restore it to grandeur and depart on another quest, or (c) share the boon with the community to restore it to grandeur then go share it with other communities.

Harry's return diverges from Campbell's model, because it is his return from his Ultimate Test that fits the monomyth, not his return to the Dursleys' as Campbell would suggest. This is because the boon he brings back has greater significance to the wizarding world than would ever interest or benefit the Dursleys or Muggles. The return phase is when he learns most from

Dumbledore or other teachers that wraps up the school year and prepares Harry for the next.

In essence, each return is in preparation for the Final Battle. The ending here is that there is no Campbellian ending. By defeating Voldemort, Harry destroys the single barrier keeping him from fully integrating with the magical world. His journey from the very beginning, then, is about his return home, which convolutes Campbell's formula further. While the books can be condensed into monomythic plot points, the transformation of the Potter heroic is actually about coming into oneself and finding wholeness, a journey that depth psychologist C.G. Jung calls "individuation."

The Individuation Process

Campbell connected myth and ritual, which is why only a select few in a social group could bridge between the group and the myth. The shaman, for instance, was typically the person within a tribe who was "different," perhaps even what modern audiences would call "crazy." This neurodivergency opens a conduit to the *numinous* and gives them the power to interpret and ritualize a myth. As noted, Campbell's observation is that myth is hidden in the modern world because it is disconnected from ritual in a traditional understanding of a ritual. As defined by Arnold Van Gannep, a ritualistic rite is a necessary step when transitioning from one state of being to another and is marked by the ritual, which is the ceremony that reenacts the transition.[24] Building off of Van Gannep, Victor Turner breaks down the ritual into a process of separation, liminality, and *communitas*. The separation takes the initiate out of the known world, stripping them of their current identity. The liminal stage is the ambiguous stage that performs the transition. *Communitas* is the reintegration into society as a new person.[25] The ritual, then, is a mirror to what is happening within the monomyth, except that one is literary and the other religious and performative.

The individuation process likewise becomes another pathway to transition. Coined by psychotherapist C.G. Jung, this process indicates achievement of wholeness and balance between the conscious and unconscious, to become "'in-dividual,' that is, a separate, indivisible unity or 'whole.'"[26] It gives psychological expression to what the hero's journey illustrates, bringing the metaphorical transformation of a myth into real world psychotherapeutic practice. In other words, Jung ritualizes therapy, except, rather than be a single ceremony, work toward individuation could take a lifetime.

The pathway toward individuation involves the analysis of dreams and dream symbolism to get to the core of the patient's connection to the collective unconscious, the layer of the unconscious that is the realm of archetype and myth that filters into the individual's unconscious through dreams. Jung's assertion is that by getting to the essence of the archetypes, one could gain awareness of and elevate unconsciousness to consciousness. In other words, one needs to identify and adjust parts of the personality that operate at the core of our personhood that can be shaped by experiences and impacted by trauma.

Like other researchers of mythology, Jung factored myths and fairy tales into his theories, asserting that they are the keys to understanding a culture's interpretation of the collective unconscious. In particular, he found his theoretical connection in alchemy, which illustrates the transformation process in greater depth than the ritual process or hero's journey by subdividing the liminality into a scientific process. Artistically, Jung recognized in the works of the alchemists a rich creative expression of the transformation with multiple layers of symbolism.

Individuation is not itself a major factor in the *Harry Potter* story, but it does pave the way for alchemy, which helped inform Rowling's narrative of Harry's own transformation.

HARRY POTTER AND THE
TRANSFORMATIVE PROCESS

Depth psychology adopted alchemical symbolism, because it provides a historical foundation and collection of symbols and metaphors that can be linked with the process of individuation. Similar to the connection between mythology and the hero's journey, this framework helps provide concrete language and imagery to the abstract concept, helping to equate the transcendent nature of individuation to a transformative process. The importance is placed not on the physical product of the work, but rather on how the process manifests in and reshapes the psyche. The product of psychological alchemy is a rich philosopher's stone that represents a tangible boon of the Self, as Jung declares at the culmination of his alchemical research: "Alchemy, therefore, has performed for me the great and invaluable service of providing material in which my experience could find sufficient room, and has thereby made it possible for me to describe the individuation process at least in its essential aspects."[27]

When applied to *Harry Potter*, Harry becomes the vessel for the readers, and his journey becomes that of the reader's. His transformation (and that of those around him) is thus our transformation. Rowling recognizes this element of the work, and through her fascination with the topic, wove alchemy thematically throughout the series. On Pottermore, she writes:

Alchemy (the search for the Philosopher's Stone, which would turn base metal to gold and give the possessor eternal youth) was once believed to be possible and real. However, the central quest of alchemy may be more complex, and less materialistic, than it first appears. One interpretation of the "instructions" left by the alchemists is that they are symbolic of a spiritual journey, leading the alchemist from ignorance (base metal) to enlightenment (gold).[28]

Through the latter half of the series, the reader follows Harry through "the coloring process."[29] This is outlined throughout *GoF*, the series' turning point, embedded within the Tri-Wizard Tournament, making the alchemical symbolism pivotal to the transformation and maturity that pushes Harry toward his final conformation with Voldemort.

Opening the Work: Selecting the Champions

Hogwarts welcomes guests from two other European schools of magic, Beauxbatons and Durmstrang, to compete in the Tri-Wizard Tournament. As Dumbledore explains:

> The Tri-Wizard Tournament was first established some seven hundred years ago as a friendly competition between the three largest European schools of wizardry: Hogwarts, Beauxbatons, and Durmstrang. A champion was selected to represent each school, and the three champions competed in three magical tasks. The schools took it in turns to host the tournament once every five years, and it was generally agreed to be a most excellent way of establishing ties between young witches and wizards of different nationalities—until, that is, the death toll mounted so high that the tournament was discontinued.30

It is arguably not an accident that the Tri-Wizard Tournament would be revived the same year that England hosts the Quidditch World Cup: Both represent the establishment of good will across international borders to hopefully reinforce social connections before the return of Voldemort. (Spoiler alert: it doesn't.) Rather, the Quidditch World Cup and the Tri-Wizard Tournament surface the Ministry of Magic's insecurities, prejudices, and xenophobia that inevitably make it susceptible to the influence of Voldemort and his Death Eaters, especially the rich and powerful (i.e., the Malfoys) who hold sway over the Minister.

Because the tournament is so dangerous, only seventh-year students may enter their names into the Goblet of Fire that, as a magical impartial party, will select the three champions, one from each school. When it comes time to select the three champions—Cedric Diggory from Hogwarts, Fleur Delacour from Beauxbatons, and Viktor Krum from Durmstrang—somehow Harry's name pops out of the Goblet. Faculty from all three schools are perplexed how Harry's name got into the Goblet. Harry is equally surprised and, as such, has a steep hill from the outset to prove his worthiness as a champion.

The Goblet of Fire is the first of two incarnations of the Holy Grail in this book, the second being the Tri-Wizard Cup to be awarded at the end of the tournament. Like the Grail's dream-like appearance in King Arthur's court, the Goblet of Fire is illusory and represents more the possibility of the coming adventure than the goal of the quest itself. The Holy Grail in alchemical terms is the quintessence, the pure essence of a substance that is a divine fifth element that unites the four elements—fire, water, earth and air—into one pure form, the Philosopher's Stone. This aspect of the quest is crucial for the alchemist to awaken to his or her potential for spiritual immortality.

Fabricius compares this stage of the work to the awakening of adolescent love, the burning uncontrollable love at the heart of medieval romances.[31] Harry and his peers, now fourteen, begin to experience the pangs of love this year and must come to terms with new feelings for the people with whom they live and study. Of the four champions, Fleur, who is part veela, is the embodiment of love. Veela in Rowling's world are beautiful sirens in the bodies of women who can bring men under their spell simply by walking into the room.[32] Cedric is very popular among the girls for his Quidditch skills and his earthly qualities. Viktor, who remains isolated whenever possible, is uneasy about love and women. Harry has these three models from whom to learn to control his own feelings. The new awakening of adolescent love is put to the test between the first and second tasks with the Yule Ball. For the first time, Harry and his peers have to cope with the events surrounding the dance: primping themselves, asking for dates, and slow dancing. Neither Harry nor his best friend, Ron, enjoy it much. Both are unable to go to the dance with their choice partners, a valuable lesson to them about asking for dates as well as acknowledging feelings.

First *Coniunctio*: The First Task (*nigredo*)

The first task of the tournament is for the champions to rescue a golden egg from a mother dragon armed only with a wand. They are awarded points for the time and effectiveness it takes to complete the task. Harry draws a particularly fierce dragon, a Hungarian Horntail. His solution is to summon his broom from his dorm room, fly after the egg, and dodge the dragon rather than fight her directly. This method draws upon his skills as a Quidditch seeker, where he regularly chases after a small golden ball, the Golden Snitch, while his teammates protect him from the other team to score points.

The *nigredo* stage, or blackening, is characterized as a symbolic death, or *mortificatio*. The *mortificatio*, Edward F. Edinger notes, is "the most negative operation in alchemy. It has to do with darkness, defeat, torture, mutilation, death, and rotting. However, these dark images often lead over to highly positive ones—growth, resurrection, rebirth."[33] The dark symbolism

Edinger describes will continue to infect the magical world after the return of Voldemort, but Rowling's use of a black dragon here primes Harry for what is ahead in his journey. Dragon symbolism is complex within mythology, and this complexity extends into alchemy as well. Across mythologies, dragons are portrayed as guardians of secrets to life or wealth,[34] which makes them attractive targets for heroes.[35] Dragons are also associated with serpents, symbolic of the cycles of life, because of the snake's ability to shed its skin, harkening back to the basilisk of *CoS*.[36]

In relation to the alchemical process, the dragon represents the root of instinct and must be slain at the start of the work to initiate the transformation. Harry realizes that slaying the dragon is beyond his skill set, prompting Professor Moody to encourage him to play to his strengths,[37] which is primarily his ability to fly a broomstick.38 The Horntail shoots fire at Harry, providing the fire of the *nigredo* phase. The burning helps to kill the impurities of the substance, leaving the essence that will move through the process.[39] For Harry, this is the moment when people begin to accept that he may have been set up for the competition, which helps Harry build allies, especially with the Ravenclaw and Hufflepuff houses who come to recognize that he is not a fame-seeker.

The fact that the Hungarian Horntail is black is worth discussing before moving on to the next phase of the work. While it is a component of the *nigredo* that the blackening is inevitable to the process, James Hillman, a post-Jungian archetypal psychoanalyst, reminds us that the color black is a non-color in the absence of light:[40]

> the color black is condemned to be a "non-color." It carries the meanings of the random and the formless. Like a black hole, it sucks into it and makes vanish the fundamental security structures of Western consciousness. By absenting color, black prevents phenomena from presenting their virtues. Black's deconstruction of any positivity—experienced as doubt, negative thinking, suspicion, undoing, valuelessness—explains why the *nigredo* is necessary to every paradigm shift. Black breaks the paradigm.[41]

Black symbolism is sprinkled throughout the series, notably in the name of Harry's godfather, Sirius Black, who appears in Harry's life long enough to help Harry through his transition from naïve Harry to the Chosen One. Sirius first appears to Harry as a big black dog, which Harry's divination teacher insists is a death omen.[42] In a way, Black's death at the end of *OotP* represents a symbolic death for Harry, helping him grow into the necessary mental state for the horcrux hunt of the next two books.

The golden egg is a symbol of rebirth and appears at the end of the first task to bring Harry out of the *nigredo* and into the next task, which includes cleansing and rebirth. The egg is the remnant of the dragon following the *nigredo* representing rebirth of the essential substance. "Retrieving the philosophical egg," according to Fabricius, "is therefore equivalent to reliving one's primal state, where subject and object are one. [. . .] By creeping into himself and becoming his own egg, the alchemist turns himself into his own hatcher. . . . "[43] With the *nigredo*, the ego has been defeated, leaving a golden essence waiting for birth. The egg and its parallel sister symbol, the Golden Snitch, signify both an alchemical birth and a spiritual death. The Snitch recurs throughout the books as the vessel of Harry's happiness. Each time he catches it, he grows a little more from a child to a true hero. At the end of the series, the Snitch becomes the vessel carrying the Resurrection Stone, an enchanted stone that can resurrect images of people who have died.[44] With it, Harry resurrects his parents and godfather who walk with him as he goes to his death, and thus his final transformation through resurrection.[45]

The Second *Coniunctio*: The Second Task (*albedo*)

To prepare for the second task, Harry has to crack the riddle of the Golden Egg, which can only be heard under water. This helps prepare Harry for the next stage of the process, the *albedo* or whitening. This whitening involves the removal of the blackness either through continued burning (the *calcination*) or a cleansing with water (the *solutio* or *ablution*); our emphasis will be on the latter.[46]

The riddle of the egg explains the next task:

Come seek us where our voices sound,

We cannot sing above the ground,

And while you're searching, ponder this:

We've taken what you'll surely miss,

An hour long you'll have to look,

And to recover what we've took,

But past an hour—the prospect's black,

Too late, it's gone, it won't come back.[47]

The task is for the champions to rescue the person most important to them at Hogwarts at that time. Harry discovers that he has to rescue his "Wheezy," meaning his best friend Ron Weasley. With a little gillyweed, a plant that enables him to breathe and swim underwater without assistance, he swims into the mermaid kingdom of the lake and finds Ron, but also Hermione, Cho (the girl he likes), and one other girl, who are all in an enchanted sleep. The mermaids prevent him from taking someone other than his assigned rescue, so Harry waits to make sure everyone is safely rescued at the risk of exceeding the time limit and failing the task.

The water of the lake holds its own philosophical symbolism. As the depth psychological symbol for the unconscious, Harry's plunge into the depths during this task offers both the opportunity to reach into himself while at the same time cleansing his essence in preparation for the upcoming tasks. According to Jung, "the philosophical water is the stone or the *prima materia* itself; but at the same time, it is also its solvent."[48] Plunging into the lake allows Harry to transition from the *nigredo* into the *albedo* by being cured and cleansed of the darkness of the blackness.

The mermaid also plays a role in alchemical symbolism. Associated with the *solutio*, mermaids help pull people into the depths of the water by the power of their song.[49] Plunging into the depths is the metaphor for diving deep into the unconscious.[50] Thus this task brings Harry face-to-face with the hidden unknowns of the deep. This includes the confrontation with the *anima*, one of the archetypes of the unconscious necessary for wholeness. Jung defines the *anima* as "a factor of the utmost importance in the psychology of a man wherever emotions and affects are at work. She intensifies, exaggerates, falsifies, and mythologizes our emotional relations with his work and with other people of both sexes."[51] Rowling's merpeople are not the beautiful ones associated in popular lore. She explains, under the guise of Newt Scamander, that the "oldest recorded merpeople were known as sirens (Greece) and it is in warmer waters that we find the beautiful mermaids so frequently depicted in Muggle literature and painting. The selkies of Scotland and the Merrows of Ireland are [ugly], but they share that love of music which is common to all merpeople."[52] The "ugly" here is Harry's edit of the phrase "less beautiful" to emphasize the creatures he encounters. Indeed, they are even hostile to him when he attempts to free the others. Rather than yield to the mermaids, Harry chooses to wait for the other champions to ensure the safety of the others. Viktor rescues Hermione, and Cedric rescues Cho, but once it seems clear that Fleur is not arriving, Harry frees both Ron and the girl, Fleur's little sister. There is some disagreement between Harry and the merpeople at this decision, symbolic of the emotional wrestle to come. The Mer-King informs Dumbledore of Harry's insistence to help the others—for which he is awarded extra points.

Rowling equates the *albedo* to the influence of Albus Dumbledore.[53] In conjunction with Hagrid (who is associated with the *rubedo* stage), they form for Harry "the ideal father figure he seeks; the former is warm, practical and wild, the latter impressive, intellectual, and somewhat detached."[54] Through *The Life and Lies of Albus Dumbledore* (a posthumous biography published in *DH*) and in *The Fantastic Beasts* films, Dumbledore is painted as very different from Harry's mentor, illustrating the bookends of the transformative process. Dumbledore struggled with the loss of his parents, the care for his siblings, and a relationship with Grindelwald with similar complicated feelings of grief and love that Harry must navigate as a part of this stage of the work.

Third *Coniunctio:* The Third Task (*rubedo*)

The third task marks the pinnacle of the rising action of the series. In this task, the champions navigate a maze, at the center of which is the Tri-Wizard Cup. The first to get to the cup is the winner of the tournament. This stage represents the *rubedo*, or reddening. Red is associated with both the Philosopher's Stone, the culmination of the work, but also with blood and life force. The maze in this task is the means to an end, as it is the events at the graveyard that follow that culminate this stage.

Mazes and labyrinths are related to mandala symbolism,[55] which, in turn, represents an "archetype of wholeness."[56] Mandalas/labyrinths appear throughout world religions as a meditative tool, and labyrinths appear throughout mythology to fulfill a similar function.[57] Its placement in Harry's journey does fulfill a meditative need. Through its twists and turns, this maze has obstructions at its crossroads that are meant to not only distract the champions, but also to eliminate them. Harry's challenges seem relatively light: he encounters a sphinx whose riddle he must answer to continue on the path, a boggart that appears as the thing a witch or wizard most fears (Dementors for Harry) that can be defeated with a dose of humor, and a magical orb that turns him upside down until he bravely takes a step to right-side himself. Nothing he encounters is beyond his skill set, which he later learns was part of the influence of Moody to make sure Harry gets to the center and the Cup first. Cedric also arrives at the same time, and the two boys agree to take the Cup together, since either way, it is a win for Hogwarts.

As they touch the Cup, it initiates a portkey, a magical transportation spell, taking the two boys to a graveyard. Two things happen here in quick succession: Cedric is killed and Voldemort is reborn through a magical process that includes Harry's blood as one of the ingredients. The reborn Voldemort fulfills the alchemical symbol of the Homunculus, the reanimated corpse.[58] In order for Harry's transformation to be complete, Harry has to confront Voldemort as his alchemical opposite.[59] There are two components associated with this stage of the work. One is the completion of Harry's transformation, which is arrested when the Cup transports Harry out of the maze. Through the next three books, Harry will continue with the work through the Final Battle.[60]

The other component involves the resurrection of Voldemort. His rebirth is done by chemicals and magic rather than through a true alchemical process.[61] His body is as distorted as his soul, corrupted by evil and its fragmentation as a result of the creation of horcruxes, a dark magic that creates vessels for encasing pieces of a soul to gain immortality. One fan theory suggests that the horcruxes may serve as individual entities, based on the fact that Voldemort does not feel their destruction, perhaps functioning more like disembodied clones.[62] Ideally, this stage of the work would be completed with the unification of Voldemort's fragments;[63] however, the destruction of the horcruxes helps Harry reconcile the fact that he, too, is a horcrux and must experience his own death in order to destroy that fragment.

Harry's *rubedo* subjects him to death and near-death experiences. Cedric's death represents a loss of innocence for Harry, which also frees him to adopt a mercurial role within Hogwarts, one that has the power to unite opposites, namely the four Hogwarts houses.[64] Jung postulates that the union of four, or the quarternity, is the actualization of the Self.[65] The Battle of Hogwarts at the end of *DH*, then, becomes the ultimate culmination of Harry's transformation.

As a modern myth, Harry's transformation becomes that of the reader in the "real" world. Indeed, literature provides a mythic metaphorical framework for personal development by being a vessel for our projections and is subject to personal interpretation rather than to a universal collective understanding. That the fan community took ownership of the books helps reinforce the mythic power of Potter. While the frenzy of the fandom has reduced, fans continue to connect with the myth.[66] Some readers came of age alongside Harry, and others turn to his adventures as guidance through a difficult period of life.

The end of the alchemical work is marked by the chemical wedding, the union of the substances into a new entity. Rowling uses the marriage between Harry and Ginny as the image for this capstone to the transformative work. This alchemical process offers an approach that unites the languages of myth, psychology, and science to reflect the journey to complete self that has helped fans come into their identity.

HORCRUXES AND THE CORRUPTION
OF THE TRANSFORMATIVE PROCESS

Much like several other popular culture artifacts of the first quarter of the 21st century, the main goal of *Harry Potter* is the mythological battle of good versus evil, but not necessarily to defeat evil, rather to bring balance and harmony. Voldemort is an embodiment of this evil, but his defeat the first time shows that the roots of his evil were planted long before he became a wizard.

As the last surviving heir of Slytherin (excluding *CC*), he is the culmination of the imbalance between the four houses and, by extension, within the wizarding world. Within the alchemical process, the purpose of the Philosopher's Stone is immortality. When taken literally, this sparks the quest for sources of immortality, such as a Fountain of Youth, in the hopes of living forever. Several stories emerge providing commentary around this perspective. Characters such as vampires and demonic creatures that live forever are not always the sympathetic heroes. In some circles, Renaissance-era alchemists joined witches as targets of witch hunts.[67]

In the 20th century, the alchemical tradition was revived by esoteric groups, such as the Rosicrucians under Frances Yates and Thelema under Alister Crowley, as the symbolic language of the new mysticism that was borne from the Spiritualist Movement. Within these movements was the quest for ritual and numinosity through alternative pathways than those governed by tradition. The quest for immortality morphed into a quest for spiritual wholeness loosely inspired by Eastern religious traditions. Characters like vampires continue to appear throughout the century, eventually becoming sympathetic heroes that showcase the struggles of living forever.

Voldemort, however, is a psychopath, blinded by his quest for power. While he is able to develop a following of worshippers, he is also tempted by the idea of living forever as a means of continual power and worship. Rowling plants very clear commentary about death versus immortality throughout the books. On the one hand, the Deathly Hallows are introduced in a fairy tale familiar to young witches and wizards, and supposedly are based on the real events of the Peverell Family, Harry's ancestors. The Deathly Hallows are about evading death, and the person who controls all three of them—the Invisibility Cloak, the Resurrection Stone, and the Elder Wand—is the master of death, as Harry ultimately becomes. This is his unique heroic trait that he brings to the trio, because it is through his humility that he understands the purpose of the Hallows in terms of life rather than of power, as was the situation with both Dumbledore and Grindelwald.

On the other hand, there are the Horcruxes. A horcrux is an object into which a Dark Wizard, such as Voldemort, embeds a piece of their soul for safekeeping. As long as the object remains intact, the wizard lives forever, which is why Voldemort did not fully disappear after Harry backfired his killing curse the first time. Voldemort developed an interest in horcruxes while still a student at Hogwarts. The topic is banned at Hogwarts, so it is unclear how Tom Riddle (Voldemort's student self) stumbled on the idea. He asks one of his instructors, Professor Slughorn, who was both potions teacher and Slytherin head of house, and thus one of Riddle's preferred teachers, about horcruxes.68

Slughorn recognizes the connection between Voldemort's power spree and this interest in horcruxes, and harbors that guilt until essentially forgiven by Harry for his role in the death of his mother. Slughorn's memory is the last piece of the puzzle both he and Dumbledore need to kick off their endgame.

In order to make a horcrux, the dark wizard has to murder an innocent, with murder here recognized as an act so horrible that it breaks the soul. Dumbledore suspects that Riddle killed children when he lived in the orphanage, opening the possibility that he might have no qualms about making horcruxes. The first known horcrux in Voldemort's timeline is the diary that Ginny Weasley succumbs to in *CoS*, with Moaning Myrtle as his victim. After that, Dumbledore suspects that subsequent horcruxes are made out of objects that would have powerful significance, such as artifacts of the four founders of Hogwarts, namely Slytherin's locket, Hufflepuff's cup, and Ravenclaw's diadem. Each of these artifacts help Voldemort connect to their legacy in a symbolic attempt to overwrite their significance with his own. Similarly, he makes a horcrux out of his grandfather's ring in a similar attempt to overwrite his family's legacy, so he can shed the skin of Tom Riddle and fully transition into Voldemort. The remaining two horcruxes, his pet snake Nagini and Harry, are risky; if the living being dies, so does the horcrux. The Nagini horcrux, however, seems to have been made as an act of desperation in full awareness of the risk that something might happen to her. Harry, of course, is an unknown, accidental horcrux.

The corruption he faces, however, is that each time he makes a horcrux, Voldemort is also losing more of his humanity. Making one horcrux is impactful enough, but seven is more than any soul should be able to handle. While it seems on the surface that these horcruxes may be an insurance policy against death, it is also indicative of his hubris and his belief that he is more than human; he is a Nietzschean *übermensch*—the highest possible affirmation of human existence, near god-like and superior, and thus the leader to bring the new order to the wizarding world. Voldemort's character is more than a metaphor: he is the benchmark for the corrupt leader that will attempt to recreate a culture in their own imperial image. He is a warning, and Harry's defeat of him is a valuable lesson that readers take from the series.

NOTES

1. James Truslow Adams, "America Faces 1933's Realities," *New York Times*, January 1, 1933, SM 1, quoted in Lawrence R. Samuel, *The American Dream: A Cultural History* (Syracuse: Syracuse University Press, 2012), 13.

2. Lawrence R. Samuel, *The American Dream: A Cultural History* (Syracuse: Syracuse University Press, 2012), 37–39.

3. Generation X, the generation in between the two, is often overlooked such that it is the observation of many memes across social media. This generation was born at a time when boomers were struggling with Vietnam and early parenthood, a shifting economy, and the more common reality of both parents working and not able to be home for their children after school. This generation's collective pessimism has helped, in many ways, balance millennial optimism, but at the cost of being unable to see the struggles of millennials as anything other than entitlement and lack of work ethic.

4. For a history of the fandom: Melissa Anelli, *Harry, A History: The True Story of a Boy Wizard, His Fans, and Life Inside the Harry Potter Phenomenon* (New York: Pocket Books, 2008).

5. Joseph Campbell, *Flight of the Wild Gander: Explorations in the Mythological Dimension* (Novato: New World Library/Joseph Campbell Foundation, 2002), 152.

6. Marshall McLuhan and Quentin Fiore, *The Medium is the Massage: An Inventory of Effects* (Berkeley: Gingko Press, 1967), 100.

7. Samuel, *American Dream*, 9.

8. In the metaphor of consumption, licensed breakfast cereal, candies and sweet treats, and juice and vitamins establish a consumptive cycle. Where the franchise literally becomes part of one's diet, nourishing(-ish) body in addition to imagination.

9. "Ultimate Funko Pop Harry Potter Figures Gallery and Checklist," The Cardboard Connection, accessed September 26, 2021, cardboardconnection.com/funko-pop-harry-potter-vinyl-figures.

10. Joseph Campbell, *Flight of the Wild Gander*, 153.

11. Campbell, 143.

12. Campbell, 7.

13. Campbell, 8.

14. J.R.R. Tolkien, "On Fairy-Stories," in *The Tolkien Reader*, (New York: Ballantine, 1986), 37.

15. Bridging both thinkers, depth psychologist, C.G. Jung found both myths and fairy tales to be potent archetypal playgrounds for understanding the collective unconscious and patient's dreams. Fellow Jungians adopt a similar approach, such as Marie-Louise Von Franz, *Interpretation of Fairy Tales,* rev. ed. (Boston: Shambhala, 1996).

16. Mircea Eliade, *The Sacred & The Profane: The Nature of Religion*, trans. Willard R. Trask (San Diego: Harcourt Brace & Company, 1959), 21–22; 68–72.

17. Christmas and Easter are Christian holidays, suggesting that this really is an attempt to incorporate different belief systems into these holidays, which is a valid argument. Additionally, these holidays come around seasonal and celestial events, the solstices, which have been ritualized across humanity since the earliest cultures. While Easter is not celebrated at Hogwarts, Christmas is—especially for the students and staff who stay at the castle over the winter holiday break.

18. Mircea Eliade, *Patterns in Comparative Religion* (New York: NY World Publishing, 1963), xiii.

19. Joseph Campbell, *Thou Art That: Transforming Religious Metaphor*, ed. Eugene Kennedy (Novato: New World Library/Joseph Campbell Foundation, 2001), 111.

20. Joseph Campbell, *The Masks of God: Occidental Mythology* (Novato: New World Library/Joseph Campbell Foundation, 2021), 464–67.

21. One popular fan theory behind the Dursleys' abuse of Harry hinges on the fact that Harry is one of Voldemort's horcruxes, because people tend to become ornery and temperamental when in the presence of a horcrux for a long period of time. This offers an interesting counter-narrative to Petunia's jealousy of her sister, suggesting something more deeply ominous about Voldemort's powers.

22. Joseph Campbell, *The Hero with a Thousand Faces* (Novato: New World Library/Joseph Campbell Foundation, 2008), 211.

23. Campbell identifies this temptation to a temptress. The equation of this character with a female character emphasizes Campbell's male-centric point of view, but also diminishes the role of women within the myth. c.f. Maria Tatar, *The Heroine with 1,001 Faces* (New York: Liveright Publishing Corporation, 2021).

24. Arnold Van Gannep, *The Rites of Passage,* trans. Monika B. Vizedom and Gabrielle L. Caffee (Chicago: University of Chicago Press, 1960), 2–3.

25. Victor Turner, *The Ritual Process: Structure and Anti-Structure* (New York: Aldine de Gruyter, 1969), 94–97.

26. C.G. Jung, *The Archetypes and the Collective Unconscious*, vol. 9, part 1 of *The Collected Works of C.G. Jung*, 2nd ed., trans. R.F.C. Hull (New York: Bollingen Foundation, 1969), 275.

27. C.G. Jung, *Mysterium Coniunctionis*, vol. 14 in *The Collected Works of C.G. Jung*, 2nd ed., trans. R.F.C. Hull (New York: Bollingen Foundation, 1970), 556.

28. J.K. Rowling, "Alchemy," Pottermore, August 10, 2015, https://www.wizardingworld.com/writing-by-jk-rowling/alchemy.

29. Jung's approach to alchemy has been accused within the Potter community of being un-spiritual [John Granger, *Unlocking Harry Potter: Five Keys for the Serious Reader* (Wayne: Zossima Press, 2007), 50–52]; however, it was actually Jung's spiritual encounter with Eastern mysticism through Chinese alchemy [C.G. Jung, *Memories, Dreams, Reflections*, ed. Aniela Jaffé, trans. Richard Winston and Clara Winston, rev. ed (New York: Vintage Books, 1959), 204] that helped provide him with the necessary language to support his work. From a Jungian point of view, individuation is more than a result of successful psychotherapy; it is the ability to transcend the ego.

30. *GoF*, 187.

31. Johannes Fabricius, *Alchemy: The Medieval Alchemists and Their Royal Art* (London: Diamond Books, 1994), 23.

32. Pottermore Wiki, s.v. "Veela," accessed August 14, 2021, pottermore.fandom.com/wiki/veela.

33. Edward F. Edinger, *Anatomy of the Psyche: Alchemical Symbolism in Psychotherapy* (La Salle: Open Court, 1985), 148.

34. Joseph Campbell, *The Masks of God: Creative Mythology* (New York: Penguin Compass, 1968), 119–21.

35. Campbell, *Hero*, 303.

36. Joseph Campbell, *The Power of Myth With Bill Moyers*, ed. Betty Sue Flowers (New York: Anchor, 1991), 53.

37. Moody's aid to Harry initially seems like that of a caring teacher taking Harry under his wing, until Barty Crouch Jr.'s identity is revealed and Harry learns that his "help" was actually to get him to the end of the tournament and to Voldemort without Dumbledore suspecting anything. This kind of betrayal from adults helps to mould Harry into someone skeptical of adults and their authority.

38. *GoF*, 343–5.

39. Jung, *Mysterium Coniunctionis*, 191.

40. James Hillman, *Alchemical Psychology* (Putnam: Spring Publications, 2014), 87.

41. Hillman, 88.

42. *PoA*, 107.

43. Fabricius, *Alchemy*, 94.

44. *ToBB*, 89.

45. *DH*, 698–701.

46. The *albedo*, according to Jung, is the "light of illumination." *Mysterium Coniunctionis,* 177.

47. *GoF*, 463.

48. C.G. Jung, *Psychology and Alchemy*, vol. 12. in *The Collective Works of C.G. Jung*, 2nd ed., trans. R.F.C.. Hull (New York: Bollingen Foundation, 1970), 235.

49. Edinger, 54; Fabricius, *Alchemy,* 32–33.

50. Jung, *Archetypes*, 5–6.

51. Jung, *Archetypes*, 70. I take issue with the understanding of the *anima* pioneered by Jung, because it assumes a binary gender with disregard to potential fluidity of attributes. As this quote emphasizes the emotional nature of the *anima*, my use of the concept divests the gender paradigm to focus on the importance of feelings. Because feelings are a complex experience, especially in the adolescent, having Harry have this emerging experience with *anima* is critical to his later success. In *OotP*, Harry grapples with the weight of the new emotions awoken during the Tri-Wizard Tournament, notably grief for the death of a peer.

52. Newt Scamander, *Fantastic Beasts and Where to Find Them* (London: Arthur A. Levine Books/Obscurus Books, 2001), 29.

53. J.K. Rowling, "Alchemy," Pottermore, August 10, 2015, https://www.wizardingworld.com/writing-by-jk-rowling/alchemy.

54. Rowling, "Alchemy."

55. Joseph Campbell, *Pathways to Bliss: Mythology and Personal Transformation* (Novato: New World Library/Joseph Campbell Foundation, 2004), xvi.

56. Jung, *Archetypes*, 387–90.

57. Campbell, *Hero*, 18.

58. Fabricius, *Alchemy*, 124.

59. Edinger, 78–79.

60. Jung, *Mysterium Coniunctionis*, 272.

61. He did attempt this kind of resurrect in *SS*, except that he failed to get the Sorcerer's Stone, which was destroyed after this event. *SS*, 297.

62. "Horcruxes: How Do They Work?" MuggleNet, last modified August 15, 2021, mugglenet.com/2012/03/horcruxes-how-do-they-work/.

63. Edinger, 58–59.

64. Jung, *Psychology and Alchemy*, 293–5.

65. C.G. Jung, *Aion: Researches into the Phenomenology of the Self*, vol. 9, part 2 of *The Collected Works of C.G. Jung* (New York: Bollingen Foundation, 1959), 223–6.

66. c.f., Chin-Ting Lee, "Keeping the Magic Alive: The Fandom and 'Harry Potter Experience' After the Franchise," in *From Here to Hogwarts: Essays on Potter Fandom and Fiction*, ed. Christopher E. Bell (Jefferson: McFarland & Company, 2016), 54–77; Bronwyn E. Beatty, "'It's a Natural Part of Us!' The Potter Generation Reflect on Their Ongoing Relationship with a Cultural Phenomenon," in *From Here to Hogwarts: Essays on Potter Fandom and Fiction*, ed. Christopher E. Bell (Jefferson: McFarland & Company, 2016), 99–122; Valerie Frankel, ed., *Fan Phenomena: Harry Potter* (Bristol: Intellect Books, 2019).

67. When one kills the witches, they kill the esoteric. Those who were accused of witchcraft were especially those who possessed knowledge beyond the comfortable Christian sphere.

68. *HBP*, 496–9.

Chapter 2

Toward a New Heroic

Just because he is a protagonist, does that make Harry Potter a hero?

Understanding the characters of a myth are as important, if not more so, than understanding the myth framework. Compelling and relatable characters become a gateway for the reader to make a personal connection by projecting innermost fantasies into how we read the characters. Having a variety of mythologies available, in the traditional sense, gives readers multiple opportunities to find those connections, which is why the representation of voices in the stories is important. When any member of a marginalized group is presented as a role less than that of the main hero, this reinforces existing cultural perceptions. The movement of myth into popular culture, as demonstrated by transmedia storytelling, allows for a variety of voices to contribute to the development and experience of a story, but they also allow for the development of different characters. In a franchised production, it is possible for multiple writers to contribute different characters. When those different characters are given central roles to the story, then they too play the part of a hero, even if they are not the central protagonist. This is the collective hero.

Millennials, more so than their predecessors, grew up surrounded by an early type of transmedia storytelling and hyperreality, with emphasis on consumption. Children's television shows and films of the 1980s had greater tie-in with their product lines than seen in previous decades. Entire seasons of shows were written around the toys that would be released at Christmas to drive the frenzy. But toys were only one part: characters could be found on lunchboxes, clothing, bathroom products, even breakfast cereal, candy, and ice cream. Fast food tie-ins had the added bonus of also creating brand loyalty to the fast-food chain; the happiness of the toy is hardwired to the food in the brain's nostalgia and comfort sectors.[1] As such, the equation between enjoyment and consumption defines this generation. Despite the extent to which millennials have faced roadblocks and economic hardship, the generation is nonetheless caught in a utopian optimism that connects the pleasure of childhood with the satisfaction of consumption.[2]

   This frames the mindset for Potter fans, who balance the complexity of "adulting" with the enjoyment of play.[3] Potter facilitates play, which is why the early fandom saw home-grown experiences that helped to fulfill fan cravings for more Potter. Reading and discussing the books brought a kind of enjoyment that felt both satisfying and reassuring, and fan interactions extended those feelings. Potter fans sought out other Potter fans through online spaces and local meetups, forming a community of like-minded individuals who, by the unwritten rules of the community, could be their avatar and live a piece of their identity that they felt necessary to hide from their immediate surroundings. They knew to live their truth, and their truth was Potter. One identity marker fans brought into the groups, and often led with, is their Hogwarts House.

THE SORTING HAT AND IDENTITY

Oh, you may not think I'm pretty.

But don't judge on what you see.

I'll eat myself if you can find

A smarter hat than me.

You can keep your bowlers black,

Your top hats sleek and tall,

For I'm the Hogwarts Sorting Hat

and I can cap them all.

There's nothing in your head

The Sorting Hat can't see.

So try me on and I will tell you

Where you ought to be.[4]

   When entering Hogwarts in their first year, all students are sorted into one of four houses that will become their primary community during their studies, often establishing the foundation of life-long friendships and relationships. There are four houses: Gryffindor, Hufflepuff, Ravenclaw, and Slytherin. The Sorting ceremony takes place the night of the start-of-term feast. The first-year students leave the train by boat and are sailed into the castle where they wait until called into the Great Hall for the Sorting. When each student is called, they sit on a stool and put the Sorting Hat on their head. "The Sorting

Hat," writes J.K. Rowling, "is one of the cleverest enchanted objects most witches and wizards will ever meet. It literally contains the intelligence of the four founders, can speak (through a rip near its brim) and is skilled at Legilimency, which enables it to look into the wearer's head and divine his or her capabilities or mood."[5] The Hat determines which house the wearer belongs in, and this decision is typically unquestioned and permanent. Harry, in fact, is the first student (that we know of) who challenged the Hat's decision and asked to not be sorted into a particular house.

Each house is associated with certain personality traits:

- Gryffindor: "You might belong in Gryffindor,/Where dwell the brave at heart./Their daring, nerve and chivalry/Set Gryffindor's apart."
- Hufflepuff: "You might belong in Hufflepuff,/Where they are just and loyal./These patient Hufflepuffs are true/and unafraid of toil."
- Ravenclaw: "Or yet in wise old Ravenclaw,/If you've a ready mind./Where those of wit and learning,/will always find their kind."
- Slytherin: "Or perhaps in Slytherin,/You'll make your real friends,/These cunning folks use any means/To achieve their ends."[6]

Initially, fans identified with the houses that they felt best described either their real-life selves or their online persona, or avatar. This allowed fans to quickly find their fellow housemates, but it also allowed fans to play out certain fantasies that lie within their shadow-selves to become someone within a new community of friends and to experiment with their identity during their transformative years. Ultimately, this helped fans learn just as much about themselves as it did about each other. If someone identifies with a certain house, it is safe to assume that they identify with certain personality traits. It is this last part that is significant to the impact of the Sorting Hat on identity formation. Through this simple act of self-sorting, young fans were able to reconcile their identities that might be divergent from the social norms of their community—and to take ownership of those identities and embrace themselves.

In the early days of Potter merchandizing, the only houses available in most products were Gryffindor or Slytherin, so they were the houses that most readers would sort themselves in to. Various Sorting quizzes appeared across the internet to help undecided fans pick a house, or to (hopefully) reinforce one's choice. One sorting, The Harry Potter Sorting Hat Personality Test,[7] was built around a personality type indicator, in which a person answers a series of questions, ranking attributes on a Likert scale from "Not at all" to "Extremely well." The 192 questions provide a comprehensive snapshot, similar to a Meyers-Briggs Type Indicator, and uses these answers to sort. Similar to Harry's Sorting, the final two questions on the quiz ask the respondent to give input on what they think their house should be or they would like to be.

As Harry Potter became more commercial, Sortings were developed as a key into the official fandom. One example is that of the Wizarding World, the website that subsumed the Pottermore website after the former's launch in 2019. One may join the fan club for free, and part of joining is a Sorting quiz, along with wand and patronus quizzes. In the early days of Pottermore, these Sortings bundled fans into certain groups that could earn house points as they completed the website's activities. At the end of a window, the house with the most points won the House Cup, which would unlock special content for members of that house. One downside is that the sorting quizzes sometimes sorted people into houses that conflicted with their self-selected houses.

Gryffindor

Gryffindors are known for their bravery and courage represented by the Lion, but this may not always manifest as their dominant trait. Harry embodies bravery and courage as a mode of survival, something he is taught by having to dodge Dudley and his school mates in the years leading to Hogwarts. Harry knew not to be on the receiving end of Dudley's fist, and realized that he could prod Dudley and run away faster than Dudley could keep up with him.[8]

Early in his journey, Harry is worried that he may have been sorted into the wrong house. He was so terrified of being sorted into Slytherin house that he begged the Sorting Hat to put him into any house *but* Slytherin. The Hat sees the possibilities in Harry that would make him a great Slytherin (perhaps due to the horcrux), but, in response to Harry's request, places him in Gryffindor. Harry carries this doubt into the Chamber of Secrets and his confrontation with Tom Riddle. In his moment of loyalty to Dumbledore, Fawkes the phoenix brings Harry both the Sorting Hat and the sword of Gryffindor, both having belonged to the founding father, Godric Gryffindor. As Dumbledore later tells Harry, it takes a true Gryffindor to pull that sword out of a hat.

Ron comes from a pure-blood wizarding family consisting mostly of Gryffindors. While it may seem inevitable for him to have bravery and courage, as the youngest son of a very large family, he has to rely on his courage to be able to step out of the shadows of his brothers. This need to establish his own identity comes from his willingness to join Harry on his adventures—which frequently involve breaking school rules or getting into situations that could lead to death. One notable moment in Ron's development is when he and Harry visit Hagrid's former pet, Aragog, and he is forced to face his fear of spiders in the Forbidden Forest. Ron has a paralyzing hear of spiders ever since his brother turned his teddy bear into one. Interviewing a spider that is the size of Hagrid's hut and being crowded by his swarm of children ignites a courage in Ron that gives him strength throughout the remainder of the series.

Another Gryffindor worth noting is Neville Longbottom. From the outset, Neville is characterized as a struggling student, serving a role in Gryffindor house as a magical klutz who can never seem to get anything right. He is on the receiving end of abuse from all fronts, even from his fellow Gryffindors and teachers, for being "too stupid." In his first year, he shares a story of how his family was convinced he might be a squib until he was dropped out of a window and bounced when he hit the ground.[9] Yet, Neville's parents were Aurors who fought bravely in the second wizarding war and were tortured into insanity by the Lestranges. That generational disconnect weighs heavily on his shoulders throughout his tenure at Hogwarts, and he locks himself into his own insecurities about his abilities. However, he shines periodically as a hero, and it becomes apparent that Neville has a great deal of courage but that it may take him a little longer to be able to manifest it. This is especially significant because Neville shares the same birth month as Harry, meaning he just as easily could have been the receiver of the Prophecy had Voldemort realized he had choices.

While the exploits of Gryffindor students often focus on Harry and his male peers, the strongest women in the series also come from Gryffindor house. Not only are they powerful and smart, but they are also willing to stand firmly behind their beliefs and values, regardless of what their friends may say. Hermione regularly proves to be one of the smartest students in the school, but how she uses her intellect is what sets her apart from Ravenclaw. While she has the ability to recall information and transfer it to new situations, she is able to humanize it in a way that keeps her grounded, especially when she is explaining things to Harry and Ron, similar to a good teacher presenting a difficult subject.

Hufflepuff

Of the four houses, Hufflepuff is held in lowest regard. Despite being fiercely loyal, Hufflepuffs are not the students who are often recognized for their talents. They have even received the perception of being a "lot o' duffers."[10] As such, they are not featured heavily throughout the books other than as side characters. The truth is that Hufflepuffs are the most fiercely loyal of the four houses and are accepting of everyone. The Hufflepuff common room is next to the school kitchens, connecting the Hufflepuffs to warmness and hospitality. Rowling has commented that Hufflepuff is her favorite house. During the Battle of Hogwarts, the

Hufflepuffs, virtually to a person, stay—as do the Gryffindors. Now the Gryffindors comprise a lot of foolhardy and show-offy people. . . . You know, there's bravery and there's also showboating, and sometimes the two go together. The Hufflepuffs stayed for a different reason. They weren't trying to show off, they weren't being reckless. That's the essence of Hufflepuff House.[11]

The pinnacle Hufflepuff in the series is Cedric Diggory. When he is first introduced in *PoA*, he is playing seeker and beats Harry in Quidditch. His initial reaction is to try to concede the win, because Harry had been distracted by the Dementors. Nonetheless, the win stood, and was celebrated as one of Hufflepuff's wins. Even Cedric's father, Amos, repeats the praise in *GoF* in front of Harry.[12]

Cedric is selected as the rightful Hogwarts champion for the Tri-Wizard Tournament. When Harry is also selected as a champion, Hufflepuff House is outraged, feeling that Harry essentially stole Cedric's victory, "a feeling exacerbated, perhaps, by the fact that Hufflepuff House rarely got any glory, and Cedric was one of the few who had ever given them any."[13] This was their time to be in the spotlight, and it ultimately had to be shared with Harry. Initially, Cedric echoes their frustration, but changes his tune after the first task when he realizes the true complexity of the tournament. When the time comes, at the center of the maze in the Third Task, the two boys get to the cup at the same time and bicker about who should take it and the win. Harry is attracted to the idea of winning, but also has enough respect for Cedric to want him to have his part in the win, prompting him suggest that they both take it—either way, Hogwarts wins.[14]

The other famous Hufflepuff is Newt Scamander. Throughout the *Fantastic Beasts* films, Scamander is painted as someone who does not fit easily within the wizarding world and is very awkward when he has to deal with people. He is clearly more comfortable with his creatures, no matter how big, small, or fierce. Scamander demonstrates his ability to remain composed in the face of an angry beast when trying to calm down Credence when he is in his Obscurus form, which helps get him under control long enough to stop rampaging through the New York subway.

When faced with a boggart in his Defense Against the Dark Arts class with Dumbledore, Scamander's fear is working in an office, and Dumbledore recognizes that Scamander is more likely to put his moral principles ahead of any social mores, which helps him develop a deeply rooted empathy for those around him, especially Muggles (No-Maj in the United States) like Jacob Kowalski, who did not have the advantage over others. Leta Lestrange, school friend and his brother's fiancée, sums him up succinctly, when she laments, "Oh, Newt. You never met a monster you couldn't love."[15]

Ravenclaw

"Hmm . . . what do you think, Harry?" said Luna, looking thoughtful.

"What? Isn't there a password?"

"Oh, no, you've got to answer a question," said Luna.

"What if you get it wrong?"

"Well, you have to wait for somebody who gets it right," said Luna. "That way you learn, you see?"[16]

The distinguishing trait of the Ravenclaw house is wisdom. This is an important distinction between why Hermione, the smartest kid in her grade, is not sorted into Ravenclaw. True wisdom is not about being smart and being able to transfer knowledge into other areas, something Hermione is expert at doing. Rather, wisdom comes from being able to see the world differently and being inquisitive enough to be open to the possibilities. This is best exemplified by Luna Lovegood, whom Rowling describes as the "anti-Hermione" when comparing Luna's free spirit with Hermione's common sense and rationalism.[17]

Luna is introduced in *OotP*, when the trio meet her on the way to Hogwarts. She is sitting in a corner seat wearing funny glasses and reading a magazine upside down. The magazine, *The Quibbler*, is known in the wizarding world for being of questionable repute. For instance, when they meet her, Luna is reading about wrackspurts (invisible creatures that float through one's ears and make the brain go fuzzy) and the glasses are to help her see them. Hermione immediately scoffs at this idea, because wrackspurts do not exist. Luna counters her skepticism with the insistence that they do. The main element to this argument is not whether Luna actually believes in the wrackspurts, but rather that she is open to the possibility that they might exist, and she is not going to discount it based on common knowledge.

Her father is the editor of *The Quibbler*, which has a reputation of printing stories about conspiracy theories, invisible animals, or tabloid speculation, and many characters consider it rubbish or a "lunatic rag."[18] Similar to Luna, Xenophilius Lovegood sees the world uncharacteristically and is recognized as an eccentric. He reveals his perspective in a dialog with Hermione:

Hermione: "I mean, you could claim that *anything's* real if the only basis for believing in it is that nobody's *proved* it doesn't exist!"

Xenophilius: "Yes, you could. I am glad to see that you are opening your mind a little."[19]

While Rowling does suggest that, upon entering adulthood, Luna came to recognize that many of her father's creatures were not real,[20] it is Xenophilius's reductionist philosophy and his persistent quest for the truth that characterizes Ravenclaw (minus his eccentricities).

Luna's wisdom also translates into a deep, authentic kindness. Even though she is made fun of at school, she never internalizes the comments and behaviors, such as when other students hide her possessions, and she has to find them before the end of the school year. She becomes a valuable character to Harry's journey, especially when she helps Harry better understand his own traumas, like when she validates the thestrals in *OotP*. Harry is now able to see these creatures because he witnessed death. Rowling here highlights that witnessing death changes one's perceptions and can make previously invisible things become visible. Harry is scared by this possibility, but Luna assures him that it is a perfectly normal part of the experience. She brings this same perspective to Dumbledore's and Dobby's funerals, always seeming to know the right thing to say and do.[21]

Slytherin

> "There's not a single witch or wizard who went bad who wasn't in Slytherin."
>
> —Hagrid[22]

As Hagrid's quote demonstrates, the Slytherins have a reputation of being dark wizards, and this is Harry's, and thus the reader's, first perception of the house, making it very easy to assume that all Slytherins are dark wizards. This is reinforced by the type of Slytherins represented throughout the series. For instance, Draco Malfoy and his friends, Crabbe and Goyle, are bullies more than they are dark wizards, who nonetheless reinforce Gryffindor prejudice of the house. Rowling addresses this perception on Pottermore, noting that the other houses also produced dark wizards.[23] One characteristic that dominates the perception of Slytherins is that they are mostly pureblood from established wizarding families, which becomes an important point in understanding the political clout they have over the Ministry, especially the Malfoys and Lestranges. More than anything, this is enough to prompt Harry to ask the Sorting Hat to not put him in Slytherin.

Slytherin characteristics include ambition and a potential for greatness. This gives them a drive to push through a challenge, one way or another (even if it involves bribery), to achieve their end goals. On Pottermore, Rowling sets up the dichotomy between Slytherin and Gryffindor, saying that the latter are "wannabe Slytherins,"[24] but they are set apart by the way their ambition manifests. Within Slytherin characteristics, there is a dedication to hard work so that they can justify earning their greatness. While some are simply born with the opportunity to be great, this work ethic demonstrates their ambitious commitments when compared to, for example, Gryffindors, who seem to rely on natural talent and sheer luck.

The fact remains, though, that Salazar Slytherin felt that magical people were naturally superior to those who lack magical abilities making Slytherin House the one that readers love to hate. When founding the school, he valued those who recognized the power of magic and were ambitious enough to use it. However, he wanted to exclude Muggle-borns, which led to his feud with Gryffindor and eventual departure.[25] This is compounded by the myth of the Heir of Slytherin being the only one to have the ability to open the Chamber of Secrets and control the monster inside (a basilisk, aligned with the snake symbolism of the house) to target Muggles. Tom Riddle resonates with this myth as a descendent of Slytherin and uses this myth to justify his power as his legacy and thus innate right.

Notable Slytherins include Severus Snape, Harry's potions teacher; Draco Malfoy, Harry's nemesis; and most of the Death Eaters and their families mentioned throughout the books. A couple, however, demonstrate that the dark wizard reputation is not an absolute: Regulus Black and Albus Potter.

The Black family is another one of the old wizarding families, with connections to the Lestranges and Malfoys. Sirius was sorted into Gryffindor, and effectively disowned by his family.[26] Regulus, however, remained devoted and even joined the Death Eaters at a young age.[27] After his family's house-elf, Kreacher, told Regulus about Voldemort's locket after helping Voldemort test the locket's defenses, Regulus, who had already been doubting the Death Eaters, determined to go after the locket himself with Kreacher's help. They swapped the locket with a fake, and Kreacher was ordered to keep the original safe. Regulus, unfortunately, died in the process.[28] As far as Sirius knew, his brother betrayed Voldemort and was executed as punishment. His opinion of his brother may have been different had he known he was helping the cause of defeating Voldemort.

Albus Potter is introduced in the epilogue at the end of *DH*, as he goes to board the Hogwarts Express for his first trip to school. He is nervous about going, and Harry reassures him that there is nothing to be afraid of: "'Albus Severus,' Harry said quietly [. . .] 'you were named for two headmasters of Hogwarts. One of them was a Slytherin and he was probably the bravest man I ever knew.'"[29] Additionally, Harry tells Albus that he can choose his house during the Sorting, as Harry did. Albus is sorted into Slytherin, which does cause some tension between father and son, making the arc in *CC* as much about Harry coming to peace with his own experience of Slytherins. What makes Albus a potent character is his relationship with Scorpius Malfoy, a fellow Slytherin.[30] The two boys become best friends, in a complete opposite of the relationship of their fathers. Much of the story is written around the two of them developing their friendship and struggling with fitting in. In an attempt to change his fate, Albus and Scorpius launch a plot meant to go back in time and rescue Cedric Diggory. This fails—Cedric was still dead—and created an alternative timeline. They do eventually correct the timeline but gain the attention of Delphi who wants to go to the time when Harry first defeated Voldemort as a baby so she can see her father. While fans would have loved to see more of a relationship develop between the two boys,[31] they nonetheless embrace the ambition and determination of Slytherin, bringing Slytherin into a new light.

House Unity

Gryffindor remains one of the more popular houses of the *Harry Potter* series. In part because, like Slytherin, it is the one most central to the series and thus easy to identify with. Even merchandising campaigns in the early years focused on Gryffindor or Slytherin. This consumer narrative pits good guys (Gryffindor) against bad guys (Slytherin), reinforcing the popular wartime binary in the aftermath of 9/11, when "us versus them" serves as a central propaganda strategy in order to maintain the support of the people. So as the *Harry Potter* phenomenon was picking up steam, its readers (especially the older ones) experienced a cultural need for a hero who can combat evil. Since Voldemort was a Slytherin, the books suggest, and because Harry's Slytherin peers are abhorrent, then the heroic good versus evil justifies an identity against a known enemy from whom Harry is the savior. Rowling plays with this in later books of the series after the Prophecy in *OotP* reveals that Harry was chosen by Voldemort to be his undoing. Harry becomes the Chosen One throughout the school and struggles with the responsibility this requires of him. Indeed, as the later books were released and the initial shock of 9/11 wore off, the idea of a clear line between good versus evil began to blur, elevating the imagery of the collective hero. In *OotP*, the trio are joined by Ginny, Luna, and Neville to go to the Ministry. In *HBP* and *DH*, Harry is joined by teachers and students to protect the school from the Death Eaters.

The Battle of Hogwarts marks a significant shift in house identity, expanding beyond exclusive membership to houses to embracing the entire school community. Rather than the single house crest, it became more common to see more "house unity" logos—the Hogwarts crest emblazoned on rainbow or purple things—alongside the traditional house items. This sends a clear message from the fan community about their value of inclusivity and acceptance.

Inclusivity refers to notion that all people and creatures deserve to belong in a social group. As a sort of social contract, groups agree to accept members by embracing their commonalities rather than focusing on their differences, which frequently leads to vitriol, disagreement, and hate. The Slytherins reflect these social mores within the walls of Hogwarts. Their emphasis on purity and wealth gives them a reason not to befriend members of different social classes. Before either boy is sorted and while they are having their robe fittings, Malfoy refers to "the other sort" and remarks that he would leave school if he was sorted into Hufflepuff.[32] This is not to separate Slytherin from the typical teenage cliques that develop in schools, with the added layer of the houses reinforcing their boundaries. Harry's story includes openness to fellow classmates that might otherwise not "fit in," such as Luna or Neville, and remains humble about his celebrity, which helps him form the relationships he does.

Rowling later reveals that Harry is descended from one of the oldest wizarding families, the Peverell family, which is the same family featured in Beedle the Bard's "Tale of the Three Brothers." While Malfoy may not have this context even with his father's deep knowledge of pure-blood wizarding families, those, such as Xenophilius Lovegood, would likely have uncovered the connection in their pursuit of the Deathly Hallows. Rowling implies at points throughout the series that Dumbledore, who researched the Hallows heavily during his friendship with Grindelwald, recognized that connection, leading him to ask James Potter if he could borrow the invisibility cloak, which is keeps in his possession until Harry comes to Hogwarts.

HARRY POTTER AND THE NEW HERO ARCHETYPE

An archetype is a universal theme or image that appears in mythology all over the world, but how it appears varies by cultural and individual interpretation. As the archetypes appear in myths, they are altered by culture, being limited or expanded upon depending on the nature of the culture, the environment, and the composition of its members. In literature, the author is the archetype interpreter, and the archetypal images they create must resonate with an audience for the work to be successful. Jung introduced the idea of archetypes as dream symbolism, connecting therapy with the interpretation of dreams that can be confusing. Thus, the therapist becomes the interpreter for an individual to help them unravel the symbols of their personal experience. Archetypes manifest differently depending on cultural patterns and the lens of interpretation. For example, a literary lens sees archetypes in different character types, such as the hero, orphan, or wise elder. The psychotherapist works with three primary archetypes, the *anima/animus*, shadow, and self, within which characters can emerge. Arguably, because of Harry's success as a mythic epic, it stands to reason that the archetypal resonance of the characters deepens that connection as both frameworks manifest throughout the series.

In his treatise on soul-making through archetypal psychology, James Hillman offers methods of seeing and applying archetypes to one's life. He suggests that archetypes are "the *deepest patterns of psychic functioning*, the roots of the soul governing the perspectives we have of ourselves and the world."[33] By this model, archetypes are held to be any universal pattern, regardless of the degree of sacred quality it possesses. They are symbolic metaphors that point beyond the normal framework of ego-consciousness, and they affect the individual on a deeply personal, emotional level. Hillman goes so far as to compare an archetype with a god in a generic, sacred sense.[34] While Harry Potter does not resemble a god in any traditional sense of the term, one could ascribe god-like energy to the franchise in reaction to the fan response. Hillman presents four categories of archetypal re-visioning: personifying, pathologizing, dehumanizing, and psychologizing.[35]

Personifying "implies a human being who creates Gods in human likeness much as an author creates characters out of his own personality" and is the process of naming the archetype.[36] Hillman relates this to the naming of experiences and feelings, to giving them a capitalized name. In the world of Harry Potter, archetypal evil is characterized by Voldemort, signifying a power-hungry, dark wizard who utilizes all avenues needed to accomplish his goals and inspires fear in anyone who is seen as opposing him. The fear of his very name creates a fear culture around it, such that many wizards refer to him as He-Who-Must-Not-Be-Named. Even Death Eaters will refer to him as the Dark Lord. Harry is one of the few in the wizarding world who is not afraid to speak Voldemort's name. Dumbledore teaches Harry and the reader that the fear of using the name incites fear of the thing. In fearing to use the name—to personify the archetype—the individual is essentially avoiding the archetype itself, creating a barrier of fear around it. This is applicable to all archetypes, both positive and negative. Giving the archetype a name and an image brings it to a level with which the individual can identify with making it represent the observable universe.

Psychologizing is particularly helpful for the readers of *Harry Potter* who get caught in the throes of mythopoetic arrest, or the passionate feeling the books garner that established the fandom. What is missing is the use of creative energy to create new myths: to live out one's personal myth as inspired by the archetypes in *Harry Potter* rather than through those archetypes. Hillman describes psychologizing as mythologizing or as "seeing through," "a process of deliteralizing and a search for the imaginal in the heart of things by means of ideas."[37] There is plenty of discussion in the fandom of the "whats" of

Harry Potter, but the dialogue falters at the "hows" and "whys" that refer to the reasons behind the significance of the series and its popularity. Whether it is through the methods of archetypal psychology, comparative mythology, or any other approach, the "seeing through" of the myth is the most crucial to its continuation, which is essential for a story to be labeled as a myth and not just a really popular story.[38] The activities of Fandom Forward, discussed in a later chapter, is an example of "seeing through." Inspired by the themes within the books, the activist group promotes spreading love and consciousness around key issues impacting marginalized groups. They are not identifying with any particular character or event within the series but bringing in and calling forth the archetypal energy from inside the organization.

Pathologizing is the psyche's reaction to an experience or behavior that manifests as an "illness, morbidity, disorder, abnormality, and suffering."[39] It follows a religious and/or medical model of cause and effect: because of "a," then "b": "We suffer, it has been customary to say, because we are either sick or sinful, and the cure of our suffering calls for either science or faith" to explain what is ailing the individual, to give it a simple, straightforward explanation with a simple, straightforward cure.[40] Both of these models "imply that pathologizing is wrong."[41] The discovery of this correlation between archetypal unrest and physical malady is the socio-psychological bridge between the onset of the problem and the path to a new enlightenment and archetypal connection.

The physicality of pathologizing is less relevant to *Harry Potter* than the tradition that shuns it. Hillman argues that pathologizing is the model for why monotheism is dangerous to the psyche, because, like science, it does not attend to the complex needs of the psyche through its simple, straight-forward explanation. Monotheism places a very thick, limited frame around archetypes and their ability to influence the psyche. In his world, Harry, as the archetypal hero, challenges the assumptions held by the Ministry of Magic regarding Voldemort and the nature of evil. The Ministry, tied to the steadfast monotheistic point of view that Voldemort was defeated the night Harry's parents died, ignore all of the signs of his return. This piece of plot demonstrates the potential damage that can come from a closed mind, or a limited point of view. Like Hillman, Harry challenges the monotheistic mentality, or "Muggle mindset,"[42] embedded in the Western tradition. To combat the Muggle mind-set means to see the people of the world as equal with equal rights, regardless of religious creed, race, gender, or culture. In other words, to break out of the monotheism that limits perspectives toward global and psychological affairs.

Furthermore, Hillman calls for a return to a polytheistic mindset, idealized by the ancient Greeks and their pantheon of gods,[43] seeing them as elements of a "nonagnostic psychology"[44] that describes various behaviors, emotions, experiences, and anything else that could not be explained by immediate observation. The monotheistic mindset birthed the modern approaches to science that strive to identify the explanation behind everything, reducing the need to accomplish the same explanation through imaginal practices. Science overshadows the imagination, evidenced in the works of Joseph Campbell, C.G. Jung, and their protégés struggling to recognize modern experiences of myth, mythic thinking, and mythic imagination. Hillman's reliance on the Greek pantheon demonstrates how studying the myths assists in identifying their psychic power, but they are exemplars rather than the guiding framework. The American mind needs an entirely new approach and library of archetypal images, because the ancient ones do not resonate with the utopian ideal foundational to the country's myths. So, while the archetypes Hillman is identifying are idealized within Greek mythology, they also manifest in various places throughout popular culture in other ways relevant to the American ethos.

The Collective Hero

As introduced earlier, Harry is part of an emergent hero type: the collective hero. This hero defies the definitions of hero that reduce this character to a central protagonist on a journey. Archetypal Harry is three-faced, like a triple goddess, because there is nothing about his journey that could have been accomplished without Hermione or Ron. Hermione is his brains; Ron is his grit. The two of them together are strong strategists, which always helps Harry formulate his plans. Without the two of them, Harry would have likely been lost early in the journey.

Becoming Ron

Harry's curiosity of the wizarding world sets his quest in motion. One of his first negative experiences is his encounter with Draco Malfoy during their robe fitting. Because Harry is new to the magical world, he is not familiar with the social hierarchies that define the culture. He learns about these prejudices from Ron, who is constantly berated by Malfoy for coming from a poor family who "has more kids than they can afford."[45] Malfoy measures relationships based on their material worth. This materiality is indoctrinated to him from his parents, who are descended from some of the oldest wizarding families, implying that there is a direct link between the "purity" of the family's bloodline and their wealth. Indeed, Malfoy's ancestry is linked to other dark wizards such as his aunt, Bellatrix Lestrange, and cousins, the Black family. Sirius Black, Harry's godfather, was shunned by the family because he chose a different path than one defined by material worth. The Weasley family also stems from old wizarding bloodlines, but they chose to stray from the materiality of the social classes to instead embrace a humanism that is welcoming of Muggles. This dichotomy is woven throughout the series: the cold-hearted, wealthy wizards who are full of prejudice are also dark wizards and Death Eaters, while the warm, loving wizards have chosen love over wealth, and established anti-Voldemort opposition movements, such as the Order of the Phoenix, simply because it is the right thing to do in the interest of the wizarding community. Although Harry grew up in a family that showered their son with all the materials he wanted, he was never given the same consideration, affecting his relationship with wealth. He grew up watching Dudley's spirit corrupted by the way his parents supported his materiality.[46]

Harry inherits a Gringott's vault full (not overflowing) of the wealth acquired by his parents. There is no backstory of the vault: It is not clear how the money was earned or inherited, if it accrued interest over Harry's lifetime, or if there were contributions along the way from fellow Order of the Phoenix members (notably Dumbledore) wanting to make sure that Harry would be taken care of when he reenters the wizarding world. Nonetheless, he is excited to discover the vault, because it is the first time that he experiences something that is solely his. Even one of his first thoughts was about the Dursleys: "All Harry's—it was incredible. The Dursleys couldn't have known about this or they'd have had it from him faster than blinking. How often had they complained how much Harry cost them to keep? And all the time there had been a small fortune belonging to him, buried deep under London."[47] When he goes shopping for his school supplies, he is tempted to get the more expensive things, but Hagrid helps guide him toward what is actually needed for school. When the trolly comes by on the Hogwarts Express, Harry seizes on the opportunity to share with Ron and buys a lot of treats. He does this not to boast to Ron that he has the money to splurge, but because this is the first time has something worth sharing, this act of companionship he never experienced with the Dursleys helps forge his friendship with Ron. His eleven-year-old self is still in awe about his escape from the Dursleys and entry into the wizarding world that he does not think twice about buying treats from the trolly on the Hogwarts Express.[48]

Ron, in turn, accepts the gifts of Harry's friendship, because, as the sixth son in a family of seven children, he is often overshadowed by his brothers, who have already done everything there is to do at Hogwarts. He is also followed by a sister, who outshines him because his mother wanted a daughter.[49] From Harry, Ron feels truly seen for the first time as himself, and not as "just another Weasley." Once Ron gets over the celebrity-shock of meeting the infamous Harry Potter, he too sees Harry as himself. This creates an unbreakable brotherhood early in archetypal Harry's journey that, despite a few growing pains, sustains Harry even in his darkest hours.

Becoming Hermione

Hermione comes into the narrative after the Troll Incident on Halloween of their first year together. They were not expecting to become friends. Hermione, also coming from the Muggle world, surrounds herself with knowledge and information in her efforts to figure out the wizarding world and carve herself a place in it. In their first couple months at school, Hermione did not yet have the type of compassion and social skills that come from children interacting with each other, suggesting that her precociousness is part of her normal experience and not an identity she adopted when coming to Hogwarts. Because of Rowling's Harry-centric writing, little is known about how the Hogwarts girls accepted her, especially those in her dormitory, but one can surmise from the scene where Ron outwardly complains about her that she perhaps was not having an easy time acclimating to the school. Ron, here, is frustrated at an experience in class where he is corrected and upstaged by Hermione's showboating: "'It's no wonder no one can stand her,' he said to Harry as they pushed their way into the crowded corridor, 'she's a nightmare, honestly.'"[50] Harry feels his frustration, but also recognizes Hermione's feelings are hurt as she runs past them. In a way, this resonates with Harry's experience of being ostracized and the feelings he experienced himself at his Muggle schools where most kids stayed away from them because they were afraid of Dudley more than interested in Harry. When Professor Quirrell rushes into the dining hall to announce the troll, Harry is the first to think of Hermione, remembering that their classmates said she was in the girl's toilet. Although Ron briefly questions Harry's heroics, he does recognize that it would be his fault if anything happened to Hermione and they go find her. Of course, they encounter the troll and use their collective ingenuity to rescue her. After their rescue, the trio is cemented. As Rowling writes, "There are some things you can't share without ending up liking each other, and knocking out a twelve-foot mountain troll is one of them."[51] After that event, the three become inseparable, and develop a shared commitment in solving the mystery of Nicolas Flamel and the Sorcerer's Stone. Collectively, they piece together the clues. Hermione relies on the books in the library, and Ron relies on his experience and information he already has. Ron is not afraid to mirror Harry's speculation, but his knowledge of the wizarding world does help close some gaps in Harry's and Hermione's assumed knowledge. Harry is convinced that Snape is the culprit looking for the Stone, and the three of them commit to stopping him from getting it.

The guardian trials set up to protect the Sorcerer's Stone require the three children using their collective skills and knowledge, even though it is ultimately Harry who faces the final task alone. This is a common feature of the books—that the three kids work together to get to the culmination of that book's story arc/hero's journey but leave Harry to face the final task alone. While, following Campbell's character catalog, this would identify Ron and Hermione as Magical Helpers who are there to support Harry along the way. They do more than just help Harry get to that final place; they become a part of him and his identity. It is his role within the trio to confront Voldemort, just as it is for Hermione to research and Ron to strategize. It is Voldemort who separates Harry, firmly believing in their one-on-one confrontation for him to enact his revenge. Harry just as easily could have brought Ron and Hermione into each battle. Magical Helpers may become close friends, but they do not become part of the hero's self-concept, such that they are enmeshed in his psyche and form his family.

Becoming Archetypal Harry

Ron and Hermione act as two halves to Harry's conscience, and together they help Harry learn how to make good decisions. Ron acts as the "bad conscience," egging Harry to break the rules, and Hermione acts as the "good conscience," trying to keep both boys in line. At the close of the sixth book, Ron and Hermione vow to accompany Harry to all ends of the earth to defeat Voldemort, despite Harry's insistence that he must go on his own. Similarly, he plays this role with each of them too, especially when they are having disagreements. Each of the children becomes the glue that holds the group together as they go through their growing pangs when they start showing interest in other boys and girls. As a group of three, if they want to stay friends, they have to figure out how to work it out, making this a stronger bond than, for example, a group of four, which can split apart because the in-fighting does not require resolution.

This mirrors Hillman's fourth category of archetypal re-visioning, dehumanizing. In essence, to dehumanize archetypes is to divest them from any cultural anchors, such as religion or science, because they are weighed down by literalism.[52] They become "good" or "bad" and shape our morals and values. They also become monochromatic. The hero invokes a specific character type, for instance, and it becomes the primary manifestation of that archetype throughout a culture's mythology. By adopting the polytheistic mindset, Hillman acknowledges that there are multiple parts to the human psyche that are not linear nor unilateral. What this also allows is for the imagination to organize archetypal images to the individual. "If human nature is a composition of multiple psychic persons who reflect the persons in myths," he writes, "then the experiencer is also in a myth. He or she is not one but many, a flux of vicissitudes."[53] Then, in order for the archetypal potency of Harry Potter to work, the archetypal images of the franchise must also be seen in multiplicity. Harry, Ron, and Hermione become a single hero.

By recognizing that they are a collective when they agree to go on the hor-crux hunt together, they realize that it is not possible to return to the Muggle world, which is the realm of the literal. At the start of *DH*, both Harry and Hermione depart the Muggle world for the last time. Harry sheds his last relationships to it when he says his final goodbye to the Dursleys. Canon does not give us a sense of him maintaining a relationship with them after he leaves but does suggest that he made at least some peace with Dudley.[54] Hermione also makes the same sacrifice, going one step further to wipe memories of her from her parents, worried that they could be used as pawns by the Death Eaters to find Harry. They choose each other, highlighting the fact that they are all faces of the same hero who just happens to be named Harry Potter. This veering from the hero's journey sets a model for countless millennials to have the courage to leave their toxic family and build their own—that the love of one's constructed family is just as valid and transcendental as blood families. Harry's constructed family is in contrast to Malfoy's blood family, when we see the next generation getting onto the Hogwarts Express during the epilogue of *DH*. Malfoy's son is similarly stiff, albeit a smidge less so, than his parents, whereas the children of Harry, Hermione, Ron, and Ginny are a motley crew of cousins who are each other's best friends.

The Role of the Adults

The adults in *Harry Potter* are largely ineffectual. While they are functional and rise to the occasion for the good of the children, they bear the burden of their own experiences as youths, as adults tend to do, and project these on to the children. Many of the adults in the immediate sphere of influence of Harry and his classmates were still in identity formation when impacted by Voldemort's first wave of power, a parallel to millennials who were like-wise in identify formation when 9/11 occurred. They default to a kind of single-mindedness that, as Erik Erikson points out, comes from wanting to never face the anxieties of their youth again.[55] When the cycle repeats with the new generations, these adults know what to do, but struggle to approach the situation differently.

Additionally, they rely on Harry to be the problem-solver, but only give him part of the information he needs to actually succeed against Voldemort. As such, he has to define his path by himself. It is for this reason that he needs to have his friends, Ron and Hermione, as well as the rest of his peers to fill in the gaps of their understanding. In many ways, this proves useful, because they access information that the adults in their lives assume that they should not have access to or do not need to know simply because they are children.

The adults in Harry Potter carry unspoken trauma and wily attitudes toward the world. Not only is the previous war with Voldemort on everyone's mind, but the first conflict with Grindelwald still resonates in the consciousness. War has an impact on a society and its ability to heal. The 20th century experienced wars in such a way that each successive generation was impacted by a new war, which, arguably, was a scaffold off the previous, compounding the layers of anxiety and trauma until, finally, someone has enough. The wizarding world divide between the adults and students extends beyond the expected generational gap, but also in terms of the depth of willingness to embrace the collectivity of the new generation, a resonate echo to the outside culture, itself experiencing generational conflict as millennials entered the workforce. Essentially, this younger generation finally had enough.

Since the series is Potter-centric, Harry's views of the adults around him influences their perception. The different types of adult each have a unique opportunity to impact him, positively or negatively; rarely both together.

Mother

James and Lily Potter represent the ideal father and mother for their orphaned son. They died in a surprise attack protecting Harry from Voldemort when he was only a year old, locking their memory into a specific point in time. When Harry learns the truth of their death, it is with glowing respect and admiration for their heroism. He also finds substitute parents in Arthur and Molly Weasley, the latter feeling especially motherly toward Harry in the absence of his actual parents. Because he never had solid parenting himself, the only way Harry really understands positive parenting is when he experiences the warmth and inclusion with the Weasley family. Molly Weasley made him a Weasley sweater for Christmas in their first year, and it was the first time Harry received presents. The gift both tagged him into the Weasley family, but it also gave him a chance to experience parental warmth.

Throughout the series, Harry learns more details about his parents and, as he comes into maturity, realizes that the archetypal parent must be different than the reality of the parents. This allows him to see their vulnerabilities, which deepens their relationship and helps inform his own direction as a parent. Parent characters reflect the role of parents in society and conflating the image with the reality can create a distortion of exceptions in the parent-child relationship. James and Lily play the role of being Harry's image of parent, much like a fictional character can inform the image of the real parent, mirroring the challenge the projection ultimately plays over time.[56] In order for Harry to move ahead in the journey, he has to release his parents. Because Harry holds his parents in such high regard, especially since they died protecting him, de-humanizing their ideal is crucial as he gets older and learns more about them. Eventually, Harry realizes he loves his parents despite all their faults. For *Harry Potter* readers, Harry's reconciliation resonates with anyone who has experienced the loss of a parent by death or by divorce. Harry helps demonstrate the importance of separating parents from the projection. As soon as Harry learns this, he is able to use his own voice and act beyond the expectations his parents' memory forces on him, and, thus, he is able to say goodbye when they appear out of the Resurrection Stone.

Because Harry is constantly forced to redefine the archetypes versus the actual people, *Harry Potter* acts as a model for the process of reconnecting to and re-identifying archetypes of the mother and father. What was once foundational to the development of children, modern society has upended the role of the parent and modified the structure of parenting such that it is easy to blame the faults of society on the parent, especially the mother. The lack of these particular archetypes, or, rather, perhaps more accurately their weak presence in American society, has enabled blaming several problems unique to the modern era on failed parenting, ranging from a breakdown of community and communication, to the various "crises" that upset the flow of society.[57]

Molly Weasley is a present parent, meaning she is allowed to be rugged and non-idyllic. She comes across frenzied and frazzled when she appears in the books, frequently because she is juggling her children and the tasks she is doing. Although she is written around stereotypical stay-at-home mother behavior (attending the children, cooking, and cleaning), for Harry, she is the emotional support he needs from a parent. In particular, Molly is equated with home and the loving (albeit cramped) Burrow. When Harry first visits the Burrow, Ron is embarrassed about how small the house is, but to Harry, it is perfect[58]—to be in a caring home is more welcoming than being in a sterile, larger home, such as the Dursleys.

In contrast, Petunia Dursley keeps a clean and orderly home, with nothing out of the ordinary. She keeps Harry safe, but does not nurture him in any sort of way. In looking at her relationship to Dudley, one might question whether she is actually capable of nurture at all. Throughout the series, the scenes involving Dudley emphasize his weight and equate it with the extent he is spoiled. Petunia consistently feeds him a mix of food and things—until Harry moves into the spare bedroom that Dudley used as storage space for the broken or forgotten toys that no longer fit in his room. In contrast to Molly, Petunia is a terrible mother, more interested in status and gossip, and infantilizing her son to keep him dependent on her as long as possible. Dumbledore, who left a letter with Harry the night he arrived at Privet Drive asking Petunia to raise Harry as her own, points this out when he picks up Harry at the start of *HBP*:

> "You have never treated Harry as a son. He has known nothing but neglect and often cruelty at your hands. The best that can be said is that he has at least

escaped the appalling damage you have inflicted upon the unfortunate boy sitting between you."

Both Aunt Petunia and Uncle Vernon looked around instinctively, as though looking to see someone other than Dudley squeeze between them.

"Us—mistreat Dudders? What d'you—?" began Uncle Vernon.[59]

Dumbledore, ever the voice of truth in the series, points out something that has been seeded as a truth throughout the series. When he points out that Dudley has suffered to his parents, and his parents react with surprise, he speaks a truth that the readers have little room to question. He does not elaborate further, but it nonetheless has an effect on the Dursleys.

Father

While the legacy of James Potter shapes much of Harry's imagination of a father figure, Harry is left with little guidance on what a positive father figure is. Vernon, as much as Petunia, was equally neglectful. In a post on Pottermore about the Dursleys, Rowling describes Vernon as "unmagical, opinionated and materialistic" when Petunia met him. He "has a perfectly correct car, and wanted to do completely ordinary things, and by the time he had taken her on a series of dull dates, during which he talked mainly about himself and his predictable ideas on the world, Petunia was dreaming of the moment when he would place a ring on her finger."[60] He was so entirely different from Petunia's family, she was eager for the change and to be out of the shadow of her sister.

Arthur Weasley is opposite to Vernon. He is not known at the Ministry as a go-getter, but he has a powerful love and curiosity of Muggles, positioning himself as an advocate for them in the wizarding world, a contrast to Vernon's prejudice and bigotry. He is a gentle parent, deferring most of the rule enforcement to Molly, and, like Molly, welcomes Harry easily into the Weasley flock. Among supporting Harry when he needs a parental figure, such as when Harry is summoned to the Ministry for underage magic, he enjoys asking Harry about Muggle items and how they work.

What Arthur cannot provide for Harry is someone who can really speak to the troubles he has. He does not confide in Arthur when his scar hurts, for instance. While Dumbledore positions himself a father-figure to Harry, their relationship is primarily that of teacher and student. Harry is mostly open with Dumbledore, but does keep some secrets to himself, even if Dumbledore already suspects them. His godfather, Sirius, ultimately fills the father role for Harry.

Sirius is Harry's godfather and was the best friend of Harry's father. He escapes Azkaban to protect Harry and to seek revenge on Peter Pettigrew for framing him. He reconciles his relationship with Harry to become Harry's closest family member. Sirius, however, does not have positive parenting to role model for Harry, and often behaves more like a brother to Harry—seemingly sometimes forgetting that Harry is not James. Harry idolizes him as a role model and reaches out to Sirius when he needs advice, which sometimes opposes Dumbledore's. During their short time together, Harry finds in Sirius the closest connection to James that he has and seeing him as a father-figure is organic and natural.

The Malfoys

Lucius and Narcissa Malfoy are, among Rowling's parents, a case study unto themselves. They do not have immediate influence on Harry, but it is evident how much influence they have over Draco, especially Lucius. Lucius appears most frequently throughout the books at convenient opportunities to exert his power as one of the school governors or to taunt the Weasleys in public. In the latter occasion, while attempting to provoke Arthur into dueling, Lucius drops Riddle's diary into Ginny's cauldron in an attempt to frame Arthur for having Dark Magic artifacts, although without knowing it was one of Voldemort's horcruxes. His character regularly looks down upon Muggles and the poor. While he is outwardly cruel, Draco's comments suggest that the two do have an active relationship, one of Lucius likely teaching Draco the kind of gentlemanly behavior appropriate for his station, as well as having conversations with him about Dark Magic and politics, grooming him as a Death Eater.

Narcissa complements Lucius in ideology and presentation, even revolving around the inner circle of Death Eaters though without becoming one herself. She does not factor heavily into the books until *HBP* when Draco is initiated as a Death Eater and given the task of killing Dumbledore. She makes an Unbreakable Vow with Snape to make sure that the task is fulfilled, even if Draco is unable to do it himself. In *DH*, Voldemort asks Narcissa to check to see if Harry is alive. She lies claiming Harry is dead, so the army will converge on Hogwarts and she can see Draco again. Even Harry recognizes her commitment to Draco and continues to feign death until they are all the way to the castle. Because she is contrasted against Lucius and Bellatrix, the commentary on Narcissa as Malfoy matriarch is in contrast to her actions in the last two books and her unyielding devotion to Draco. Unlike Petunia who kept Dudley close by constantly feeding him, Narcissa kept Draco close with her love. She could have easily betrayed Harry saying he was alive, but at that point, whether Harry was alive or dead was immaterial to her—her focus is only on her son. Harry telling her Draco is alive gives her hope and a purpose.

In the Malfoy household, Lucius clearly is the *paterfamilias*, with Narcissa the quiet wife at his side. Given the patriarchal nature of the household,

Draco was given more voice than Narcissa, which is not surprising given the stature of the Malfoys in wizarding society. Not only are they one of the wealthiest families, but they are also one of the few pure-blood families left, collectively known as the Sacred Twenty-Eight, the twenty-eight wizarding families listed in the "Pure-Blood Directory" who could still claim the purity of their bloodline.[61]

Mentors

Beyond role models, Harry recognizes mentors within some of his teachers. These mentors serve a different function from the parental figures, because they are more involved in the transformation of the hero rather than in the shaping of them. Here, they are available to help Harry and his friends grow through learning and advice and are especially open when asked difficult questions. They share just the right amount of information for the moment in time, giving the children the space to work out solutions on their own.

Harry's primary mentor is Albus Dumbledore. From the earliest chapters of the series, Dumbledore is heavily invested in Harry's growth and experiences, more so than a school headmaster may be. For Harry, he fulfills the archetypal wise old man role (literally), who is both master and teacher with the wealth of information to impart on the hero.[62] In the first five books, Dumbledore helps Harry comprehend each adventure he has and contextualize the events within the larger history of Voldemort. As an archetypal image, the wise old elder represents the collected wisdom of all generations with a broader sight than parental figures who are more confined in the near-present. This vantage point positions Dumbledore as the knowledge keeper, and his one fallacy is that he withholds some information from Harry out of compassion for him rather than any egoistic motivation to keep the apprentice subservient, as seen in Voldemort's relationship with his followers. Had he been more forthcoming with Harry, certain details about the Deathly Hallows may have changed the entire plot of *DH.* Going into *HBP*, Dumbledore knew his death was imminent as Dark Magic from the Resurrection Ring's horcrux slowly infected him, and so he used private lessons with Harry to teach as much as possible about them to prepare Harry to defeat Voldemort. During their King's Cross exchange, Dumbledore releases Harry, acknowledging his growth into manhood, which was difficult to admit—even though Harry was "of age" within the wizarding world, he was still that little boy in Dumbledore's eyes. For Harry, hearing Dumbledore acknowledge his growth also proves to be a turning point moment in his own self-concept, giving him renewed courage to finish the fight against Voldemort.

Hagrid, the half-human/half-giant groundskeeper of Hogwarts, is an unyielding supporter of Dumbledore. He takes an interest in Harry because

Dumbledore takes an interest in Harry, and because he is the one who brought baby Harry to the Dursleys, is the first to bring him back into the wizarding world, is the one to escort him from the Dursleys for the last time, and is the one to carry him out of the forest. Harry looks to him as a mentor for advice, but Hagrid mostly reiterates the rules and supports Dumbledore's teachings. He is the earthliest character of the series, other than perhaps Professor Sprout, because, as groundskeeper, he is most connected to Hogwarts' land and creatures. As Harry grows, Hagrid remains an adult friend, especially as Harry works more closely with Dumbledore. Thus, Hagrid becomes more of an emotional mentor to balance Dumbledore's rational mentor. In *SS*, Rowling plays with this by writing Hagrid as Norbert's mummy and how his wand is embedded in a pink umbrella. In the films, Hagrid may appear in a pink apron while baking or tending to other domestic chores, especially with Norbert.[63]

Remus Lupin becomes an unexpected mentor for Harry. They bond in the third year over memories of James and Patronus lessons, and again when the Order of the Phoenix is reunited after Voldemort's return. Lupin is a balance to Sirius, especially since he has been discriminated against by the wizarding world his entire life. He does not have the perspective that comes with Sirius's privilege, which may have also been resonate with James's privilege. As such, Lupin conveys a compassion for the marginalized throughout the war, until he struggles with marriage and parenthood. At that moment, Harry becomes the mentor, reminding Lupin that not having a father is far worse than having one that is a werewolf.

With all three of these mentors, Harry learns what he needs from them, but ultimately, they are his childhood mentors. With *DH* and the defeat of Voldemort, Harry and his friends transition into their own adulthood, having been tried, tested, and scarred by the cause of hunting the horcruxes. Each mentor has his own perspective on the previous war with Voldemort, and that knowledge proves valuable in helping Harry watch for the signs and flags of Voldemort's influence, so the friends are not caught off guard.

TO HOGWARTS WITH LOVE

One of the dominant themes of the *Harry Potter* series is love: romantic love between two characters, platonic love between two friends, parental love between an elder and a child, and inter-species love between a human or creature and a being from another species. Throughout the series, Rowling treats love as a force beyond all others that will always triumph over evil. Love is positioned as the key to Harry's survival. As Dumbledore explains to Harry in his debrief of the events at the Department of Mysteries in *OotP*: "You would be protected by an ancient magic of which he knows, which he despises, and which he has always, therefore, underestimated—to his cost. I am speaking of course of the fact that your mother died to save you."[64] Dumbledore's gambit of placing Harry in the care of his aunt (his closest blood relative) is the deep magic of love as represented by a mother's self-sacrifice to save her son. Harry's ability to love is also what differentiates him from Voldemort: "You are protected, in short, by your ability to love!" said Dumbledore loudly. "The only protection that can possibly work against the lure of power like Voldemort's! In spite of all the temptation you have endured, all the suffering, you remain pure of heart."[65]

Harry learns that he and Voldemort share a childhood orphaned by their parents and raised in a neglectful environment from which they are rescued with their Hogwarts letter. Even at age eleven, Dumbledore suspected that Voldemort (Tom Riddle) was already leaning toward a desire for power, whereas in Harry he recognized a desire for belonging. When Draco tries to recruit Harry before the Sorting in *SS*, Harry easily chooses creating friend-ships based on warmth and genuine care, rather than those who would like to benefit from his fame.

Thus, when Harry and his friends explore the Department of Mysteries in *OotP*, they are unable to unlock one room. Its door would not respond to unlocking spells nor Harry's pocketknife skeleton key. In her 2008 interview with fan site the Leaky Cauldron, Rowling describes the Love Room: "I think what's in the Love room, it's the place where they study what love means. So that room, I believe, would have at its center a kind of fountain or well containing a love potion, a very powerful love potion."[66] This love potion, *amortentia*, is so powerful, she describes, that it can essentially change a person. It can inspire heroism, or it can lead to foolishness. The behavioral transformation can be unpredictable, making it dangerous if misused, such as the assumed situation between Merope Gaunt and Tom Riddle Senior, Voldemort's parents.

Love between two people, whether it is *platonic*, *agape*, *eros*, or *amor* (the four primary categories of love as defined by the ancient Greeks), brings the two together and incites a transformation within the psyche of the individu-als. As previously discussed, the language and imagery of alchemy provides a metaphorical model of the impact of love, in which the *coniunctio* melds together the alchemical gold and silver to create the Philosopher's Stone, fabled as the key to immortality and symbolically connected within depth psychology to the process of individuation.[67]

Plato imagined love as so dangerous that it could threaten the gods. In the *Symposium*, Plato describes early humans as round androgynes who were essentially two people stuck together back-to-back. There were three such pairings: man to man, woman to woman, and man to woman. "In strength and power," he writes, "they were terrible; and they had great ambitions. They made an attempt on the gods [. . .] they tried to make an ascent to heaven so as to attack the gods."[68] The gods decided to punish their hubris by separating the people at their backs, making individuals who felt intense longing for their previous companion. The crux of human nature, then, is to find that other half: "And so, when a person meets the half that is his very own, whatever his orientation [. . .] then something wonderful happens: the two are struck from their senses by love, by a sense of belonging to one another, and by desire, and they don't want to be separated from one another, not even for a moment."[69] With this foundation, alchemy allowed through the chemical process to replicate the sensation of loss and loneliness through the transformative work. Modern depth psychologists, following Jung, surmise that this process was never about the work itself, but about the psychological impact of it. This rests on the hypothesis that a sense of wholeness follows the process, when one fully becomes individuated, or, literally, in-divid-ual. Within Jung's archetypes, the *anima/animus* represents the lost half from Plato's allegory. When meeting someone, human tendency is to project the *anima/animus* onto a romantic partner, temporarily equating the two in the transference.

Transference is temporary, according to Jung, because eventually the unconscious will awaken to the conscious, and the wily energies can be kept under control.[70] The *anima/animus* is seeking the *heiros gamos*, the sacred marriage of opposites: male/female, conscious/unconscious, Sol/Luna, symbolized in alchemy by the *coniunctio*.[71] This is an essential part of individuation or the hero's quest, because without it, the Philosopher's Stone will never be purified.

Before the process can get to the *coniunctio*, the *prima materia* must first be isolated. Harry Potter is the saga's *prima materia*, and the start of the alchemical work involves separating him from his non-magical, mundane existence. Initially, the "*prima materia* [was] thought of as a composite, a confused mixture of undifferentiated and contrary components requiring a process of separation."[72] To isolate and purify its components, the *prima materia* undergoes a *separatio*. The chemical components that make up a substance provide complexity; the *separatio* provides simplicity—a sort of *tabula rasa* on which to project the work.[73] The mythic hero must be separated from their homeland in order to fulfill the hero's task and find the boon. For the reader or participant engaged with the myth, this literary separation provides a metaphor for the work, breaking the transformation into discrete parts, a stage that Jung recognized as "a withdrawal of the naive projections by which we have moulded both the reality around us and the image of our own character."[74] At the beginning of each book, Harry receives his Hogwarts letter and leaves the Dursleys to go to Hogwarts. The Dursley house serves as a nexus to Harry's transformation. He returns every summer, but starts each new year leaving from the Muggle world to the magical, and each year he progressively matures as he grows toward individuation.

The next step of the work is the *mortificatio*, a death that removes any lingering ties to its original form and forces it into a liminal state of being and non-being. Edinger associates this with the first stage of the "coloring process," the *nigredo, albedo,* and *rubedo*.[75] This spiritual death is more intense than the *separatio*, because it prevents the *prima materia* from reverting to its original state. This is necessary prior to the *coniunctio* because the contamination of original substances can prevent the successful union with new substances. As if to illustrate this point, Rowling places a scene at the end of *HBP* when Harry, on the threshold of his greatest adventure to date, breaks up with Ginny Weasley, because his work "saving the wizarding world" is not complete until he is finished hunting Voldemort.[76] They are prevented from being together because of Voldemort and the trail of horcruxes he has left behind. *DH* follows Harry through the horcrux hunt, culminating in Harry's own death, necessary to achieve the degree of maturity in order for the *mortificatio* to take.

The three coloring stages help purify the *prima materia* to make the Philosopher's Stone, or the chemical wedding of completion. This latter result is imagined in alchemical texts as a metaphorical representation of love, or the union of Plato's opposites.

Harry is capable of love, even though he never experienced it while living with his foster family. Because of his cruel upbringing, Harry is able to distinguish behaviors he never liked and chooses not to behave that way. When he arrives at Hogwarts, he is exposed to an entire gamut of different people, some of whom go on to become his best friends. He and Ron immediately clicked on the train to Hogwarts just through their conversation with each other. Both boys wound up in the same compartment with each other (Ron to avoid his brothers). Ron and Hermione give Harry his first real feelings of family and belonging, which helps to establish Hogwarts as Home for Harry.

Rowling gives Harry a special power, the "power of love" that protects him from harm, especially from Voldemort, who is incapable of understanding love. The power comes from a deep magical protection placed on Harry when his mother sacrificed herself to protect him from Voldemort. Harry later repeats this when he likewise sacrifices himself for his schoolmates and teachers during the Battle of Hogwarts. Voldemort challenges Harry to face him in the Forbidden Forest away from his friends and teachers. Before leaving the castle, Harry rescues Snape's memory before he dies. This memory gives Harry the final pieces of the puzzle that Dumbledore laid out for him, but it also gives Harry a powerful lesson in love and sacrifice:

Dumbledore opened his eyes. Snape looked horrified.

"You have kept him alive so that he can die at the right moment?"

"Don't be shocked, Severus. How many men and women have you watched die?"

"Lately, only those whom I could not save," said Snape. He stood up. "You have used me."

"Meaning?"

"I have spied for you, and lied for you, put myself in mortal danger for you. Everything was supposed to be to keep Lily Potter's son safe. Now you tell me you have been raising him like a pig for slaughter—"

"But this is touching, Severus," said Dumbledore seriously. "Have you grown to care for this boy, after all?"

"For *him*?" shouted Snape. "*Expecto Patronum!*"

From the tip of his wand burst the silver doe: She landed on the office floor, bounded once across the office, and soared out of the window. Dumbledore watched her fly away, and as her silvery glow faded he turned back to Snape, and his eyes were full of tears.

"After all this time?"

"Always," said Snape.[77]

The silver doe represents Lily Potter, and that his patronus takes her form represents a deep emotional connection to her.[78] Earlier in Snape's memories, Harry learns about how Snape and his mother were childhood friends and how their friendship suffered under their adolescent differences during their time at Hogwarts. Harry learns that it was Snape who alerted Dumbledore of Voldemort's plan to go after the Potters. And he learns that Snape turned spy for Dumbledore to atone for his involvement in her death.[79] This peek into Snape's memories gives Harry insight into not only the multifaceted character of Snape, but also into the chthonic power of love. Snape learned too late that love needs to be experienced as a union, rather than an obsessive, unrequited feeling. He and Lily were as opposite as could possibly be, but he allowed his Slytherin parroting to destroy their friendship when he called her a "mud-blood" out of frustration and jealousy for her friendship with James Potter, Snape's biggest bully.[80]

Armed with this new insight, Harry readies himself to confront Voldemort in the forest. Harry knows that he is going to die, as that is a crucial line in the Prophecy: " . . . and either must die at the hand of the other for neither can live while the other survives."[81] Dumbledore bequeathed Harry the first ever

Golden Snitch he caught in a Quidditch match. This golden ball holds the key to the life-force that culminates Harry's transformation. He pops it into his mouth, which is how he caught it in that first match, and it opens to reveal the Resurrection Stone/Gaunt's Ring. Harry uses the stone to call the spirits of his parents, his godfather, and their best friend. Flanked by James, Lily, Sirius, and Lupin, he enters a grove and is hit with the killing curse.

Harry finds himself in a liminal state that resembles London's King's Cross Station, his threshold between the Muggle and magical worlds, thus making King's Cross a threshold between life and death. There is an ugly, child-like thing crying in pain, and Dumbledore sits with Harry explaining the meta-physical meaning behind Harry's "death." Harry survived the killing curse before because of his love shield, and this helps him survive this curse too. This time, because Voldemort absorbed some of the protection when he used Harry's blood to resurrect in *GoF*. The child is the piece of Voldemort's soul that lodged into Harry the night his parents died, turning him into a horcrux. This little piece of soul bonded to Harry's, and along with the blood bond, bound the two wizards' destinies beyond anything previously known in the wizarding world, and this bond has to be severed before either wizard can die. King's Cross holds both Harry and his horcrux in limbo, but the curse that brought them there helped loosen that bond. That piece of Voldemort's soul is a dark pollutant that Harry needs to acknowledge in order to release himself from its powers. Dumbledore's presence here helps give Harry clarity of heart and mind to comprehend his own power against Voldemort. Harry is seated at a crossroad, with the choice to live or die. Dumbledore tells Harry that he is truly the master of death, because "the true master does not seek to run away from death. He accepts that he must die, and that there are far, far worse things in the wizarding world than dying."[82] One of those worse things, Dumbledore alludes, is living without love. Harry suffered his whole life because of Voldemort; however, he also grew into the hero figure by necessity of this connection. When he could have succumbed to the same temptations that plagued Voldemort, it was his ability to love and be loved that prompted his growth and transformation. Voldemort's lack of love, on the other hand, prevents him from ever being more than a broken soul. He is even incapable of seeing the devotion of his Death Eaters (especially from Bellatrix) as any-thing more than their obligation to him.[83] Dying, while it would release its suffering, would give Voldemort the upper hand in the fight.

Harry also learns from Dumbledore that he has the power to choose to live because of the nature of his death, a willing sacrifice to save his friends. Love is a necessary emotion for all humans because it connects people with each other. The first experience of a child is, usually, the love of the mother. Voldemort's mother suffered under the weight of an abusive father and unre-quited love for Tom Riddle Senior. Dumbledore believes that Merope Gaunt used a love potion on Riddle, given both the potency of the potion (hence it being locked in the Department of Mysteries) and also the romantic appeal of using it to lure Riddle into some kind of marriage.[84] For reasons unknown, Merope freed Riddle from the enchantment, perhaps believing that her pregnancy would convince him to stay with her.[85] He returned home, abandoning her, leading Dumbledore to guess that she gave up on magic after his departure, eventually dying from a broken heart after Voldemort was born.[86] This abandonment, coupled with the grim surroundings of the orphanage, left Voldemort unable to learn love—though perhaps it was in his nature given the inability to love that characterized the Gaunt family. Had Merope died with an ounce of compassion for her son, it is possible that he may have been primed for love.

It is the role of the mother that establishes the contrast between Harry and Voldemort. Even though Harry was raised by the Dursleys, he had a year to be loved by his parents before their death. He also was infused with the power of love by his mother's sacrifice. With the death of Voldemort, Harry is then free to love without constraint. The epilogue of the seventh book shows Harry as an average father, married to Ginny Weasley, sending his middle son off to school for the first time. His *coniunctio* is represented literally by his marriage, his *hieros gamos*, when Rowling brings them together at the end of his journey. Symbolic of the psychology of transformation, this is the union between the conscious and the unconscious, and the actualization of one's whole identity. At the time of each book's publication, Rowling gave permission to her readers to embrace their unique selves and transform along with Harry. This is why first-generation readers feel such an affinity for the saga and all of its offshoots. Through the power of love and the strength of the Boy Who Lived, readers came into their identity, even if it deviated from illusory social norms. While identity politics is not unique to Potter fans, they rallied around their newly formed community and avatars to declare that any attempt to negate one's truth is a violation of their rights to equity and inclusion.

These archetypal connections with the characters give the series its dynamism. As mentioned previously, readers have a wide variety of characters to connect with, and that connection could manifest in the different creative outlets that mark the fandom. As technology has advanced, it has afforded new opportunities for connecting with the characters, even with the ability to create a unique digital avatar that is not constricted to the primary characters.

One side effect of the variety of characters is that it has garnered criticism around representation, especially how certain traits are leveraged and who is missing from the group. Rowling does rely on stereotype, a common feature of children's and young adult literature, to quickly convey a point, such as with Hagrid and his pink umbrella. On the other hand, the way that she portrays Molly Weasley and Dudley Dursley reveals a latent concern about fat people—Molly is dumpy, and Dudley is spoiled. Similarly, while the books are respectful of anyone who has a disability or other affliction, prejudice creeps into the description. For example, the wizarding world is written such that squibs, those in the wizarding world with no magical ability, are outright banned from any meaningful life within the magical community.[87]

In any archetypal read of a mythology, it is important to both acknowledge the cultural context of the characters and symbols and evaluate their purpose within the story. While some will necessarily be problematic as cultural values continue to progress and evolve, one must question whether or not that devalues their meaningfulness. It is also possible that some characters and symbols are frivolous and distracting, and that is also the by-product of writing an entire world into creation.

Academic interpretation requires that readers, affectionately called "aca-fans,"[88] hold tension between interpreting the meaning and their own enjoyment of the stories, especially as the franchise itself grows and morphs into its own organism beyond the grasp of its founding author.

NOTES

1. Eric Schlosser, *Fast Food Nation: The Dark Side of the All-American Meal* (New York: Perennial, 2002), 49–51.

2. This is a generalized blanket statement overall that ignores disparities in privilege that have always been a struggle for BIPOC and is a fundamental flaw in intergenerational research that has bundled groups into lumps of mainstream membership. It is a post-millennial perspective that not only recognizes the limitations of this bias but also actively challenges it.

3. Christopher Noxon, *Rejuvenile: Kickball, Cartoons, Cupcakes, and the Reinvention of the American Grown-Up* (New York: Three Rivers Press, 2006).

4. *SS,* 117.

5. J.K. Rowling, "The Sorting Hat," Pottermore, August 10, 2015, https://www.wizardingworld.com/writing-by-jk-rowling/the-sorting-hat.

6. *SS,* 118.

7. Personality Lab, "Find Your Hogwarts House: The Harry Potter Sorting Hat Personality Test," accessed September 25, 2015, https://www.personalitylab.org/tests/bessir4w5_hogwarts.htm.

8. Rowling emphasizes this in her characterization of the two boys: one lean and the other frequently described as fat, one of many instances that researchers have pointed out reflect fat phobia.

9. *SS,* 125.

10. *SS,* 80.

11. Pottermore, "Why You Should Fall In Love With a Hufflepuff," February 14, 2018, https://www.wizardingworld.com/features/why-you-should-fall-in-love-with-a-hufflepuff.

12. *GoF,* 72.

13. *GoF,* 293.

14. *GoF,* 632–35.

15. *FB:CoG*, 236.

16. *DH*, 587.

17. Pottermore, "Things You May Not Have Noticed About Luna Lovegood," February 12, 2018, https://www.wizardingworld.com/features/things-you-may-not-have-noticed-about-luna-lovegood.

18. *DH*, 299.

19. *DH*, 411–12, emphasis original.

20. Harry Potter Wiki, s.v. "Xenophilius Lovegood," last modified July 30, 2021, https://harrypotter.fandom.com/wiki/Xenophilius_Lovegood.

21. Pottermore, "The Kindness of Luna Lovegood," January 11, 2016, https://www.wizardingworld.com/features/the-kindness-of-luna-lovegood.

22. *SS*, 80.

23. Wizarding World, "You're a Slytherin," accessed September 27, 2021, https://www.wizardingworld.com/outcome/slytherin.

24. Wizarding World, "You're a Slytherin."

25. *CoS*, 150.

26. *OotP*, 111.

27. *DH*, 187.

28. *DH*, 609.

29. *DH*, 758.

30. Wizarding World, "Celebrating Albus Potter and Scorpius Malfoy: The Next Generation of Slytherin," May 6, 2019, https://www.wizardingworld.com/features/celebrating-albus-potter-and-scorpius-malfoy-the-next-generation-of-slytherin.

31. Among other criticisms, the fan community accused the authors of "queerbaiting," which Ellen Ricks defines in her post on *The Mary Sue* as "hinting at non-heterosexual characters or relationships without explicitly making them a part of the story." This attempt at writing diverse stories helps incorporate inclusion without offending the cis/hetero audience. Ricks points to the importance of representation and how queerbaiting is insulting and upsetting. She writes, "I would love nothing more than to see a queer character like myself on the page or on screen in the Harry Potter world, but that will never happen until Rowling admits that her books were not as diverse as they could have been. The problem with Rowling is that she's trying to retroactively fix things in the past while continuing to make the same mistakes in new projects. Harry Potter was a product of its environment—white, '90s England—and it was still groundbreaking, even if it doesn't meet our diversity standards today." Ricks's observations resonate with the transphobic tweet storm, described in a later chapter. Ellen Ricks, "Harry Potter and the History of Queerbaiting," The Mary Sue, March 21, 2018, https://www.themarysue.com/harry-potter-and-the-history-of-queerbaiting/.

32. *SS*, 77.

33. James Hillman, *Re-Visioning Psychology* (New York: HarperPerennial, 1975), xix, emphasis original.

34. Hillman, xix.

35. Yes, this is another possible framework for analyzing Potter. When coupled with transmedia storytelling, Hillman's archetypal soul-making creates a transformative experience between the franchise and the fan that transcends the established frames used in this project. There is a personal aspect necessary to this kind of work that requires inputs from fans and merits a separate project.

36. Hillman, *Re-Visioning*, 12.

37. Hillman, 136.

38. It is very simple for a myth to be discarded before it passes into subsequent generations. The modern Western mentality of a disposable culture constantly bounces from myth to myth, object to object, person to person. There is little room for mythic blooming in an age of too much information.

39. Hillman, *Re-Visioning*, 57.

40. Hillman, 57.

41. Hillman, 57.

42. A term coined by the Harry Potter Alliance several years ago. Henry Jenkins, "'Cultural Acupuncture': Fan Activism and the Harry Potter Alliance," *Transformative Works and Cultures* 10 (2012), https://doi.org/10.3983/twc.2012.0305.

43. Hillman leverages ancient Greek symbolism in support of his analyses. Mention here follows his framework and is not implying that this is exclusive of other models.

44. Hillman, *Re-Visioning*, 167.

45. *SS*, 108.

46. *SS*, 19–22.

47. *SS*, 75. In a post on Pottermore, Rowling reveals that when Vernon met James, he commented that wizards must live on unemployment: "James explained about Gringotts, and the fortune his parents had saved there, in solid gold. Vernon could not tell whether he was being made fun of or not, and grew angry." J.K. Rowling, "Vernon & Petunia Dursley," Pottermore, August 10, 2015, https://www.wizardingworld.com/writing-by-jk-rowling/vernon-and-petunia-dursley.

48. *SS*, 101–2.

49. *DH*, 375–76.

50. *SS*, 172.

51. *SS*, 179.

52. Hillman, *Re-Visioning*, 169.

53. Hillman, *Re-Visioning*, 177.

54. Before leaving the house, Dudley and Harry have a brief exchange where Dudley admits that he values Harry more than Harry thought, especially after Harry saved him from the Dementors in *OotP*. *DH*, 38–41.

55. Erik H. Erikson, *Childhood and Society* (New York: W. W. Norton & Company: 1950), 404.

56. Bruno Bettleheim, *The Uses of Enchantment: The Meaning and Importance of Fairy Tales* (New York: Alfred A. Knopf, 1977), 68–70.

57. Erikson, 288–289.

58. *CoS*, 32.

59. *HBP*, 55.

60. Rowling, "Vernon & Petunia Dursley."

61. Pottermore Wiki, s.v. "Pureblood," last modified January 2, 2014, https://pottermore.fandom.com/wiki/Purebloods.

62. Jung, *Archetypes*, 35.

63. By itself, the implication of the symbolism is problematic in context with Rowling's expressions of her trans views; however, the use of these gendered stereotypes helps convey the point succinctly. The pink umbrella prompts readers to think of Hagrid as odd, but it also reveals that he is not stiffly rational, allowing some color and play into his life.

64. *OotP*, 835–36.

65. *HBP*, 511.

66. Melissa Anelli, "PotterCast 131 J.K. Rowling Interview Transcript," The Leaky Cauldron, January 02, 2008, http://www.the-leaky-cauldron.org/2008/01/02/pottercast-131-j-k-rowling-interview-transcript/.

67. Jung, *Archetypes*, 555.

68. Plato, *Symposium*, trans. Alexander Nehamas and Paul Woodruff (Indianapolis: Hackett Publishing Company, 1989), 26.

69. Plato, 28.

70. C.G. Jung, *The Practice of Psychotherapy: Essays on the Psychology of the Transference and Other Subjects*, vol. 16 of *The Collected Works of C.G. Jung*, trans. R.F.C. Hull, 2nd ed. (New York: Bollingen Foundation, 1966), 170–71.

71. Jung, *Psychology and Alchemy*, 37. The binary structure here is inherent in the research. Modern depth psychology scholars and practitioners recognize that this binary is not an accurate reflection of the modern human experience. Expanding the binary into a spectrum is a necessary next step to embracing the collective hero archetype.

72. Edinger, 183.

73. Edinger, 183–87.

74. C.G. Jung, quoted in Marie-Louise von Franz, *Alchemy: An Introduction to the Symbolism of Psychology* (Toronto: Inner City Books, 1980), 195.

75. Edinger, 147. The "coloring process" has been analyzed by Potter teacher John Granger as the fundamental formula for an alchemical interpretation of Harry Potter, but this is limiting when considering the myriad descriptions of the alchemical process that incorporate more steps. What this also shows is that there is no one definitive version to provide a formula. This project follows a Jungian and post-Jungian depth psychology lens, which it is worth noting. Granger felt that this "psychological understanding of alchemy and position that alchemists were 'Gnostics' is a case of historical projection of one's own empiricist and anti-religious beliefs into the past." The venom continues: " . . . in Jung's assumption that the alchemist was primarily a gold seeker who experienced individuation (by contact with the archetypes of change in the collective unconscious) the psychoanalyst was 180 degrees off." Granger, *Unlocking*, 50.

76. *HBP*, 646–47.

77. *DH*, 687.

78. J.K. Rowling, "Patronus Charm," Pottermore, September 22, 2016, https://www.wizardingworld.com/writing-by-jk-rowling/patronus-charm.

79. *DH*, 659–90.

80. *PoA*, 356–57; *OotP*, 640–49.

81. *OotP*, 841.

82. *DH*, 721.

83. Melissa Anelli, "J.K. Rowling Web Chat Transcript," The Leaky Cauldron, July 30, 2007, the-leaky-cauldron.org/2007/7/30/j-k-rowling-web-chat-transcript. In *Harry Potter and the Cursed Child*, we learn that Bellatrix conceived a child with Voldemort. This child, Delphi, was orphaned after the Battle of Hogwarts and taken into an uncaring home. Her motivations to time travel and change the past are entirely motivated by wanting her father. Harry prevents their meeting, and she is never given the chance to meet Voldemort.

84. *HBP*, 213.

85. *HBP*, 214.

86. *HBP*, 262.

87. Maureen Saraco, "Squibism Disability and Having a Place at Hogwarts School of Witchcraft and Wizardry," in *Cultural Politics in Harry Potter: Life, Death and the Politics of Fear*, ed. Rubén Jarazo-Álvarez and Pilar Alderete-Diez (New York: Routledge, 2020).

88. Henry Jenkins, ed., "Acafandom and Beyond: Week Two, Part One (Henry Jenkins, Erica Rand, and Karen Hellekson)," henryjenkins.org, June 20, 2011, http://henryjenkins.org/blog/2011/06/acafandom_and_beyond_week_two.html.

Chapter 3

The Media of the Boy Wizard

The popularity of *Harry Potter* and the extended Potterverse is only possible thanks to the fandom that grew up around the books. This is not simply a bunch of people enjoying the book at a Book Club, but rather the full embodiment of the story as consumable culture in response to the archetypal potential explored in the previous chapters. Henry Jenkins recognizes *Harry Potter* as an example of "convergence culture," defined as "the flow of content across multiple media platforms, the cooperation between multiple media industries, and the migratory behavior of media audiences who will go almost anywhere in search of the kinds of entertainment experiences they want."[1] The reciprocal relationship between Rowling and *Harry Potter* fans became a social contract determining where her place as the author ended and where the fandom's ownership began, challenging the limits of copyright, intellectual property, interpretation, and appropriation. A fan who designs a craft project or who writes a song based on the Potter franchise is not doing so to try to take money from the author; their intent is not to profit off of Potter popularity. It is about the fundamental need to connect with the characters and somehow immerse into the story.

Regarding Potter fandom, Jenkins writes:

> Storytellers now think about storytelling in terms of creating openings for consumer participation. At the same time, consumers are using new media technologies to engage with old media content, seeing the Internet as a vehicle for collective problem solving, public deliberation, and grassroots creativity. Indeed, we have suggested that it is the interplay—and tension—between the top-down force of corporate convergence and the bottom-up force of grassroots convergence that is driving many of the changes we are observing in the media landscape.[2]

The process of storytelling used to be a one-way street, or "top-down force," to use Jenkins's words. The storyteller, here including the corporate machine in addition to the author, was never obligated to the audience, allowing for a creativity flow that inspired many great works. This also created a mystique around the stories. Millennial consumption was fully ensconced in that one-way storytelling but found potent playgrounds for the imagination within the stories. Mass-produced culture allows products to proliferate, and a mass-media culture continually provides material to mass-produce. Media is on an endless cycle and is continually accessible. With the launch of cable television and video technology, media was always "on," and millennial viewers are never "off." The consumption cycle is continually moving and flowing, expanding to include the means of consumption not just the things.[3]

Because media is both the means of consumption and the conveyance of storytelling, the playing field between storytellers and consumers is leveled, such that the consumers themselves are the storytellers. Each fan has a story to tell about their entry into the franchise, and this story becomes the springboard with which they make their connections with each other and the storyteller. Myth and reality are constantly collaborating to define culture with the tools available to society, and media and constant consumption accelerates the cycle, which allowed *Harry Potter* to quickly take over the fan consciousness. As American mores have eased and waned, the media helped millennials find their voices and how to use them to share Harry's message of love, and the Internet provided an accessible platform for discourse and change.

MYTH AND MEDIA

The nature of media allows for rapid growth and change as the stories jump between formats and the fan dialectic. In recognition of this new storytelling, Jenkins proposes the concept of transmedia storytelling: "Stories that unfold across multiple media platforms, with each medium making distinctive contributions to our understanding of the world, a more integrated approach to franchise development than models based on urtexts and ancillary products."[4] The key in Jenkins's definition is *franchise development*, because this is the uniquely contemporary (and corporate) facet of modern mythmaking. Inherent in this construct is the acceptance that the owner of the myths is not necessarily working within the symbolic collective unconscious or archetypal realm, but that they are transcribing archetypal images into multi-layered experiences of story. These stories, Jenkins notes, are world makers: "To fully experience any fictional world, consumers must assume the role of hunters and gatherers, chasing down bits of the story across media channels, comparing notes with each other via online discussion groups, and collaborating to ensure that everyone who invests time and effort will come away with a richer entertainment experience."[5] The fictional, mythic worlds of this media construct the real-world fan communities. The performative aspect of the story is no longer reduced to ritual but can be seen in ritualistic fan behaviors. The narrative structure is complex and multivocal such that it no longer can fit in established constructs. While the previous analysis helps contextualize Potter within familiar frameworks that have frequented Potter analysis, the remainder of this book relies on the understanding of a transmedia—or trans-mythic?—cultural narrative.

Jenkins outlines four functions of transmedia storytelling, of which the content should serve one or more of the following: "1. Offers back-story; 2. Maps the World; 3. Offers us other characters' perspective of the action; 4. Deepens audience engagement."[6] This parallels the four functions of mythology outlined by Joseph Campbell, with the clear difference that Jenkins's four functions emphasize the co-creation of the myth rather than the unilateral direction of traditional mythology. Modern media has replaced the storyteller, transforming the role into someone who is on the other end of a screen or pages of a book. More specifically, the "storyteller" is now a collective of many voices working in concert in a feedback loop between corporate and consumer where the initial source text in modern media resonates loudly with the audience, who then create the participatory fan culture that surrounds it, thus prompting the author or originator to expand beyond the original scope of the creation. Harry Potter helped establish this synergy for the Internet Age, and many source texts have been given a transmedia green light before establishing their presence in the media realm, allowing for immediate response that can change the direction of the franchise as it is rolling out.

One of the largest challenges that has surrounded Potter is bringing the experience to life. From films to video games to theme parks, building an extra-literary experience has proven difficult given that the magic of the books defies the scientific laws that prevail in the Muggle world. Transmedia storytelling makes it possible to experiment with different experiences and media, because this does not require a single investment (or storyteller) in the hopes that fans will accept it. Additionally, where Potter has struggled is in the role of the audience fan in the experience. Since the rebranding of Warner Brothers' and Pottermore's brand into the Wizarding World, the story has expanded beyond Potter and introduced other characters and generations for fans to interact with.

Taking a look at each of Jenkins' functions demonstrates how Potter and transmedia storytelling intersect.

Offers Backstory

Interwoven throughout the narrative of *Harry Potter* is a creation story of sorts through the backstory of the previous generations. The backstory is not a creation of the wizarding world, but rather the creation of the current conflict.

Through each book of the series, Rowling unravels another piece to the puzzle, creeping back further and further in time to pinpoint moments in history that eventually play significant roles in the development of Voldemort's and Harry's shared storylines. Harry learns about the Order of the Phoenix and how the group, including his parents and their friends, came to be unified against Voldemort and the Death Eaters. To learn why the Order of the Phoenix was established, Harry needed to travel further back into the early life of Voldemort while still a student at Hogwarts. Dumbledore curated this story through collected memories (many were his own) to highlight parallels between Voldemort's and Harry's childhoods to emphasize the importance of one's choices. Going back further still, Harry learns about Dumbledore's relationship to Grindelwald, arguably the prototype for Voldemort. The *Fantastic Beasts* film franchise is meant to further develop the backstory with more depth and detail around the Dumbledore/Grindelwald relationship. At the time of this writing, the series is still in progress.

Maps the World

There are layers of maps that are noteworthy. The first is Harry's map. At first, the view of this map is limited to what Harry knows of London and, eventually, of Hogwarts. But, as Harry spends more time in the wizarding world, the map continues to expand giving insight into otherwise unknown corners. In the midst of his adventures, Harry acquires a literal map, the Marauder's Map, which provides insightful details of Hogwarts including secret passages and who can be found where. Harry receives the map from Fred and George Weasley, who themselves stole the map from Filch's office. Later, it is revealed that the map was created by Harry's father and his friends as a way to sneak in, out of, and around Hogwarts. The only room not included on the map is the Room of Requirement, which is intentionally unplottable.

The other map is the map of the fandom world. From the books, the world expanded to the fan and fan fiction sites. These webpages brought fans together who wanted to discuss every angle of the books. Two key fan sites, The Leaky Cauldron and MuggleNet, also posted news related to all things Potter; hosted podcasts that mixed news, theory, and interviews; and provided hubs for discussion via message boards, instructions for crafts, and links for purchasing various Potter paraphernalia. As Potter expanded into films, theme parks, video games, and other merchandise, fan websites likewise expanded into conventions and conferences that brought the fans together to continue the discussions begun online, reinforce camaraderie, and—of course—buy merch. Because the wizarding world situates within the Muggle world, places in Harry's world frequently intersect with real locations. Some have embraced the Potter recognition. For instance, King's Cross Station in

London has a sign for Platform 9 ¾, with a luggage trolley stuck in the wall serving as a photo opportunity for the wandering tourist. Other places have been constructed and form the core of theme park and related experiences, discussed below.

Offers Other Characters' Perspectives

The richness of the series is that the story is not lived just through Harry's perspective. While his is the primary lens, other characters also offer insights and counterpoints. The school setting aids in this aspect, because those perspectives are infused with Harry's learning. We, the readers, learn these perspectives alongside Harry, including when to recognize that perspectives are limited when seen through a single character's experience. Part of Harry's journey, then, is to piece together the bits of information to try to get to the most comprehensive understanding that he can. Again, Ron and Hermione are key here, because their own unique perspectives balance Harry's to provide dimensionality to the puzzle.

Deepens Audience Engagement

The overall franchise experience is a web connecting the various outlets of engagement. The more immersive these are, the more engagement the audience will give to the franchise. This works primarily because the immersive environment not only gives one the ability to absorb the world but also to ingest and become a part of it. Each iteration of these immersive environments attempts to use popular media formats to connect with the audience in an attempt to renew their engagement that might wane as older experiences stagnate and stop being fresh. Moving beyond the books, films, and fan sites mentioned already, Rowling and Warner Brothers invited audiences to immerse into the Wizarding World in other ways, notably through Pottermore, mobile games, the theme park, traveling museum exhibitions, spin-offs, and a shopping haven.

Pottermore

The Pottermore website evolved from J.K. Rowling's personal website to separate her Rowling work from Potter work. It launched in 2011 as a hub of Potter news and as the primary seller of the e-books and audio books. On its initial launch, Pottermore was an interactive site, in which users could sign up as Hogwarts students, get Sorted, and "play" through the books, casting spells, brewing potions, and earning points toward the House Cup. The main value of the website was that occasionally players would come across unpublished material about the characters and places, helping to establish more history of the wizarding world than what appeared in the books. The site was iterated in 2015, maintaining content and house Sorting, but removing much of the interactive component, until it was finally closed in 2019 and all content was ported over to the new Wizarding World website. The website continues to carry content, news, and activities, and is also now the launch point to the official Wizarding World web shop, featuring a comprehensive catalog of Potter products.

Mobile Games

Creating a successful game-based virtual Potter experience has been difficult. Video games on the major platforms allow players to play through the films and wizarding world, but they did not resonate with fans and were never over-whelming successes. Mobile technology has offered opportunity for games that fans can play on their phones, often using popular game formats such as hidden pictures or match-3 to draw them in. These games are meant to be pas-times rather than something to take seriously. However, two games serve as notable examples in the attempt to make Potter portable and are developed in tandem with Warner Brothers' gaming label, Portkey Games: *Harry Potter: Hogwarts Mystery* (developed by Jam City, Inc., released in 2018) and *Harry Potter: Wizards Unite* (developed by Niantic, Inc., released in 2019). In both of these games, players build their own character avatar, are Sorted into a house, cast spells, and brew potions, much like the initial Pottermore plat-form, but now with new story supporting the experience.

- *Hogwarts Mystery* is set before Harry's time, focusing on the gen-eration between the Marauders and Harry. The player's character is unique to them, and the story adapts based on the choices the player makes throughout the game. There are two layers to the game play: the day-to-day class element and the overarching story. The classes help the player develop their skills while also building relationships with classmates. The overarching story revolves around the player's missing brother and cursed vaults, unfolding throughout chapters across seven years. The game can be played solo, or the Dueling Club allows players to duel other users.
- *Wizards Unite* used augmented reality (AR) to add magic to the Muggle world. Players could explore real-world areas to find magical resources, potion ingredients, magical beasts, or partners to duel. The game was inspired by the success of *Pokémon, Go!*, which involves players wandering areas to catch Pokémon. While *Wizards Unite* was not the immediate success of *Pokémon, Go!*, it nonetheless brought more of

the Potter magic into Muggle pockets. For this game, players joined the Statute of Secrecy Task Force to help solve the mystery of The Calamity, which spread traces of magic throughout the Muggle world. Here, again, the plot was unique to the game and adapted based on the choices one makes.[7]

Harry Potter: The Exhibition

The exhibition is an opportunity for fans to have backstage tours of the Potter films. Using immersive technology, the intent is to navigate a constructed environment that both displays artifacts from the movies while bringing the magic to life. The exhibit travels around the world to major cities and museums, staying on display for a period of time before moving on. The limited run of the exhibit creates a scarcity that is meant to bring fans flocking to their nearest museum, necessitating the producers to go beyond a typical exhibit—which may already be themed to increase audience engagement—to create an experience comparable to the other immersive Potter experiences, which are located in singular places that might not be accessible for the average fan. The touring exhibition brings a little Potter closer to home.

Fantastic Beasts and *Cursed Child*

Rowling expanded Potter early in the run of the series by releasing two "text-books," *Fantastic Beasts and Where to Find Them* and *Quidditch Through the Ages*, proceeds of which were donated to charity. The story of the author of *Fantastic Beasts*, Newt Scamander, provides the principle plot for the eponymous film franchise. Going beyond the pages of the book, the films tell a history of the wizarding world that was teased in *DH*, notably the relationship between Dumbledore and Grindelwald. The first film, *Fantastic Beasts and Where to Find Them*, was released in 2016 and grossed over $800 million worldwide.[8] The second film, *Fantastic Beasts: The Crimes of Grindelwald*, released in 2018 and has grossed around $650 million worldwide.[9] The series is planned to have five films, with the third film, *Fantastic Beasts: The Secrets of Dumbledore*, scheduled for release in 2022. The films underperformed to expectations and are marred in controversy, discussed in a later chapter, that may still impact the trajectory of their development.

Harry Potter and the Cursed Child springboards from the epilogue chapter of *DH* and revolves around the generation following Harry and his friends, notably Harry's middle son, Albus, and his friendship with Draco Malfoy's son Scorpius. The story was developed as a partnership between J.K. Rowling, John Tiffany, and Jack Thorne for the stage, premiering in 2016. Critically, the play received good reviews, but fan response was divided. There were concerns about some of the casting choices, especially the casting of a young black woman for Hermione, prompting Rowling to tweet: "Canon: brown eyes, fizzy hair and very clever. White skin was never specified. Rowling loves black Hermione."[10] Additionally, facets of the play read more like fan fiction, raising concerns about the quality and validity of the work. As such, some of the fandom reject the play as canon.[11] Since 2016, the play as moved from productions in London and New York to Melbourne, San Francisco, Hamburg, Toronto, and Tokyo.[12]

The Wizarding World of Harry Potter at Universal Studios (WWoHP)

The culmination of the fan experience occurs in the construction of simulated spaces that provide immersion into the fantasy world. Theme parks have dominated this corner of the industry, building spaces of entertainment and hyperreality so absolute that it feels like walking into the movie, breaking the fourth wall, and becoming a character in the story. The success of theme parks rests at the intersection between hyperreality and capitalism, because they reflect the need for a place to escape from reality. Disney defined the potency of theme park experience beginning with the 1955 opening of Disneyland in Anaheim, California. The mantra Walt Disney instilled into his Imagineers (a portmanteau of imagination and engineers) was that Disneyland should be a place where parents and children could play together. He also wanted the park to be so encapsulated that park guests could "leave the real world" outside and delve fully into the experience.

When Universal Studios announced the WWoHP, it was the first American experience that created immersion into Harry's world. Part one of WWoHP opened at Universal Studios in Orlando, Florida, in 2010, designed to imitate the wizard village, Hogsmeade, as seen in the films. Nestled in the back of the Islands of Adventure park, Hogsmeade allows fans a chance to be citizens of the magical world. Guests can drink butter beer in the Three Broomsticks, buy all sorts of Potter candy from Honeydukes, and weave in and out of crowded shops filled with wands, house gear, toys, and other souvenirs. Guests can waive an Interactive Wand in special spots to augment the magic of their experience by casting spells that make buildings, plants, and other décor talk. The primary attraction of this area is Harry Potter and the Forbidden Journey housed within Hogwarts Castle. The queue line weaves and winds through the hallways of the castle filled with projected footage of the characters, moving portraits, and iconic scenes from the films. The ride story is unique to this attraction, with the guests flying with Harry and Ron around the castle, chasing a dragon, visiting the Forbidden Forest, and fending off Dementors.

Part two of WWoHP opened in 2014 in the main Universal Studios park themed around Diagon Alley. Much of the experience mirrors that of Hogsmeade, because guests have to purchase tickets to both parks to see both areas. As such, the parks are divided such that the same products and shopping experiences are available in both places in case a guest is only visiting one park. The main attraction here is Harry Potter and the Escape from Gringotts built into Gringotts Bank. Guests have the opportunity to tour the bank in the queue line, and the ride joins Harry, Ron, and Hermione has they escape from Gringotts after breaking into Bellatrix's vault to find a horcrux.

The two areas are connected by the Hogwarts Express, which recreates the train ride from King's Cross to Hogsmeade. The story differs depending on the direction the train is going. From King's Cross to Hogsmeade, a Dementor enters the train; from Hogsmeade to King's Cross, various characters run or fly by, including Fred and George Weasley.

The experience is meant to make the wizarding world seem as real as possible, placing the guest into the heart of Harry's magical experiences, and they are successful as immersive experiences. Universal has since constructed versions of WWoHP at their California (2016), Japan (2014), and Beijing (2021) parks.

Harry Potter Store New York

In 2021, a new Harry Potter experience and store opened in New York's Times Square. Taking the thematic highlights from the theme parks, HP:NY gives a physical storefront to the Wizarding World webshop. In addition to being a massive store with photo opportunities sprinkled throughout, HP:NY also includes two virtual reality (VR) experiences: one to help Dobby catch magical creatures around Hogwarts and the other battle Death Eaters with Hagrid.[13] The store also has hidden surprises for members of the Harry Potter Fan Club, who can find Enchanted Keys using the fan club app.[14]

CITIZEN HUMANITIES

One other contribution that the Harry Potter fandom made to transmedia experience is the extent to which the fans leverage digital media to offer commentary and critique about the Potterverse, in what Michelle Markey Butler calls "citizen humanities." Similar to citizen science, in which members of the public collaborate on real-world problems using science, citizen humanities refer to a public collaboration around literary criticism, especially through memes and similar engagements.[15] Before memes, it was blog posts and web groups that threaded conversation between an initial post and comments.

This is significant to the shaping of the fandom, because it inspired fans to engage in the kind of deep criticism that is often left to the aca-fans, such as the most minute details of the books such as the significance of Lily Potter's eyes and their importance to the ending. In the lead-up to the release of the final novel, discussions around the significance of Harry having Lily's eyes came up in multiple forums, with fans picking up on the multiple references to their eyes throughout the series. In fact, they are referenced so often that Harry gets annoyed at the constant reminder, even more visibly so in the film adaptations.

This kind of criticism allows fans to become the "experts" of the stories as they are adapted to other platforms or media and take ownership of the content in a way that is different than participating in fan culture. This goes to a new level when comparing the film version with the original book version to see how "correct" it is. As an example, Katharine McCain describes how one particular line in *GoF* was delivered differently in the film version, and how this riled up the fans. The scene is where Dumbledore asks Harry if he put his name in the Goblet of Fire. In the book, he asks "calmly," but in the film, actor Michael Gambon as Dumbledore poses the question harshly and roughly, and uncharacteristic from the more calm, soothing Dumbledore played by Richard Harris in the first two films.[16] While this may seem like a small change, it nonetheless lit up the fandom, and the memes and GIFs that followed the film's release afforded fans the opportunity to comment on the scene or even "fix" it. The memes themselves become the meta text for critique.

Additionally, memes and GIFs are a type of communication that has the capability of carrying a heavy message in short, micro-bursts, giving everyone the chance to weigh-in on an issue. This becomes especially prevalent as the fandom moves into a new frame of cultural dynamics, one that recognizes the flaws in J.K. Rowling and the influence they had on the plot. One such meme features a picture of Professor McGonagall with the caption, "JK Rowling at The [sic] start of The [sic] decade," versus a picture of Professor Umbridge with the caption, "JK Rowling at The end of the decade."[17] The meme conveys a transformation in the perception of J.K. Rowling from being a rational person to someone with a closed mind as commentary on her exclusionary Twitter posts. Another one posted on Reddit shows two clips of first-year Hermione, both from the scene in *SS* when Hermione corrects Ron's pronunciation of the *Wingardium leviosa* charm. The first says, "Besides, you're saying it wrong," followed by "It's TRANSPHOBIA, not 'defending biological sex."[18] This reflects a fandom that has continued to grow and develop their perspectives through their collected use of the Internet, which itself has grown and shifted as a consumer tool over the years especially as a means for participation. Fans have moved away from discussing the tiny details and sharing their love of Potter into a greater sense of activism and purpose.

On the other hand, the 2016 presidential election awakened a smoldering rage in a lot of people's hearts. In so many ways, the outcome of the election is the clear result of a consumptive society heavily invested in the media— such that the candidate who is a media presence known for business and wealth became the president, as though elevating the archetypal image of this society into consciousness. Through every controversy and Twitter gaffes, the Trump presidency itself became a meme generator, and the Potter fandom did not disappoint with the memes. One meme shows Trump in profile, but with Voldemort on the back of his head, à la Professor Quirrell, with the caption, "Ever wonder what's under Trump's hair?"[19] In another example, there is a picture of Voldemort above a picture of Trump. The caption reads, "One of these men is feared by all, ruins everybody not with him, and nobody likes him. The other man is Voldemort."[20]

In a popular quote fans love to share, Henry Jenkins describes fan fiction as "a way of the culture repairing the damage done in a system where contemporary myths are owned by corporations instead of owned by the folk."[21] Memes and GIFs, as micro–fan fiction, help to repair damage through humor and satire, or at least to ease the pain of the damage.

HARRY POTTER AND THE CYCLE OF CONSUMPTION

In the shadow of the fandom, the providers of Harry Potter—Rowling, Scholastic, Warner Bros.—recognize that the organism of *Harry Potter* has grown larger than they had anticipated. In trying to profit off of the fandom, the marketing departments observed and analyzed fans to identify ways to continue to feed the hunger, and their methods have grown and evolved to adapt to consumer behaviors. In particular, the fan behaviors around their Potter purchasing serves what Baudrillard terms a "mark of membership" into the community of like-minded fans.[22] The culture this forms itself becomes the object of consumption, such that all the markers of one's Potter affiliation has just as much value as one's declared membership in the group. The mass production of Potter products, then, helps reinforce the cycle of consumption. In order for this relationship to continue, the products of consumption need to retain their meaning.

One of the challenges of a consumer culture is the constant need to continue consuming, which means that someone needs to continue manufacturing the objects of consumption. If all that is available is a limited array of products, the enthusiasm for the brand will die down. As evidenced by contemporary franchises, the constant restocking of product and experience inventories with new and different things keeps the community thriving. Positive consumption fills one with joy with a healthy diet that listens to the desires of the body and fills it just right. An unhealthy diet filled with consumption can lead to negative consumption and overconsumption. On a cultural level, negative consumption or overconsumption are themselves difficult to codify until the economic balloon bursts, which is there many millennials find themselves. American society outlines the rules of consumption: what things are con-sumed, how they are consumed, and at what cost. In a consumer society like the United States, where essentially everything is an act of consumption, the essentials are often taken for granted, such as electricity or Internet access, with focused attention instead on the ludic. But the balance between play and need tipped out of balance when the narrative that debt was an acceptable means of consumption failed to balance with the realities of the economy.

As such, the importance of community membership changes to align with the realities of its members to consume. If products or experiences are given a seasonality to inspire demand, then it becomes more appealing to invest in short bursts, keeping the flow of consumption going. This is a far cry from the earlier days of fandom when the means of consuming Potter included the hard work of individual creation and the opportunity to share the results with other members. One other reality that is a factor is the satisfaction of the consumer to continue supporting the franchise. In light of Rowling's controversial stance on the rights of trans women, many Potter fans opted to boycott the products. That means no longer buying the toys, the different versions of the books with different cover art, and no longer affiliating with any aspect of the franchise that directly revolves around Rowling. The Harry Potter juggernaut is large enough that such a boycott will not have immediate impact beyond the satisfaction of the fan for taking a stance. That does not mean that Rowling and Warner Brothers have free reign to jam the mythos, but it does slow the intended consequences of the intent. That is clear sign that the consumption cycle continues to thrive, but that is not a guarantee that the potency of the myth sustains.

NOTES

1. Henry Jenkins, *Convergence Culture: Where Old and New Media Collide* (New York: New York University Press, 2016), 2.

2. Jenkins, 169.

3. Ritzer, *Enchanting*, 202–3.

4. Jenkins, *Convergence Culture,* 293.

5. Jenkins, 21.

6. Maria Dicieanu, "*Harry Potter*, Henry Jenkins, and the Visionary J.K. Rowling," in *Transforming Harry: The Adaptation of Harry Potter in the Transmedia Age*, ed. John Alberti and P. Andrew Miller (Detroit: Wayne State University Press, 2018), 95.

7. As of 2020, the game introduced the Knight Bus to help players play the game virtually in response to COVID-19. This was intended to be a continuing feature beyond the pandemic. *Harry Potter: Wizards Unite*, "All Aboard the Knight Bus! Next Stop, Hogwarts Fortress," April 20, 2020, https://www.harrypotterwizardsunite. com/post/knightbus/. The game closed in 2022.

8. Box Office Mojo, "Fantastic Beasts and Where to Find Them," IMDbPro, accessed September 27, 2021, https://www.boxofficemojo.com/release/rl3696264705/.

9. Box Office Mojo, "Fantastic Beasts: The Crimes of Grindelwald," IMDbPro, accessed September 27, 2021, https://www.boxofficemojo.com/title/ tt4123430/?ref_=bo_se_r_1.

10. J.K. Rowling (@jk_rowling), "Canon: brown eyes, fizzy hair and very clever. White skin was never specified. Rowling loves black Hermione," Twitter, December 21, 2015, https://twitter.com/jk_rowling/status/678888094339366914?lang=en.

11. "As a longtime 'Harry Potter' enthusiast myself, I regretfully agree with the vocal minority who did not enjoy 'Cursed Child' and would rather it wasn't part of Harry Potter's story." Kim Renfro, "Some 'Harry Potter' Fans Are So Disappointed With the New Story that They're Refusing to Call It Canon," *Business Insider*, August 1, 2016, https://www.businessinsider.com/harry-potter-cursed-child-reactions-2016-7.

12. Wizarding World, "J.K. Rowling's Harry Potter and the Cursed Child," accessed September 27, 2021, https://www.harrypottertheplay.com.

13. Harry Potter New York, "Virtual reality Experiences: Become Part of the Adventure," accessed September 27, 2021, https://www.harrypotterstore.com/ vr-experiences/.

14. Wizarding World, "The Harry Potter Flagship Store in New York is Now Open," accessed September 27, 2021, https://www.wizardingworld.com/news/ harry-potter-new-york-store-opening-this-summer.

15. Michelle Markey Butler, "*Harry Potter* and the Surprising Venue of Literary Critique," in *Transforming Harry: The Adaptation of Harry Potter in the Transmedia Age*, eds. John Alberti and P. Andrew Miller (Detroit: Wayne State University Press, 2018), 148. Also: Katharine McCain, "*Epoximise!* The Renegotiation of Film and Literature through *Harry Potter* GIF Sets," in *Transforming Harry: The Adaptation of Harry Potter in the Transmedia Age*, eds. John Alberti and P. Andrew Miller (Detroit: Wayne State University Press, 2018).

16. McCain, 120–1.

17. Know Your Meme, "#IStandWithMaya - Beginning/End of Decade," December 19, 2019, https://knowyourmeme.com/photos/1677427-istandwithmaya.

18. u/KredibleKarma, "I just found out what terf means and about Jk Rowling's tweets so I will substitute my boycott with fan fiction," Reddit, June 17, 2020, https://www.reddit.com/r/NonBinary/comments/ haphys/i_just_found_out_what_terf_means_and_about_jk/.

19. Slow Robot, "What's under Trump's hair," Pinterest, accessed October 01, 2021, https://www.pinterest.com/pin/145944844153492280/.

20. Jessica Pineda (sometimesvegan), "Image tagged in funny, hilarious, trump, donald trump, harry potter, voldemort," Pinterest, accessed October 01, 2021, https://www.pinterest.com/pin/105975397466486157/.

21. Amy Harmon, "In TV's Dull Summer Days, Plots Take Wing on the Net," *New York Times*, August 18, 1997, https://www.nytimes.com/1997/08/18/business/in-tv-s-dull-summer-days-plots-take-wing-on-the-net.html.

22. Jean Baudrillard, *The Consumer Society: Myths and Structures*, rev. ed. (Thousand Oaks: Sage Publications, 2017), 127.

PART II

Harry Potter and Social Politics

Chapter 4

Lessons Learned from the Boy Wizard

CONSUMING POTTER

The popularity of Potter awakened familiar questions about the impact of media on the trajectory of our perceptions. Because *Harry Potter* was marketed at children, questions of the series' influence on children were raised to ensure they are learning the appropriate messages, prompting to larger discussions of the role of popular culture—especially while the nascent Internet spread like a global virus—in the social development of Americans and the establishment of community. For this second part, analysis will pull back from textual analysis and focus on the broader social context of the series and its impact as a millennial mythos.

The power and influence of media rests in the sheer saturation of it in the American post-war experiment. Radio, television, and print evolved into streaming services with 24-hour access, phone apps, and Internet sites of varying flavors of storytelling and news reporting. Advertisements cover the landscape and branded products extend the corporate reach into the consumer identity. Consumerism helped fuel a new leisure culture, one accessible (in theory) to members of all social classes, and the entertainment industry wasted no time in manufacturing experiences both within leisure experiences and responsibility institutions. One works to have fun, so the workplace takes on facets of fun to be encouraging. One learns to be able to work, but training is more engaging when it is entertaining. Entertainment has to distinguish itself from the everyday to continue to maintain the gold standard for simulated environments and hyperreal realities. As Neil Postman cautions, "What is peculiar about such interpositions of media is that their role in directing what we will see or know is so rarely noticed. A person who reads a book or who watches television or who glances at his watch is not usually interested in how his mind is organized and controlled by these events, still less in what idea of the world is suggested by a book, television, or a watch."[1]

The perceived passive reception of media is indeed a valid concern, echoed especially among analyses of children and media.[2] The argued concern is that children, in particular, lack the skills to distinguish media from reality, especially when advertisement is involved. The latter can influence the consumptive behaviors and brand loyalty of the child as they grow into adults. Millennials are especially primed for a life of permanent merger between media and consumption. On the one hand, they are "the product of affluence and abundance," but they are also responding to "uncertain, anxious times—the terrorist attacks of 2001, followed by infectious disease scares, a convulsing stock market, war overseas, and natural calamities."[3] In other words, the anxieties and uncertainties that tend to push millennials to the comforts of childhood. Given that *Harry Potter* appeared at a crucial time of generational identity formation, its particular influence has attracted a variety of criticism. For example, in her memoir of the Harry Potter fandom, the Leaky Cauldron webmistress Melissa Anelli notes that the *Harry Potter* books "were most heavily challenged between 1999 and 2003, coinciding with the Harry Potter fandom's incubation period. In 2000, the ALA [American Library Association] alone received 646 challenges, a 50-percent increase from 1999, which [ALA Office of Intellectual Freedom director Judith] Klug says was largely because of Potter."[4] Similarly, Henry Jenkins described "the Potter wars" as conflict over "what rights we have to read and write about core cultural myths—that is, a struggle over literacy."[5] He adds that "literacy is understood to include not simply what we can do with printed matter but also what we can do with media."[6]

From Jenkins's perspective, the controversies surrounding Potter are tied to the controversies around who controls the curriculum. While teachers continually find opportunities to use Potter or Potter-inspired pedagogy in their classrooms, members of conservative and religious groups often lead the cries for banning the *Potter* books for teaching magic and witchcraft. One such vocal supporter is Georgia parent, Laura Mallory. Mallory began her crusade in 2005 to have the *Harry Potter* books removed from the libraries of her local school district, citing that they "promote the Wicca religion and use of them by the Local Board violates the First Amendment of the United States Constitution."[7] Despite numerous appeals and escalations, Mallory's efforts are continuously denied because she often fails to provide concrete evidence for her claims. For instance, while the books describe witchcraft, they have no connections to Wicca. Throughout her initial two-year crusade, fan-led news sites The Leaky Cauldron and MuggleNet reported on her efforts through their websites and in their podcasts. This culminated in an in-person interview with Melissa Anelli.[8] The interview reinforced the fan perspective that Laura Mallory's claims were unfounded, even rooted in ignorance. Key to the interview was Anelli calling out Mallory for not reading the books, yet still going ahead with her crusade. Mallory responded that she had been guided not to read the books through her prayers.[9] Even Rowling was perplexed by the whole affair, noting that "Fundamentalism in any form, in any religion, is intolerant, and tolerance is the only way forward."[10] In 2012, MuggleNet reported that Mallory reignited the fight that had been dormant for four years.[11] A comment responding to an Adams State University blog post about the same story, captures the overall sentiment of the Potter community's response to Mallory:

> If anything is promoting evil, its [sic] this woman. She's spreading hate for something innocent. I've loved Harry Potter since I was little and there is absolutely nothing wrong with me. The deaths in the books do not scar young children, they help teach them that death is natural and not to be afraid of it. This woman is a real life Voldemort, trying to ruin the childhood of children by spreading her nonsense. There is absolutely nothing wrong with Harry Potter.[12]

One aspect that stands out about the Anelli/Mallory interview is that, from their perspectives, both women are right; Harry Potter means a specific thing to them and they cannot be persuaded otherwise. The "agree to disagree" debate outcome is a fundamental fallacy at the root of American discord. Just as "good" and "evil" are not clearly defined in a post-post-modernist America, neither is the line between "right" and "wrong" clearly delineated. If we hold sides in an "us versus them" tension, we can never find balance. Although the epilogue suggests a happy ending, *Harry Potter and the Cursed Child* shows that the balance is temporary. The victims of the emotional trauma of the war—and the first generation following—seek psychological resolution across the entire generation, without which the cycle keeps repeating.

The Laura Mallory example is the kind of event that inspires the fandom to collectively "eye roll," but it is also sparks actions and activism among the fans. This part of the book focuses on the lessons learned from *Harry Potter* and how this translates into real life experiences with the aim to demonstrate that there is more to Potter than cultural exegesis. Thanks to the series' mythic nature, readers of the books absorb lessons and bring them into their own experiences. From this vantage point, it makes reasonable sense that Potter would garner so much attention and criticism. The love of Potter can challenge the established status quo and shift the balance of cultural power and who owns it. The chapters in this section pivot from the narrative and fandom into the events of the first quarter of the 21st century and how *Harry*

Potter helped millennials navigate them: the political lessons learned from the series, the role of education, and the social activism Potter inspires.

POTTER PLAYS AT POLITICS

Harry Potter and the Half-Blood Prince opens with the recently sacked MoM, Cornelius Fudge, paying a visit to the Muggle Prime Minister to bring him up to speed with the events around Voldemort's return. The arrangement allows the MoM to visit the Muggle Prime Minister to liaise between the magical and Muggle world, especially if there is something happening that has the potential to impact Muggles. This is to help maintain the secrecy of the wizarding community.[13] While the Prime Minister remains unnamed, it is worth noting that Tony Blair and the Labour Party led the United Kingdom from 1997–2007, essentially the release cycle of the series. While the focus on this book is *Harry Potter* in America, it would be surprising if Rowling's tone toward politics did not partially echo the trajectory of Blair's leadership.[14] Initially, this administration was met with the optimism that accompanies the party change in a democratic society—in this case from conservative to the more liberal-leaning Labour Party—but, as with American politics, that optimism was affected by the 9/11 attacks. As British forces aided the Americans in the Middle East, a campaign that conflated revenge for the 9/11 attacks and unreconciled dislike of Saddam Hussein's dictatorship of Iraq, the optimism waned, as we see reflected in this opening chapter of *HBP*. As Todd J. Ide notes, "Regardless of whether a political leader can control events or not, events do influence the popularity and support that leader enjoys, even if he or she is seen to stumble in response to those events, the result can damage a politician beyond the ability to recover."[15] The two ministers meeting becomes a commentary on the multiple faces of a political leader: the political (the Prime Minister) and the public (the Minister of Magic). Fudge recounts for the minister all of the events that occurred over the last year, prompting the Prime Minister to exclaim, "Now see here, Fudge—you've got to do something! It's your responsibility as Minister of Magic!" To which Fudge responds, "My dear Prime Minister, you can't honestly think I'm still Minister of Magic after all this? I was sacked three days ago! The whole Wizarding community has been screaming for my resignation for a fortnight. I've never known them so united in my whole term of office!"[16]

Although Rowling's commentary is targeted at British leadership, the sentiments resonate with American readers as well, who were navigating a social shift from the liberal-leaning Democratic party that led the country through the prosperous 1990s to the conservative-leaning Republican party with the

2000 election. President George W. Bush was not in office a full year before the 9/11 attacks, which accomplished two things for his administration.[17] First, it gave the Bush Administration clearance to further a conservative agenda that tightened social restrictions while loosening government corporate regulation. The former helped foster a sense of assurance (reassurance) that the government was protecting its people. The passing of the Patriot Act in October 2001 gave the government more power to fight terrorism by expanding existing law enforcement tools into the reaches of counter-terrorism.[18] In defense, then-senator Joe Biden, a Democrat, observed that, "the FBI could get a wiretap to investigate the mafia, but they could not get one to investigate terrorists. To put it bluntly, that was crazy! What's good for the mob should be good for terrorists."[19] Similarly, the Transportation Security Agency (TSA) was created to enact stricter security measures to help support the air industry and passenger confidence in same.[20] Increased security measures included (and continue to include) reinforced security screening as passengers enter the airport concourse, more in-depth screening of checked bags with restrictions on what can be brought onto the plane, and limited public access to parts of the airport. Other countries adopted similar measures as the United States threatened to restrict international travel from countries that chose not to follow these measures. In the immediate 9/11 fury, the American public willingly accepted these changes as common belief rests on the compromise of losing some freedoms if it helps get the country out of crisis.[21]

The other "gift" to the Bush Administration is that, regardless of the public's perception, President George W. Bush's legacy was cemented as a "wartime president." Throughout American history and mythology, the president fulfills the perception of the ultimate American individual and carries the image of national wholeness:[22] "The President was immediately identifiable—something few senators or congressmen were. He was a handy symbol, a personification of national ideals and desires, as well as of his own or his party's policies, programs, and ideals."[23] The "success" of a president depends on their ability to unite the people and the perception of how they handle crisis. Wartime presidents have the added responsibility of keeping the country and its people safe. However, for Bush, he inherited an America that was jaded with war. The glory and optimism that followed World War II gave way to pessimism and distrust in the shadow of the Vietnam War. In addition, as is hopefully clear at this point, the Internet and the development of online communities defined a new, more immediate feedback loop between the American people and the country's leadership. As the War on Terror trudged on, as more government funding was shifted to support the military and the private corporations that were supplying the war, the trust in the government waned. This coincides with Harry's own growing into political awareness, which helped provide the knowledge tools that millennials turned into election ballots and social justice groups. It also helped prepare them for the realities of an uncertain future that could be captured into a single image in the collapse of the housing market in 2007 and the Great Recession that followed. Millennials never financially recovered from that period, and Harry's lessons help arm a generation for the fallacies and foibles of the coming administrations.

THE GIERZYNSKI LESSONS

In 2013, political science professor Anthony Gierzynski, with colleague Katheryn Eddy, published the results of a survey of students that began at the University of Vermont and expanded to schools across the country. From this survey, Gierzynski noted six political lessons Potter teaches millennials. The project relied on two key assumptions/observations. One is that "the stories in our entertainment media can affect generation after generation [but] some stories, because of their timing, have their largest effect on one single generation."[24] The other is that Harry Potter's impact is greatest on the millennials, noting that while "the story of Harry Potter may continue to affect subsequent generations, its biggest impact will likely have been on the generation that experienced the series while growing up during the ten plus years the series literally dominated the culture."[25] For current purposes, Gierzynski's five lessons help provide a framework of understanding the millennial mindset and how it seeps throughout American culture, social media, and across digital spaces. One could perhaps claim that it is an exaggeration to say that *Harry Potter* dominated the culture as Gierzynski describes, but to those living through the phenomenon, *Harry Potter* was, in fact, the primary lens for seeing the world, which is why, even after more than a decade since the release of the seventh book, the series continues to show up in the news or in academic conferences: there are *still* new things to discover about the legacy of Harry and his conquest against Voldemort.

Lesson 1: Diversity and Acceptance

"A constant lesson throughout the books and movies is acceptance of those who are different from ourselves."[26]

Harry Potter and Identity Politics

A fundamental binary exists in the wizarding world: Magical people and non-magical. In this world, magic is an awesome innate power that some are born with. In its simplest sense, magic is an elemental force—it needs to be controlled otherwise it becomes an element unto its own. In the *FB* film, this is visualized as an *obscurus*, caused when a child, an Obscurial, represses their magical abilities.[27] From the research of Newt Scamander, we learn that an obscurial will often die before their tenth birthday.[28] *FB* character Credence Barebone is an exception, surviving well into his teen and young adult years, generating such a great energy that it attracts Grindelwald to New York. In this particular case, Credence is adopted by an anti-witchcraft group, the New Salem Philanthropic Society, indoctrinating him in an intense hatred for magic that manifests into a form that causes distruction in its wake.[29] The level of power this pent-up magic possesses is magic at its most destructive, and is an extreme, rare manifestation in this binary. Rowling's world paints this as a negative chaotic that cannot be controlled, only subdued. In the right hands, however, the power can be harnessed to fuel powerful magic, the sort Rowling equates with evil and the dark magic of Grindelwald.

Thus, magical children need to be taught how to control their magic. Controlling magic, Rowling suggests, is not instinctual for young witches and wizards. Those fortunate enough to grow up in the wizarding world have a cultural container to help model behavior. They may even learn some rudimentary skills to be able to navigate aspects of wizarding society. Muggle-born witches and wizards are not given the same opportunity, so when odd things happen to them, they could either be passed off as oddities or, as Harry experienced, the cause for abuse for not fitting into the normal mould.[30] These experiences (the Dursleys' abuses) prime Harry for his entry into the wizarding world. One of Harry's first encounters in the wizarding world highlighting the division between magical and non-magical people is while he gets fitted for his school robes at Madame Malkin's Robes for All Occasions during his Diagon Alley shopping trip with Hagrid. During his fitting, Harry is standing next to another future Hogwarts student, who we later learn is Draco Malfoy.[31] Draco, parroting things his parents would say, probes Harry about his parents to ensure he comes from a wizarding family. Draco, seemingly talking for the sake of talking, tells Harry, "I really don't think they should let the other set in, do you? They're just not the same, they've never been brought up to know our ways. Some of them have never even heard of Hogwarts until they get the letter, imagine. I think they should keep it in the old Wizarding families. What's your name anyway?"[32] Harry is rescued from this awkward conversation by the completion of the fitting, but Malfoy's statement does not sit well with him. Even though he is from a wizarding family, he internalizes Malfoy's statement about not knowing he was a magic user until he received his letter. However, when approached by Malfoy on the train to join forces with his cronies, Harry retorts, "I think I can tell who are the wrong sort for myself, thanks."[33] In this moment, Rowling cements the perspective of the story through Harry's lens of the "wrong sort." Throughout the series, Harry frequently stands against any establishment that purports to have power over others, including magical creatures. This also means that Harry is always on the wrong side of the Death Eaters, whose purpose is to retain a prejudiced stance against Muggles, an age-old debate within the magical community given Malfoy's nonchalant comments in the robe shop that demonstrate the normalcy of the perspective.

The magic versus non-magical debate is further subdivided within the wizarding community and the presence of non-magical witches or wizards, or squibs. While squibs appear throughout the wizarding world in support roles, they seem to be barred from magical education. As Maureen Saraco observes, the Hogwarts letter is the gateway to acceptance: "Barring certain types of children from school is an early and powerful sign that they do not belong and is a way to preserve a system of domination by ensuring that the dominated never gain access to the tools they need to escape second-class status."[34] Rowling acknowledges this prejudice through the story of Angus Buchanan, posted on Pottermore. Buchanan did not receive a Hogwarts letter, but crashed into a Sorting Hat ceremony: "The horror of the moment when the Hat announced kindly that the boy beneath it was a good-hearted chap, but no wizard, would never be forgotten by those who witnessed it. Angus took off the hat and left the hall with tears streaming down his face."[35] Having this division helps serve as a reminder that social binaries are never so simple and often come with complexities.

Those messages of tolerance are taken to heart by the fan community. Throughout the series, Rowling paints the underdog characters as sympathetic and supportive of Harry and his cause,[36] while the others are marked as bigots and their vitriol include hateful and despicable undertones.

When the Death Eaters take over the Ministry in *DH*, Rowling is quick to note that this immediately changed the lives of the wizarding world. Muggle-borns were under constant threat of laws that would take away their wands, and even vocalizing support for Harry could lead to swift punishment. When the Trump Administration rose to power after the 2016 election, similar laws targeting specific groups, notably women and BIPOC, resonate with the shifting dynamic in wizarding politics. Here, the comparison between Death Eaters and the Trump Administration (and their respective supporters) is firm.[37]

Trump famously built his platform on disparaging the Other. In some cases, this was through mockery in a public or press event. In others, it was through language and actions associated with a culture of hate and white supremacy. While Trump and his staff (and family) would defend their actions as not hateful, they very carefully never publicly divested themselves from the white supremacy moniker. One such example occurred during the first 2020 presidential debate between incumbent Trump and Democratic nominee Joe Biden. Responding to a question asking Trump to condemn white supremacists, Trump emphatically responded, "Proud Boys, stand back and stand by."[38] This phrase spun the media world into hyperdrive, analyzing what this could possibly mean within the spectrum of Trump's other presidential gaffes. In subsequent interviews, he never explained nor renounced this statement, leaving people to assume his intent and insert meaning into a phrase that stands without any supporting context.

The Proud Boys are a white supremacist group, one dedicated to furthering a mission for a white America, with deep roots into American racism and parallels to other global racially/ethnically superiority complexes. To evoke them on a public platform is like a call to arms, something that seemed to ignite into the coup attempt of January 2021. There are multiple white supremacist groups across the United States, united under the "conservative agenda" of "Making America Great Again." When bubbling into the public eye, we see these groups leading the charge in Othering the marginalized, often claiming their own victimhood as justification of their actions and beliefs.

It is an easy leap to assume that this hate culture, always present just below the surface of American society, is a response to the social media hashtag culture that has gained traction since *DH* was published. From #blacklivesmatter to #metoo, the tolerance for mainstream abusive behaviors has gone by the wayside. Millennials and other like-minded Americans use the Internet and social media platforms to vocalize historically silent (and silenced) sentiments. When something goes viral, it gains enough traction that it is no longer a singular movement. When #blacklivesmatter launched in 2013, it was in protest of the acquittal of George Zimmerman who killed teenager Trayvon Martin in 2012.[39] It evolved from hashtag into a global movement "whose mission is to eradicate white supremacy and build local power to intervene in violence inflicted on Black communities by the state and vigilantes."[40] In other words, the culture shift associated with Potter's publication gives language against Death Eaters for the betterment of all people. This foray into social justice has manifested in fan-led activism groups as well, discussed in a forthcoming chapter.

Lesson 2: Political Tolerance and Equality

> "In the Harry Potter world, the protagonists are constantly objecting to,
> and fighting against, these injustices that deprive classes of individuals
> their rights, equal treatment, and freedoms while it is the antagonists who
> continually practice intolerance and evince the companion disposition of
> authoritarianism."[41]

Harry Potter and Diversity

As already seen in Lesson 1, one key aspect of Potter is embracing difference.
This applies within the political sphere as well. The inherent prejudices magical people hold against non-magical people and other creatures manifests as
a desire to overthrow the Statute of Secrecy and exert dominance over the
Muggle world rather than coexist as they currently do.[42] The International
Statute of Wizarding Secrecy, according to Rowling, was adopted by each
country's Ministry of Magic to ensure the safety of the wizarding community
rather than engage in war with Muggles in response to their anti-magic brutal-
ity.[43] Grindelwald especially campaigned to overthrow the statute as a means
of exerting his power. In a rally in France, Grindelwald tells the crowd:

> You came today because of a craving and a knowledge that the old ways serve
> us no longer. . . . You came today because you crave something new, something
> different. It is said that I hate Les Non-Magiques. The Muggles. The No-Maj.
> The Can't Spells. I do not hate them. I do not. For I do not fight out of hatred.
> I say the Muggles are not lesser, but other. Not worthless, but of other value.
> Not disposable, but of a different disposition. Magic blooms only in rare souls.
> It is granted to those who live for higher things. Oh, and what a world we could
> make, for all of humanity. We who live for freedom, for truth and for love.[44]

Grindelwald's speech could be used to rally against any common Other. The
magical versus non-magical plays as a metaphor for any differences, giving
it the flexibility to support attitudes of tolerance and equality, as identified by
Gierzynski. The key to the success of Grindelwald is that he infuses his message of magical superiority with claims of not being motivated by hate, using
language that very carefully masks the prejudice he harbors.

   This hidden prejudice manifests throughout the series when magical
people make declarations against magical creatures. The fountain statue in
the Ministry of Magic, titled *The Fountain of Magical Brethren*, depicts a
witch and a wizard surrounded by a centaur, a goblin, and a house-elf looking
up at them adoringly.[45] Here, at the seat of magical power in Britain stands
a testament to the superiority of witches and wizards over the natural world,

here represented by three magical creatures, one of whom—the centaur—is a species of astronomy and divination, suggesting the position that magical people have control over the future. While Harry watches, he notices witches and wizards passing the fountain in a passive acceptance of its message. When Harry and his friends visit the Ministry in *DH*, the statue (destroyed in a battle with Voldemort at the end of *OotP*) is replaced with an ominous statue of a witch and wizard sitting on thrones staring down at ministry personnel.[46] The previous message suggesting community is replaced with the more fascist "Magic is might," giving symbolic interpretation to the different power dynamics of a ministry in the hands of Death Eaters and supporters of their cause.

The perceived superiority of magical people is why there is traction behind a movement to bring the Statute of Secrecy to an end. Without this legal barrier, the wizarding world could exert a power over Muggles as a sort of retribution against medieval Muggles whose witch hunts inspired the Statute of Secrecy in the first place. In their King's Cross meeting in *DH*, Dumbledore tells Harry his belief that Grindelwald's motivations stemmed from an early interest in finding the Deathly Hallows, three legendary tools (a wand, a stone, and an invisibility cloak) that could give the owner power over Death, the ultimate key to power that could justify social power as well.[47] With these tools, Dumbledore reveals, Grindelwald could have the Elder Wand (an unbeatable wand) so no one could overrule him, and with the Resurrection Stone he could raise an army of Inferi (the undead). He would be unstoppable! His friendship with Dumbledore was based on this fascination with the Hallows, but Dumbledore saw the "revolution" and subservience of Muggles differently. After his break from Grindelwald following an argument that led to the death of Dumbledore's sister, Dumbledore turns his ambitions and skills toward promoting a greater good for all people and creatures. The revelation of his early ambitions is presented not to destroy the memory of Dumbledore, but to reveal his vulnerabilities, a gift the dead are not afforded after the publication of a tell-all posthumous biography that attempts to defame him. Dumbledore admits to Harry that he learned from Grindelwald that he could not be trusted to control the seductive nature of power and that he could easily have gone the path of Grindelwald.

The fundamental difference between Grindelwald and Voldemort is the lack of careful consideration Voldemort puts into his cause. Voldemort is motivated entirely by his own quest for immortality, making the power over Muggles less a "glorious revolution" and more of a totalitarian dictatorship built around the worship that he believes he deserves.

An American Coup

January 6, 2021, started as a normal day, despite tensions looming in the air. This was the day when Congress would certify the presidential election results with a formal count of Electoral College votes. The 2020 election, though close, voted in favor of Democratic nominee, Joe Biden, defeating incumbent Donald Trump. From the get-go, Trump contested the integrity of the election, using any legal means necessary to prove it. Violence was expected at some point in the transition process, but what actually transpired caught Washington, DC, and the nation offguard.

It is common that when groups who have an issue that they want to make visible to the public, they have a gathering or a march in Washington, DC, in the symbolic center of American politics. Often, they are non-violent demonstrations, although sometimes there may be some violence as occurred when Trump called the National Guard against Black Lives Matter protesters during the summer of 2020. But these demonstrations are not mob riots, upholding a respect for the sanctity of the sacred halls of government.

While the votes were being counted, a mob breached the US Capitol building, forcing senators, representatives, and media personnel to shelter. They broke windows, carried the Confederate flag throughout the halls, and shot tear gas and guns. Some broke into offices to take selfies or damage property. Throughout the riot, people shouted chants supporting Trump and threatening anyone who challenged their mission, even calling police officers "traitors" for trying to stop them.

Although the Ministry of Magic is eventually filled with Death Eaters and supporters of Voldemort, the magical public is not really involved in the unbalancing of power. The magical coup is facilitated through discreet actions rather than mob riots. In fact, many witches and wizards abhor the kind of violence associated with this behavior. This is best illustrated at the Quidditch World Cup at the start of *GoF*. While fans are celebrating the game's outcome, several hooded Death Eaters parade through the campsite antagonizing Muggle landowners and Muggle supporters inciting chaos and causing damage. Although, at this point in the plot, the return of Voldemort is unknown, these people are acting according to their perceptions of what he would want, demonstrating that the followers of a leader can be just as dangerous as the leader—if not more so because of their numbers. The terrorists behind the coup represent a vocal subset of the American public. Unlike Death Eaters who keep their previous association quiet, MAGA ("Make America Great Again") supporters are proud of their affiliation. The outcome of the coup would have been very different if they all showed up on January 6th.

While domestic terrorism is not a foreign concept to Americans, 9/11 was perhaps the most televised and imprinted on the American memory. The 1995 bombing of the Oklahoma City federal building and the 1999 Columbine High School shooting were still being processed in the culture's psyche, as were other bombings and shootings repeated in the nightly news and expanding cable news cycle. Rowling may have written the *GoF* Death Eater scene in response to the zeitgeist, but this scene, in the opening events of the middle of the series and turning point, made an impact on young readers who watched these events transpire on television through Harry's lens. Already familiar with witnessing through television, Rowling's detailed language made the event something worthy of national news.

While the Ministry swooped in quickly to quell the disturbance, the children had already seen too much. Harry, in particular, is separated from the Weasleys and has his wand stolen, which was used to cast the Dark Mark (the symbol of the Death Eaters) into the sky. When Harry is found, Ministry official Barty Crouch initially tries to scapegoat Harry for casting the mark. The other adults around him support the accusation, except for Arthur Weasley, who reminds them that Harry is just a child and does not have that kind of magic. This is a glaring mark on Ministry leadership that Harry retains throughout the series that eventually cements into a distrust in politicians.

Lesson 3: Don't Be an Authoritarian Git

"Authoritarian fears are alleviated by defense of the collective normative order: positive differentiation of the in-group, devaluation and discrimination against out-groups, obedience to authorities, conformity to rules and norms, and intolerance and punishment of those who fail to obey and conform."[48]

Harry Potter and the Culture of Fear

The authoritarian mindset comes from a place of fear in response to perceptions of the decay of society caused by politics of inclusion and diversity (i.e., change in the very nature of the social order).[49] A culture of fear is a cornerstone of American psychology, one that is a constant driver of social trajectories, yet remains a fundamentally and chronically repressed trait.[50] Fear leads people to associate with the public figures who speak to those fears, acknowledging them and seemingly offering assurances and solutions. This support is indicative of a perception that the leader will maintain the status quo—conformity and normalcy—and makes it easy to overlook the reality of their authoritarian message that suggests that this power figure is a shepherd taking care of their flock.

When Dolores Umbridge first addresses the Hogwarts student body at the start of term feast in *OotP*, most of the students tune out her speech. This is not just reflective of teenagers sitting through a speech, but also of how easy it is to miss the underlying message of authority. Rowling, here, makes a connection between education and anti-authoritarianism, noting that the teachers and Hermione, symbols of education and intelligence throughout the series, are listening carefully to Umbridge's every word.[51] After the speech is over, Hermione shares her notes with Harry and Ron, who are initially dismissive:

> "Did it?" said Harry in surprise. "Sounded like a load of waffle to me."
>
> "There was some important stuff hidden in the waffle," said Hermione grimly.
>
> "Was there?" said Ron blankly.
>
> "How about 'progress of progress's sake must be discouraged'? How about 'pruning whenever we find practices that ought to be prohibited'?"
>
> "Well, what does that mean?" said Ron impatiently.
>
> "I'll tell you what it means," said Hermione through gritted teeth. "It means the Ministry's interfering at Hogwarts."[52]

As a psychological trait, fear becomes a natural filter for the information of survival. A careful oration can provide reassurance while masking a hidden agenda. Harry and Ron easily tune Umbridge out, because they do not believe that she is speaking to anything relevant to them, such as the resurrection of Voldemort. The information Hermione distills for them reflects the dangers of communication. Had Hermione been a different kind of student, such as a Slytherin, she may have interpreted Umbridge's speech favorably, echoing Malfoy's comments that Dumbledore is a problem for Hogwarts. Because this interpretation comes from Hermione, a trusted character, it establishes the problem of the Ministry's involvement in Hogwarts; in other words, the intervention by government on education and curriculum is a key step in the ability for authoritarian leaders to rise to power. Similarly, Grindelwald's speech in *FB:CoB* has a similar effect. His charismatic message of love engages the audience but lures them into poetic compliance. Scamander and Tina Goldstein hear right through the rhetoric, but Queenie is sold on it. In a significant moment between Queenie and Jacob, Queenie chooses to join Grindelwald, saying "Jacob, he's the answer. He wants what we want."[53] Although she walks willingly into Grindelwald's circle, she too is acting from fear. While she felt lost and alone in Paris, it was Grindelwald who provided her comfort when her sister did not. When the love spell over Jacob is broken, Grindelwald is the one who validates her magical empowerment over the Muggle in the name of love.

Umbridge and Grindelwald deliver two different kinds of speeches with essentially the same political message. Authoritarianism and its political cousins, totalitarianism and fascism, help nurture the anxieties of the people, but they also seed social instability that, like the increasing control Umbridge assumes over Hogwarts or Grindelwald over his movement, can create myopia and amnesia in a populace that refuses to or is unable to listen through to the latent messages of the speech.

Lesson 4: Violence and Torture Are Bad

"Another frequent theme in the Harry Potter stories is that using violence freely and indiscriminately is characteristic of bad people. The protagonists avoid violence, using it only when it is necessary—and sometimes, as with Harry, not even then—and abhor torture."[54]

Harry Potter and the Disarming Charm

Harry experiences abuses throughout his early years at Hogwarts, including physical and emotional abuse from a teacher, but his first real experience of violence and torture comes during the Quidditch World Cup.[55] After the World Cup, during the euphoria of Ireland's win, a group of Death Eaters parade through the campgrounds: "High above them, floating along in midair, four struggling figures were being contorted into grotesque shapes. It was as though the masked wizards on the ground were puppeteers, and the people above them were marionettes operated by invisible strings that rose from the wands into the air."[56] Once at school, Harry learns about the three Unforgiveable Curses, spells so dangerous that the Ministry has enacted laws against their use. These three spells give the witch or wizard total control over another being, including death. From this, Harry equates the senseless violence he witnessed at the World Cup with Death Eaters, but it is not until his fifth year when he experiences torture for himself, changing his entire view.

After witnessing the Ministry's response to the return of Voldemort and the cover-up of the real reasons Cedric died, Harry becomes vocal in his distrust of the Ministry, especially in DADA classes with Umbridge, who, thanks to Hermione's warning, Harry recognizes as a part of the cover-up. His outspokenness earns detention with Umbridge, whose reason for punishment is Harry's "spreading evil, nasty, attention-seeking lies."[57] For his detention, he has to write "I must not tell lies" over and over, with a magical quill that etches the phrase into his hand using his blood as ink.[58] At the end of the evening, Umbridge checks Harry's hand rather than his lines: "'Tut, tut. I don't seem to have made much of an impression, yet,' she said, smiling. 'Well, we'll just have to try again tomorrow evening, won't we? You may go.'"[59] This detention repeats throughout the school year until the phrase leaves a scar on Harry's hand.

This is not the only time Rowling uses this form of torture. In *DH*, Bellatrix Lestrange tortures Hermione at Malfoy Manor after the trio is caught by Death Eaters.[60] In the film adaptation, Bellatrix carves "mudblood" into Hermione's arm. The impact of Hermione's and Harry's scars is that they become a living testament to the evil they experienced. After the series' end, Rowling allows these moments to fade into memory, a missed opportunity to share the memory with their children in either the epilogue or *CC*.

It is noteworthy that, after all he has experienced, Harry still avoids needless violence. He does use a violent spell against Malfoy during a duel that he learns from the Half-Blood Prince's potion book, but uses it without knowing its affect.[61] This curse, *sectumsempra*, is noted in the marginalia of the textbook as "For enemies."[62] When Harry later learns that the curse was created by Snape to use against his father and friends,[63] his attitudes toward the Prince's "help" throughout the school year changes to disgust for the violent intents.

When Harry uses the curse against Malfoy, "blood spurted from Malfoy's face and chest as though he had been slashed with an invisible sword. He staggered backward and collapsed onto the water-logged floor with a great splash, his wand falling from his limp hand."[64] There are times before the Battle of Hogwarts when Harry tries to use violent spells, but his heart is not in it after this horrifying incident. As much as he dislikes Malfoy, it is never his intent to kill him as this spell seems to do. Harry's inability to kill is a trait Rowling intentionally equates with her hero, a philosophy emphasizing that violence is not the answer. Lupin echoes this philosophy when he tells Harry that disarming is a thing of the past, that he should at least Stun if not going to kill.[65] Harry refuses to agree with Lupin challenging his pessimistic views of war throughout the final book. Indeed, when the moment comes to defeat Voldemort, Harry does it with the disarming charm, *Expelliarmus*, causing Voldemort's death curse to backfire on him.[66]

Lesson 5: Government Leaders Are Corrupt, Incompetent, and Fixated on Maintaining Power

> "The series' implicit critique of government, however, is limited to the individuals who are in charge. There is an accepted need for the regulations of the Ministry of Magic to keep the magical world hidden from the Muggle world and to maintain a responsible use of wizarding powers."[67]

Harry Potter and the Case of Government Corruption

Harry learns early in his exposure to the wizarding world to question, if not fully distrust, government leaders:

> "There's a Ministry of Magic?" Harry asked before he could stop himself.
>
> "'Course,' said Hagrid. 'They wanted Dumbledore for minister, o'course, but he'd never leave Hogwarts, so old Cornelius Fudge got the job. Bungler if ever there was one."[68]

In fact, the only Ministry official Harry comes to trust is Arthur Weasley, who works in the Misuse of Muggle Artifacts office. It is his fascination with Muggles and his kindness to Harry that solidifies his trust even after the Order of the Phoenix is revived.

Throughout the series, every encounter Harry has with Fudge becomes more like a publicity stunt rather than a government leader taking an interest in Harry's well-being. When Harry calls him out for his flip-flop actions, Fudge chalks it up as changing times rather than admit his growing bias against Harry as is especially apparent when he learns of Dumbledore's Army in *OotP*. Fudge is increasingly paranoid of Dumbledore's influence and learns of Dumbledore's Army through Umbridge.[69] During this questioning, Fudge and Umbridge reveal unorthodox investigation processes, including letting a petty criminal off their charges in exchange for information about Harry. "'Blatant corruption!' roared the portrait of the corpulent, red-nosed wizard behind Dumbledore's desk. 'The Ministry did not cut deals with petty criminals in my day, no sir, they did not.'"[70] Dumbledore also points out that a number of educational decrees outlining new rules for the school were not actually put into effect until after Harry's alleged crimes.[71] This first-hand witness to Fudge's corruption and incompetence cements Harry's attitudes of distrust against the MoM.

His distrust carries over to new leadership as well reinforcing the idea that a well-run government is necessary, but that a bad leader makes a bad government. When Harry meets Fudge's successor, Rufus Scrimgeour, he does nothing to ease Harry's distrust. Scrimgeour visits Harry, Ron, and Hermione at the Burrow to execute Dumbledore's will, which included leaving some gifts for the three. Harry is quick to notice that Scrimgeour's visit comes a month after Dumbledore's death:

> "Isn't it obvious?" said Hermione, before Scrimgeour could answer. "They wanted to examine whatever he's left us. You had no right to do that!" she said, and her voice trembled slightly.

"I had every right," said Scrimgeour dismissively. "The Decree for Justifiable Confiscation gives the Ministry the power to confiscate the contents of a will—"

"That law was created to stop wizards passing on Dark artifacts," said Hermione, "and the Ministry is supposed to have powerful evidence that the deceased possessions are illegal before seizing them!"[72]

Hermione also points out that the statute of limitations on the confiscated items was up and barring no evidence of dark magic, they had to be legally released to the recipients.[73] The trio witnesses another instance of the MoM bending its own rules out of suspicion of Dumbledore's motives for Harry.

On the other side of the Atlantic, the president of MACUSA (the Magical Congress of the United States of America) casts a different image of government leaders. The MACUSA was formed as a result of the International Statute of Wizarding Secrecy with two main purposes: (1) "to rid the continent of Scourers, corrupt wizards who had hunted their fellow magical beings for personal gain"; and (2) to provide law enforcement over "the number of wizarding criminals who had fled to America from Europe and beyond, precisely because of the lack of organized law enforcement such as existed in their own countries."[74] The role of the president, then, is less about leading the Ministry, but more about enacting the Laws of the Congress. The MACUSA is modeled on the United States' government and its branches, but the president is still given the final decision. The president Newt Scamander meets in *FB*, Seraphina Picquery, is more focused on maintaining wizarding secrecy, such that she ignores Scamander's warnings about the Obscurus. After the Obscurus destroys much of New York and Newt Scamander helps soothe the unleashed Credence, only then does the president offer a slight apology and thanks for his help.

Harry Potter and Political Entrepreneurs

Bethany Barrett defines a *political entrepreneur* as someone with the "political skill and personal charisma [. . .] able to organize citizens with common interests into a coherent and effective movement."[75] Furthermore, their power rests in their ability to "validate discriminatory actions" by claiming that "they are merely a response to something perpetrated by the targeted group."[76] Herein is the crux of how Donald Trump, not politically skillful *per se* but overwhelmingly full of charisma, speaks to the political latent fears of swaths of "ignored" Americans. His ability to communicate to this constituency was misunderstood by all political players leading up to the 2016 election. Convinced he had no way to win, commentators were frequently surprised when he won various electoral benchmarks throughout the primaries. It likely should not have come as a surprise when he won by a narrow victory in 2016.

Since the 2000 election, the GOP have worked to discredit the Democratic Party, who in turn discredited the Progressives in 2016 enough to rally the necessary votes in the Electoral College for a Trump win.

Despite the propaganda otherwise, Trump's presidency stood on an unstable platform. The only way it could maintain was to perpetuate the perception of villainous Others doing America harm, reinforcing his role as the one to restore the country. His campaign to build a border wall between the United States and Mexico spoke to those afraid of illegal Mexican[77] immigrants coming into the country to take jobs and other welfare services. He helped perpetuate misconceptions of Black Lives Matter by turning the message into one of reverse racism that victimizes the white population. When the protests in 2020 turned violent (often at the hands of someone outside the movement) the message focused on the violence and destruction, rather than the systemic inequities behind the protests. When the violence came to Washington, D.C., during the attempted coup, it was justified as a part of Trump's "movement."

The biggest challenge came against the Democrats for their "witch hunt" to defraud Trump's election. In many ways, this is exactly the sentiment of Pure-bloods against those in the wizarding community who support Muggles. By calling the investigations a "witch hunt," Trump evoked the same kind of fear as the Pure-bloods who challenged both the Statute of Secrecy and the power plays against Muggles. This is especially prevalent in the character of Dolores Umbridge, whose name is derived from the word *umbrage*, meaning the reaction at a perceived offense or annoyance. She is one of the few instances within the series of a Ministry official participating in the establishment of rules and regulations. When we first meet her, these are situational educational "decrees" to control Hogwarts in the name of the Ministry. In *DH*, we see her writing pamphlets in support of the Pure-blood movement that is also connected to Voldemort's movement through the Death Eaters involved at the Ministry. Many of these pamphlets elevate the importance of magical purity and explain why Muggles needed to be cataloged.

In contrast to Umbridge, there is the New Salem Philanthropic Society in *FB* who speak and campaign against magic at a time in American history when the Spiritualist movement was declining and the Anti-Spiritualist movement was growing. The organization was led by Mary Lou Barebone, a descendent of Bartholomew Barebone, an 18th century No-Maj who saw magic as evil and made a large effort to explore the wizarding world.[78] As his descendent, Mary Lou likely shared the same hatred, and with her small family of three adopted children, organized regular meetings and distributed information pamphlets to encourage the exposure and destruction of the magical community.[79] They also made an effort to gain the support of the popular senator, Henry Shaw Junior, to help legitimize their organization. While he was initially uninterested, he was killed by the Obscurus during an attack at his fundraiser, prompting his father to become more interested in the movement.[80]

The New Salem Philanthropic Society represents a different kind of witch hunt. Rather than being about one politician, this witch hunt is about villain-izing another group, such as the liberals who are not supportive of Trump. As witches are often symbolically linked with liberalism and education, this reaction from the voting constituency is more than an act of support for their leader; it is the narrative of the cultish behavior that underscores the MAGA movement.

Lesson 6: Be Skeptical, Not Cynical

> "While the protagonists maintain a healthy level of skepticism, they never become cynical. They try to get to the truth, to hold onto hope, to see the good in most everyone, and to trust those who have shown themselves trustworthy."[81]

Harry Potter and Healthy Skepticism

This culminating lesson is the heart behind the previous five. Being skeptical is to question everything and to be mindful of what to take for granted. The cynicism, especially that of Lupin, fosters a narrow mindset that automati-cally errs away from hope and a positive outlook for the future. Lupin's cyni-cism is positioned as a generational opposition to what is seen as the naiveté of youth. He struggles to trust and to love, even after he marries Tonks and their son is born. His view, it is worth noting, is informed by an entire life of prejudice for being a werewolf. His closest friendships were formed to give him inclusion, making the death of James Potter and the betrayal of Peter Pettigrew that much harder to rebound from. Having been on the receiving end of prejudice that convinces him he is unworthy as a werewolf, Lupin greets even personal interactions with cynicism. This is a far cry from the Lupin of *PoA*, who, for one glorious year, was treated as an equal. Rowling notes that Lupin's lycanthropy is

> a metaphor for those illnesses that carry a stigma, like HIV and AIDS. All kinds of superstitions seem to surround blood-borne conditions, probably due to taboos surrounding blood itself. The wizarding world is as prone to hysteria and prejudice as the Muggle one, as the character of Lupin gave me a chance to examine those attitudes.[82]

One additional barrier to acceptance of werewolves is that the wolfsbane potion is difficult to brew.[83] The system of prejudice is seemingly set up to fail the werewolves. Lupin's cynicism mirrors the first of Gierzynski's lessons of equality and tolerance. The people Lupin admires most are those who unconditionally accept him. The only one left of Lupin's core supporters is Harry, who becomes baby Teddy's godfather and becomes his parental figure after the deaths of Lupin and Tonks, a hopeful indicator of a post-Voldemort future.

WHAT DOES HARRY LEARN?

In the end, after the defeat of Voldemort, Harry is faced with a choice. After everything that happened, Harry becomes the master of the Elder Wand, the Deathly Hallow that had driven the power-hungry Grindelwald and Voldemort.[84] With his wand, Harry becomes the legendary master of death, Dumbledore's greatest ambition. He loses the ring in the forest but decides to leave it lost. He chooses to keep the ever-helpful Invisibility Cloak. But he decides to get rid of the Elder Wand. In the book, Harry decides to return the wand to Dumbledore's tomb, under the assumption that if he dies a natural death, "it's power will be broken, won't it? The previous master will never have been defeated. That'll be the end of it."[85] In contrast, the film adaptation shows Harry breaking the wand and throwing it into a gorge. Visually, this accomplishes a more dramatic impact than the closing of the novel. In the novel, Harry chooses to repair his wand before reburying the Elder Wand, whereas the film seems to make a bolder statement about Harry's rejection of power. Indeed, as Cassandra Bausman suggests, Harry's rejection of the wand shifts the priorities of power as characterized by Voldemort to a concept of power that welcomes love and embraces selflessness—Dumbledore's power.[86]

By removing the Elder Wand from circulation, Harry makes a heroic choice for all of humanity. Pottermore describes the Elder Wand as "'dispassionate' and 'ruthless' in its need for power, forming no true bond with the wielder."[87] Additionally, "The secret of the Elder Wand is that it's more sentient than any other. It can identify the caster of any spell that touches it and keeps tally of which wizard has beaten which, giving tis allegiance to the one it judges the victor. Physical possession is irrelevant."[88] The metaphor is that power is not a possession, a tool that can be wielded. Harry recognizes this when he rejects wielding the wand, because his most powerful tool—his ability to love—is innate.

These lessons are sprinkled throughout the series, informing and transforming the readers. While the years after the series' publication were fraught with economic instability, the country settled into a cautious optimism united under President Obama's single-word campaign slogan: HOPE. The country experienced a pivot with the 2016 election, a period of time when these lessons of Harry Potter were put to the test.

NOTES

1. Neil Postman, *Amusing Ourselves to Death: Public Discourse in the Age of Show Business* (New York: Penguin Books, 1985), 11.

2. c.f. Neil Postman, *The Disappearance of Childhood* (New York: Vintage Books, 1994); Nicholas Sammond, *Babes in Tomorrowland: Walt Disney and the Making of the American Child, 1930–1960* (Durham: Duke University Press, 2005); Henry A. Giroux and Grace Pollock, *The Mouse That Roared: Disney and the End of Innocence*, rev. ed. (Lanham: Rowman & Littlefield, 2010).

3. Noxon, *Rejuvenile*, 10.

4. Anelli, *Harry, A History*, 185.

5. Jenkins, *Convergence Culture*, 170.

6. Jenkins, 170.

7. State Board of Education, State of Georgia, *Laura Mallory, Appellant, vs. Gwinnett County Board of Education, Appellee, Case No. 2006–84, Decision* (Atlanta: GaDOE, December 2006).

8. Anelli, *Harry, a History*, 177–201.

9. Anelli, 201.

10. Anelli, 200.

11. Keith Hawk, "Laura Mallory Appears To Be At It Again—Claiming 'Harry Potter' Books Promote Evil," MuggleNet, January 19, 2017, mugglenet.com/2012/02/laura-mallory-appears-to-be-at-it-again-claiming-harry-potter-books-promote-evil.

12. Joe, February 16, 2012, comment on Rachel Decker, "Harry Potter Books Charged with Supporting Witchcraft," *The Paw Print at Adams State University* (blog), https://blogs.adams.edu/thepawprint/harry-potter-books-charged-with-supporting-witchcraft/.

13. *HBP*, 6.

14. Todd J. Ide, "The Dark Lord and the Prince: Machiavellian Elements in Harry Potter," in *Critical Insights: The Harry Potter Series*, eds. Lana A. Whited and M. Katherine Grimes (Ipswich: Salem Press/Grey House Publishing, 2015), 180.

15. Ide, "The Dark Lord," 182.

16. *HBP*, 15.

17. Whether intentional or not is the matter of conspiracy theories.

18. United States Department of Justice, "Highlights of the USA PATRIOT Act," accessed August 21, 2021, https://www.justice.gov/archive/ll/highlights.htm.

19. United States Department of Justice, "Highlights."

20. The Transportation Security Agency, "Transportation Security Timeline," Accessed August 21, 2021, https://www.tsa.gov/timeline.

21. James Oliver Robertson, *American Myth, American Reality* (New York: Hill & Wang, 1980), 335–8.

22. Robertson, 310.

23. Robertson, 311.

24. Anthony Gierzynski and Katheryn Eddy, *Harry Potter and the Millennials: Research Methods and the Politics of the Muggle Generation* (Baltimore: Johns Hopkins University Press, 2013), 4–5.

25. Gierzynski and Eddy, 5.

26. Gierzynski and Eddy, 12.

27. Rowling, *FB,* 150.

28. Rowling, *FB,* 151.

29. Harry Potter Wiki, s.v. "Credence Barebone," accessed August 21, 2021, https://harrypotter.fandom.com/wiki/Credence_Barebone; Pottermore, "Magical Abilities That Don't Sound At All Fun," August 16, 2018, https://www.wizardingworld.com/features/magical-abilities-that-do-not-sound-all-that-fun.

30. *SS,* 24–25.

31. *SS,* 76–79.

32. *SS,* 78.

33. *SS,* 109.

34. Maureen Saraco, "Squibism Disability and Having a Place at Hogwarts School of Witchcraft and Wizardry," in *Cultural Politics of Harry Potter: Life, Death and the Politics of Fear*, eds. Rubén Jarazo-Álvarez and Pilar Alderete-Diez (New York: Rutledge, 2020), 23.

35. Pottermore, "Everything You Need to Know About Squibs," April 24, 2017, wizardingworld.com/features/everything-you-need-to-know-about-squibs.

36. Gierzynski and Eddy, *Harry Potter and the Millennials*, 12.

37. This is not to say that Trump is equal to Voldemort. He is closer to Grindelwald, which suggests one possible foreshadowing of the direction American society is heading.

38. Rev, "Donald Trump & Joe Biden 1st Presidential Debate Transcript 2020," September 29, 2020, https://www.rev.com/blog/transcripts/donald-trump-joe-biden-1st-presidential-debate-transcript-2020.

39. Howard University School of Law Library, "Black Lives Matter Movement," accessed August 21, 2021, library.law.howard.edu/civilrightshistory/blm.

40. Black Lives Matter, "About."

41. Gierzynski and Eddy, 18.

42. Gierzynski and Eddy, 11.

43. Pottermore, "How Do Wizards Keep Themselves So Secret From Muggles?," January 24, 2018, wizardingworld.com/features/how-do-wizards-keep-themselves-so-secret-from-muggles.

44. *FB:CoG*, 245–6.

45. *OotP*, 127.

46. *DH*, 241–2.

47. *DH,* 716.

48. Gierzynski and Eddy, 18.

49. Gierzynski and Eddy, 18.

50. William Graebner, *The Age of Doubt: American Thought and Culture in the 1940s* (Long Grove: Waveland Press, 1991), xii; Mary Lynn Kittleson, "Coming

Home: Hyper-Images of the Hero and Child in America," in *The Soul of Popular Culture: Looking at Contemporary Heroes, Myths, and Monsters*, ed. Mary Lynn Kittleson (Chicago: Open Court, 1998), 102.

51. *OoTP*, 213.

52. *OotP*, 214.

53. *FB:CoG*, 256–258.

54. Gierzynski and Eddy, 21.

55. One word used to describe Harry throughout various sources is *resilience*, suggesting that his ability to stand above his abuses is heroic. This is a constant problem within American culture that vocalizing abuse is seen as whiny and victimizing rather than becoming a heroic survivor. It is not until *DH* that Harry embraces the violence he's experienced and draws from it to fight for social change. For those not written into a hero story, acknowledging their truth and associated mental health struggles should never be reduced to resilience.

56. *GoF*, 119. The Death Eaters, especially Lucius Malfoy, are later admonished by Voldemort as disappointing and unfaithful for this and other actions (or lack of them) in the name of Voldemort. *GoF*, 647–51.

57. *OotP*, 265.

58. *OotP*, 266–7.

59. *OotP*, 268.

60. *DH*, 463–7.

61. The Half-Blood Prince's potion book helps Harry through potions class in his sixth year. Harry had not registered for potions under the assumption Snape was teaching it but jumped on the opportunity to take the class under Slughorn. Potions, while his least favorite subject, is a prerequisite for entering the Auror (dark magic law enforcement) profession, something Harry is interested in becoming.

62. *HBP*, 447–8.

63. *HBP*, 603–4.

64. *HBP*, 522.

65. *DH*, 70.

66. *DH*, 743–4.

67. Gierzynski and Eddy, 25.

68. *SS*, 64–65.

69. *OotP*, 610–21.

70. *OotP*, 614.

71. *OotP*, 615.

72. *DH*, 123.

73. *DH*, 124.

74. J.K. Rowling, "The Magical Congress of the United States of America (MACUSA)," Pottermore, October 6, 2016, wizardingworld.com/writing-by-jk-rowling/macusa.

75. Bethany Barratt, *The Politics of Harry Potter* (New York: Palgrave MacMillan, 2012), 53.

76. Barratt, 68.

77. The term used here in the racist way of the Southern border states to be inclusive of all Latin and South American cultures, echoing language used in the media.

78. Harry Potter Wiki, s.v. "Bartholomew Barebone," last modified September 27, 2021, https://harrypotter.fandom.com/wiki/Bartholomew_Barebone#Exposing_wizarding_world.

79. Harry Potter Wiki, s.v. "New Salem Philanthropic Society," July 26, 2021, https://harrypotter.fandom.com/wiki/New_Salem_Philanthropic_Society.

80. Harry Potter Wiki, s.v. "Henry Shaw Junior," May 5, 2021, https://harrypotter.fandom.com/wiki/Henry_Shaw_Junior.

81. Gierzynski and Eddy, 27.

82. J.K. Rowling, "Remus Lupin," Pottermore, August 10, 2015, wizardingworld.com/writing-by-jk-rowling/remus-lupin.

83. Brendan G.A. Hughes, "The HIV Metaphor: J.K. Rowling's Werewolf and Its Transformative Potential," in *Wizards vs. Muggles: Essays on Identity and the Harry Potter Universe*, ed. Christopher E. Bell (Jefferson: McFarland & Company, 2016), 60.

84. Dumbledore became its master after he defeated Grindelwald. When Malfoy disarmed Dumbledore, he became its master, but it was buried with Dumbledore. Voldemort stole the wand, but it never worked right for him. Harry disarmed Malfoy and took his wand, so when he confronted Voldemort, Harry was the master of the Elder Wand. "In general," wandmaker Ollivander tells Harry, "where a wand has been won, its allegiance will change." *DH*, 493.

85. *DH*, 749.

86. Cassandra Bausman, "'Elder' and Wiser: The Filmic Harry Potter and the Rejection of Power," in *Transforming Harry: The Adaptation of Harry Potter in the Transmedia Age*, eds. John Alberti and P. Andrew Miller (Detroit: Wayne State University Press, 2018), 51.

87. Pottermore, "Everything We Know About the Elder Wand," November 17, 2017, wizardingworld.com/features/everything-we-know-about-the-elder-wand.

88. J.K. Rowling (@jk_rowling), "The secret of the elder wand is that it's more sentient than any other. It can identify the caster of any spell that touches it and keeps tally of which wizard has beaten which, giving its allegiance to the one it judges the victor. Physical possession is irrelevant," Twitter, February 19, 2018, https://twitter.com/jk_rowling/status/965566203694649344?lang=en.

Chapter 5

Wizarding Decrees and the Defense Against the Dark Arts

The influence of *Harry Potter* on its readers was quickly noticed by teachers and librarians who professionally resonated with Potter and recognized the series' educational value. On one hand, the series promoted literacy and encouraged children to read for fun.[1] Additionally, those same teachers and librarians noticed social connections between the books and their young learners such that they developed pedagogical frameworks inspired by Potter that were entertaining.[2] For example, chemistry lessons became Potions class, or history classes became the History of Magic. Quickly, classrooms and libraries became their own Hogwarts, with lessons about "magic," literacy, and life.

One of the rich elements of Rowling's epic series is the commentary on the education system writ large. The setting in a specific, private boarding school is simply the overlay to a broader commentary about the role of education in shaping the social perceptions of students, including targeted focus on the rules and behaviors of teachers, the curriculum and different learning styles, and the influence of external factors on the education of children—and how they use that education for social change. The series, then, is more than a bridge between teachers and students; it is a conveyance for socialization, which in this case is highly political and thus arms students for being adults in a period of darkness and uncertainty.[3] As author Stephen King notes, "If teaching life-lessons is one of the jobs books do, then the Potter novels teach some fine ones about how to behave under pressure."[4] In addition, even for learners who are not actively reading, the books are still "taught" to them through repeated exposure in fandom channels that reinforce the lessons and messages of the series.[5] This deep immersion into Potter, it stands to reason, fostered the political perspectives of readers, including, as discussed here, the value of educational institutions versus the authentic learning that comes from experience.

THE ROLE OF THE TEACHER

We know very little about Harry's school life prior to going to Hogwarts. There are a few anecdotes that come up in relationship to weird magical events, such as finding himself on the roof of the school to escape Dudley, or how he was often ignored at school because people were afraid of upsetting Dudley by becoming Harry's friend.[6] Dudley plays the role of the prototypical bully, and it would seem from the way Rowling establishes the story that the teachers really did not interfere with Dudley's bullying of Harry; in fact, we know that Dudley was praised by his parents, Vernon and Petunia, whenever he had a chance to bully Harry. When Dudley is accepted to attend Smeltings, Uncle Vernon's *alma mater*, the Dursleys vocally support that school's practice of giving students sticks to use on each other in the hallways.[7] When Vernon or Dudley found Harry disagreeable, Dudley was encouraged to poke Harry with the stick.[8] Initially, the Dursleys planned to send Harry to Stonewall High, the local state school, but changed the narrative when Harry started attending Hogwarts, saying that he went to St. Brutus's School, "a first-rate institution for hopeless cases."[9] Again, the teacher is de-emphasized, so when Harry goes to Hogwarts and develops relationships with his teachers, his concept of whether or not they can be trusted may already be questionable.

Certain teachers quickly earn Harry's respect: Dumbledore, Hagrid, Professor McGonagall, and Professor Lupin. These teachers place a strong emphasis on experiential learning rather than traditional rote coursework by encouraging students to experiment (within reason) and learn practical applications. McGonagall could be described as the most traditional of these instructors with a teaching philosophy firmly rooted in the belief that in order for one to know, one has to do. Similarly, Harry's other favorite teachers subscribe to a similar teaching style. One key difference between McGonagall and Hagrid versus Dumbledore and Lupin is that the latter tailor their lessons to the individual student, meeting them where they are to facilitate learning. This approach gives students authority and ownership over what and how they learn, creating essentially "wicked students" prepared to tackle "wicked problems."[10] This authority happens when students learn knowledge while simultaneously applying skills. There is a play element inherent in this aspect of education. Play, here understood as the creative interactivity involved in shaping the immediate world, helping establish rules and social norms, and teaching how to apply them in social situations.[11] The merging of education and play garners cautionary statements from cultural critics,[12] but it helps promote authentic learning in an "enchanted" society enmeshed in hyperreality surrounded by simulacra. Rather than reinforcing the entertaining, play in its purest form disrupts the norm. It is, Erikson hypothesizes, the need of the ego to "master the various areas of life, and especially those in which the individual finds his self, his body, and his social role wanting and trailing."[13] Play's success relies on the fact that it is the opposite of work, thus the synthesis of all aspects of life becomes an active engagement rather than passive absorption.[14]

Hogwarts teacher, Professor Binns, is a traditional "sage on the stage" during his History of Magic lectures, never wavering from his script. His main distinguishing characteristic is that he is a ghost, having died in the teacher's lounge during a nap. Heavily committed to teaching, his ghost simply got up to go to class, leaving his body behind. While this may seem like praise for his dedication to the craft, it is in contrast to the students' perception of his class as the most notoriously boring in the entire school.

While he is vexed about going off-script, Binns is the only Hogwarts teacher to share information about the Chamber of Secrets. He stresses to Hermione that his expertise is facts rather than myths, but is persuaded to tell the story when Hermione counters by noting that all legends have a basis in fact.[15] His account not only provokes the students, who were already scared of the Chamber, but Binns' lecture helps provide some fundamental history of Hogwarts, especially the conflict between the four Hogwarts founders about their admission practices (Muggles versus magic).[16] This brief exchange demonstrates an acknowledgement that students are worthy of the extra details, but he is otherwise disinterested in their education.

In contrast, the teachers who Harry admires do make an investment in his education. For example, Hagrid is not a good instructor, but he teaches Harry how to take risks through his encouragement and mentorship. He is rewarded, in turn, by Harry's support during Care of Magical Creatures classes, especially when he blunders and the Slytherins blast him for it.

The challenge, however, is that Harry conflates these teachers with the mentorship and friendly adult roles that he craves from a childhood deprived of nurture. That makes the impact of their faults that much more difficult for Harry to process, especially those who are members of the Order of the Phoenix. For instance, Harry learns excellent strategies against the Dark Arts from Lupin—not the least of which is the Patronus charm that helps define Harry during his battles with Voldemort's forces. Yet, he struggles with Lupin's lack of resiliency to the new era of Voldemort and his lack of commitment to his newly formed family. Harry maintains that there is a better way for the good to overcome the evil, but Lupin refuses to see anything beyond the white and the black. Similarly, Harry develops a relationship with Mad-Eye Moody during the Tri-Wizard Tournament, especially since Moody takes an active stance against Harry's bully (he turns Malfoy into a ferret) and also encourages him to play to his strengths through practical applications of magic that he already knows. In other words, when it seemed like the odds are stacked against Harry, Moody gives him the positive reinforcement he needs. What Harry later has to reconcile is that the Moody who helps shape his success during his fourth year is a Death Eater imposter, and that he does not have a proper relationship with the real Mad-Eye Moody.

Dumbledore is written throughout the series as one willing to break rules and challenge norms. Frequently, when outsiders are visiting Hogwarts, they remark on Dumbledore's unorthodox practices as the school's headmaster. This unorthodoxy, however, is highlighted as positioning Dumbledore as a supreme teacher. He is willing to see sides of a student or teacher that others may not quite understand. For instance, when he is teaching a young Newt Scamander during a Defense Against the Dark Arts lesson, Dumbledore places Scamander in front of a boggart—much like Lupin does for Harry's class—and encourages Scamander to face his fears. Part of the allure of the boggart as a teaching device is that the spell to overcome it, *riddikulus*, turns the boggart into something that can be laughed at. Scamander's greatest fear is working behind a desk. His banishment turns it into a mechanical dragon— very appropriate for a future magizoologist.[17]

In *HBP*, Dumbledore becomes increasingly vulnerable, losing some of his idol's shine as he and Harry work together to better understand the horcruxes. It is incredibly difficult for teachers and students to not form some kind of attachment, and Dumbledore's attachment to Harry causes him to hold back on some of the puzzle pieces Harry needs for success, notably the Prophecy. Nonetheless, Dumbledore continually helps Harry grow and prepare for what he predicts will be Harry's biggest adventure. It is not that he has any special foresight, but that Dumbledore, like any good teacher, knows how to read people and adjust his curriculum accordingly.

In stark contrast to Dumbledore is Snape. From the first moment that they laid eyes on each other, Harry and Snape harbor a mutual dislike. Harry is initially unsure what Snape has against him, and he is convinced that Snape is out to get him after his first Potions lesson. Harry's father and his friends, we later learn, were known bullies to Snape, often abusing and embarrassing him in front of the rest of the school. In *PoA*, Snape confronts Sirius for his part in luring Snape to the Shrieking Shack while Lupin was in werewolf form. Sirius defends himself by claiming that he saved Snape from harm and claims the plan was primarily James's idea. Snape, however, is so wounded from their torment that he is unable to separate blame for James and Sirius regardless of their level of involvement. Snape made his displeasure about Lupin well known to anyone who was willing to listen, even teaching the class about werewolves when he substitutes for Lupin's class.

Snape's treatment of Harry and his friends is nothing short of deplorable and is clear that he never forgave the Marauders for their abuse nor for James's ability to snatch Lily away from him. Snape is not popular among the students, except the Slytherins for whom he is the head of house. Snape struggles with Harry because he looks so much like his father. In *The Great Snape Debate* (released prior to *DH*, predicting the trajectory of the character in the final book), Berner and Millman pose an obvious question: If Snape was in love with Lily Potter, as we learn in *DH* he is and always has been, why not treat Harry better?[18] They conclude that: "His teachers at Hogwarts rewarded the students who tormented him while brushing him aside as unimportant. Voldemort was the first authority figure to accept Snape for who he was and welcome him, giving him a position of responsibility and a place in the world. Snape would despise the mere idea of his Dark Lord's defeat and thus hate Harry as the boy who could cause it."[19] On the other hand, the authors also speculate that Snape is conflicted by his remorse for Lily's death.[20] Until the last pages of *DH*, the question remained whether Snape is a good or bad character; however, in spite of his redemption in death and Rowling's reward of the character in the name of Harry's son Albus Severus, it is a reasonable conclusion that he is a terrible teacher who gives up on students who he does not like (Harry, Hermione) or who show little promise (Neville).

He regularly goads Malfoy and the Slytherins whenever they have the upper hand against the Gryffindors, especially where Harry, Ron, and Hermione are concerned. For example, during a pre-class mini-duel outside Potions class, Hermione is hit with a spell that makes her teeth grow. In response, Snape sends a Slytherin to the hospital wing, but refuses to send Hermione, telling her, "I see no difference."[21] He is also known for threatening to poison students to test their potion antidotes. This is a negative experiential learning that is more about power than it is about the actual learning. Although he treats potions-making like a fine art, he seems utterly convinced that students are incapable of being able to brew potions on their own, because he holds his own talent in high regard. His level of abuse seems like the kind of behavior that would not be tolerated by school districts, but such teachers do exist, creating a negative experience for the students outside their favor. And this does not need to be overt behavior; it can appear through microaggressions. It could be as simple as neglect of the student and their abilities, to as complex as bringing the teacher's own bias into the classroom and projecting it on certain students. Snape's loathing toward Harry has nothing to do with Harry at all, but rather with unresolved anger toward his father and an unrequited love for his mother.

One last teacher to briefly mention is the one most clearly positioned by Rowling as Harry's worst teacher, Sybill Trelawney. Professor Trelawney teaches Divination, a questionable addition to the Hogwarts curriculum, but one deemed valuable enough for students to experience as an elective course. Her introduction to the class reinforces a perception that Divination may not be the most valuable subject:

So you have chosen to study Divination, the most difficult of the magical arts. I must warn you at the outset that if you do not have the Sight, there is very little I will be able to teach you. Books can take you only so far in this field. [. . .] Many witches and wizards, talented though they are in the area of loud bangs and smells and sudden disappearing, are yet unable to penetrate the veiled mysteries of the future.[22]

Rowling presents a skepticism in the subject from the outset, but, since prophecy is an important plot point in the later books of the series, she has Harry and Ron suffer through the classes. This skepticism is in contrast to fellow Gryffindors Lavender Brown and Parvati Patil, who immediately embrace Divination as their favorite subject. They are also marked as less-than-authentic classmates from the eyes of Harry, Ron, and Hermione.[23]

Trelawney is one of the first teachers Umbridge seeks to purge when she assumes control over Hogwarts to address what is seen as low standards at the school as the result of Dumbledore's failings. In one of her first tasks as High Inquisitor, Umbridge does a classroom observation of Trelawney, something familiar to Muggle educators, and sufficiently disrupts Trelawney's ability to teach.[24] She is ultimately fired by Umbridge, who determined that her abilities with Divination were insufficient qualifiers to continue teaching: "Incapable though you are of predicting even tomorrow's weather, you must surely have realized that your pitiful performance during my inspections, and the lack of any improvement, would make it inevitable you would be sacked?"[25]

The case of Trelawney raises questions about teacher credentials, from academic training to practical experience. Dumbledore clearly favors practical experience: Trelawney told him the Prophecy about Harry, prompting Dumbledore to keep her close; Hagrid has so much more expertise with magical creatures than other potential faculty that it outweighs his non-wizard status. Curiously, Dumbledore keeps Snape from teaching Defense Against the Dark Arts until Harry's sixth year, despite the rumor that DADA was the class that he really wanted to teach. Dumbledore assumed that Snape might relapse into his old Dark Arts ways,[26] but this concern paled to his need for Slughorn's memory of horcruxes and Voldemort. Using Harry as bait, hiring Slughorn to teach Potions for a year would keep him close while Dumbledore and Harry worked through their investigation.[27] Again, Dumbledore weighs experience and need over credential and expertise.

DADA AND EDUCATIONAL DECREES

As mentioned, the series places a strong emphasis on experiential learning. The main concept behind this learning model is that students, regardless of their learning style, can learn by doing (and by doing it in a small group of social reinforcement) according to one's strengths and learning styles. This model attempts to break rote teaching that rewards knowing facts and details in favor of teaching that emphasizes skills and competencies. If done well, the degree of skill transference is higher if a student has learned through experience rather than if a student has learned through memorization.

Ultimately, this is why Harry feels prepared to leave Hogwarts before the start of his seventh year. To that point, he has learned much through his experiences fighting different forms of Voldemort, searching for horcruxes, and solving challenging puzzles. In fact, in each of his years, it is the lessons he learns outside of the classroom that get him closer to Voldemort. For instance, beginning in his third year, Harry receives supplemental instruction from his teachers in direct response to a looming threat. In *PoA*, Lupin teaches Harry the complicated Patronus charm that school-aged witches and wizards rarely perform to help Harry defend himself from the Dementors. In *GoF*, Moody helps Harry pass the tasks by helping Harry see his strengths. *OotP* has Snape teach Occlumency, an ability to protect one's mind from charms that can penetrate it for memories or other information. Dumbledore helps Harry in *HBP* with his horcrux lessons. While Harry does not master all of these skills, they nonetheless help prepare him for final confrontation with Voldemort.

When Umbridge restricts the curriculum for Defense Against the Dark Arts, Harry's classmates turn to him to teach them how to defend themselves from Voldemort. Umbridge's restrictions are the result of the Ministry intervention. Although not all of them are named in either book or film, Umbridge's actions are backed by "Educational Decrees," official Ministry statements establishing (or frequently overturning) school rules. The first decrees to impact Hogwarts, Educational Decree Twenty-Two (allowing the Ministry to appoint a teacher if the headmaster is unable to find a suitable candidate) and Educational Decree Twenty-Three (creating the position of Hogwarts High Inquisitor), establish Umbridge's authority.[28] The rationale from the Ministry is that Fudge is responding to concerns from student parents who are anxious about the prior year's events at the school: the Tri-Wizard Tournament and the death of Cedric Diggory.[29] The more manifest concern is Dumbledore and his "eccentric decisions" in particular with faculty staffing and what they are allowed to teach.[30] Umbridge, as the DADA instructor, intends to teach a curriculum that is "carefully structured, theory-centered, Ministry-approved."[31] The outcomes of her course, as Hermione observes, make no mention of using defensive spells:[32]

- Understanding the principles underlying defensive magic.
- Learning to recognize situation in which defensive magic can legally be used.

- Placing the use of defensive in context for practical use.[33]

Harry and the other fifth-year students are preparing for their O.W.Ls, or Ordinary Wizarding Levels, school-wide exams to help students career-plan for life post-Hogwarts and to identify the remaining courses they need for this specialization. While arguably a theory-based approach can help inform their exams, the Hogwarts students have also witnessed in varying degrees incidents when a practical approach would make a difference. They recognize that Umbridge's limited curriculum will not provide them the right skills for practical use of defensive magic.

Politicizing education is not unique to the wizarding world. State School Boards all around the country outline the guidelines that must be addressed within the curriculum to prepare students for the state assessments that determine the funding allocated to schools. Two recent events, for example, have affected public education at the national level: the Textbook Debate and Critical Race Theory.

The Textbook Debate

In 2009, a well-publicized[34] debate plagued the Texas Board of Education around forthcoming updates to the state textbooks and associated curriculum. Central to this, in particular, was the Social Studies curriculum. This debate circulated in academic circles for two main reasons: One was that the proposed changes were positioning a revisionist history that diminished the roles of key Founding Fathers like Thomas Jefferson in favor of promoting other figures, such as Moses, to counter-balance a perceived liberal bias in the curriculum.[35] This is not a new endeavor within the state's educational history, but in the newly digitized social media Internet, this was the first time that Texas's national impact on the textbook market was called into question by audiences outside academia. Because of the expense of the publication market, textbook publishers write with California and Texas in mind so they are not publishing multiple textbooks that may or may not get adopted for school use. "After California," Alexander Stille writes in 2002, "Texas is the biggest buyer of textbooks in the United States, accounting for nearly 10 percent of the national market."[36] Texas also passed its own "Educational Decree" in 1995 that allowed rejection of proposed textbooks on grounds of "factual inaccuracy."[37] The concept of "factual inaccuracy" aligns itself along party lines. The conservative stance is that a "liberal" education (here understood as equated with the Democratic party) is un-American and un-Christian in how it teaches concepts of diversity, climate change, and evolution. In a Letter to the Editor of the *New York Times*, Daniel Czhrom, one of the authors of a book banned by Texas in 2002 observes: "Many conservatives are simply unwilling to accept how much the writing and teaching of American history have changed over the last 40 years. [. . .] They prefer a pseudo-patriotic history that denies the fundamental conflicts that have shaped our past."[38]

Similar to the Defense Against the Dark Arts, the textbook becomes a political tool for the ownership of curriculum. The apparent hope seems to be the unravelling of unsavory history at the lowest levels of education to age them out of the cultural consciousness. In his controversial[39] *People's History of the United States*, Howard Zinn questions this myopic perspective of history. Calling the work of the historian an ideological distortion, Zinn outlines the power of historians to filter the "hard histories" simply by presenting some facts in passing mention and others as central to the narrative. In other words, the bias of the historian is an inevitable truth of the field, but one in continual need of challenge:

> My view point, in telling the history of the United States, is different: that we must not accept the memory of states as our own. Nations are not communities and never have been. The history of any country, presented as the history of a family, conceals fierce conflicts of interest (sometimes exploding, often repressed) between conquerors and conquered, masters and slaves, capitalists and workers, dominators and dominated in race and sex. And in such a world of conflict, a world of victims and executioners, it is the job of thinking people, as Albert Camus suggested, not to be on the side of the executioners.[40]

A post-Potter world recognizes, thanks to efforts of characters such as Umbridge, the value of a broader perspective on society and history. When not occurring within the classroom, people take DADA to social media, which helps further confirm their bias about "factual inaccuracies" in the entire spectrum of political parties.

One such use of social media called attention to an egregious factual inaccuracy in a Texas-approved geography textbook. In a section about "Patterns of Immigration," the textbook describes slaves brought to the United States through the slave trade as "workers," diminishing the horrific history of slavery to sound more like a labor exchange.[41] While the publisher did apologize for their oversight, this example reinforces the power of language on shaping a narrative. In response to a question on the use of language to disempower, Noam Chomsky remarks that, "the terminology we use is heavily ideologically laden, always. Pick your term: If it's a term that has any significance whatsoever—like, not 'and' or 'or'—it typically has two meanings, a dictionary meaning and a meaning that's used for warfare."[42] The Southern mythology built around slavery is so strong that the racist ideology informing perceptions of American history manifests in aspects of unconscious bias.[43] Using language such as "immigration" and "workers" softens the history by burying it behind the curtain of "inclusiveness." "Fear of the name increases fear of the thing itself," Dumbledore tells Harry after his first confrontation against Voldemort.[44] To call it "slavery" is to face the reality of America's dark history. Similarly, Mad-Eye Moody tells the class, "the sooner you know what you're up against, the better. How are you supposed to defend yourself from something you've never seen?"[45]

Critical Race Theory

"By order of The High Inquisitor of Hogwarts

Teachers are hereby banned from giving students any information that is not strictly related to the subjects they are paid to teach.

The above is in accordance with Educational Decree Number Twenty-Six."[46]

Fast-forwarding a decade, the 2020 election raised another attempt to revise American history. Media is a proven and powerful information tool, making it an easy target for political polarization. Throughout its time in office, the Trump administration embarked on a strong propaganda campaign to discredit facts and information that did not come from "approved" sources, such as the social media accounts of Trumpian conservatives, Fox News, Breitbart, and others, as "fake news." This is because the Trump Administration knew how to weaponize social media, and how these newer media lend themselves to "niche-oriented media."[47] This fragmentation of information aligns with McLuhan's observation of the affect new technologies have on fragmenting the senses: "It is simpler to say that if a new technology extends one or more of our senses outside us into the social world, then new ratios among all of our senses will occur in that particular culture. [. . .] And when the sense ratios alter in any culture then what had appeared lucid before may suddenly be opaque, and what had been vague or opaque will become translucent."[48] In this case, what became "translucent" was that the through line of American racism had burrowed a deeper network on the contemporary psyche than the optimistic media of the 1980s and 90s wanted everyone to believe. So deeply infiltrating is this mythos that a narrative emerged of a "post-racial society" claiming that "we don't see race" while at the same time reinforcing a social infrastructure that pervasively marginalizes people of color.

Critical Race Theory (CRT) wound its way into the realm of subject matter "not strictly related" to the educational goals of conservative politics. At the core of CRT is a close review of the systematic inequities that have supported American racism since emancipation, especially noteworthy following the Civil Rights Movement of the 1960s. CRT pioneers Derrick Bell and Alan

Freeman shared a common concern that, by the mid-1970s, racial reform was slow and that the familiar approaches to reform were simply ineffective due to the complex nature of modern racism.[49] Rather than behave as though racism no longer exists, CRT accepts that racism is deeply entangled in the American mythos. As such, CRT further aims to deconstruct and reconstruct the surrounding narrative from one of race-based oppression to one of equity and opportunity. In October 2020, the Trump Administration passed an Executive Order banning diversity trainings within federal entities and contractors.[50] These "harmful ideologies" and "divisive concepts" furthered the Administration's propaganda in support of a new American whiteism to "Make America Great Again." This Executive Order opened doors of possibility to protest the teaching of these "divisive concepts" in schools. While these "harmful ideologies" extend beyond Trump's four-year window, media projects such as the 2016 film *13th* and 2019's launch of the *1619 Project* touched a sensitive spot in the American psyche, one that Trump was all too eager to continually poke into aggression. These media challenge the core of the American identity at a time when the media (in particular, social media) situates as the central battleground for ideological warfare.

The fire against CRT is less about the theory itself, but more about reinforcing the racist mythos while also protecting individuals, particularly white individuals, from feeling distress or guilt on account of their race, with blatant disregard for the BIPOC (Black, Indigenous, People of Color) population who have faced profiling, marginalization, social inequity, and systemic discrimination.[51] Nonetheless, state legislatures took up the debate and issued their own decrees banning CRT in state schools. Leading into the 2021–2022 school year, Texas joined the growing list with House Bill 3979 that restricts what content teachers may include in their curriculum under auspices of the "essential knowledge and skills" of the state Social Studies competencies.[52]

As an illustration of the implications of the CRT issue, this bill eliminates the core tenants of a humanistic civic education. Teachers would not be allowed to say:

1. That one race or sex is superior to others;
2. That an individual of a certain race or sex is inherently "racist, sexist, or oppressive," making note to be inclusive of unconscious behavior.
3. That one should face discrimination because of their race or sex.
4. That one race or sex should not/cannot "attempt to treat others without respect to race or sex."
5. That one's moral character is a by-product of race or sex.
6. That an individual bears responsibility for the actions of those committed in the past.

7. That no one should feel discomfort, guilt, anguish, or any other form of psychological distress because of their race or sex.
8. That a meritocracy or hard work ethic is racist or sexist, or was established to oppress members of another race or sex.
9. That slavery is essential to the true founding of the United States.
10. That racism and slavery are anything other than deviations from "the authentic founding principles of the United States."[53]

The vitriol parallels that of Umbridge's decrees. While those were rescinded when she left Hogwarts, they had the desired effect that allowed the Ministry to eventually be "taken over" by the Death Eaters. Umbridge, while not a Death Eater, continues her work in the Ministry leading a commission on registration of Muggle-borns.

At the time of this writing, the ripple effect of these CRT bans has yet to be fully realized. It is safe to say that the legal backing of educational content is a significant shift in the American narrative. Although regulation has long existed, as have state standards and outcomes, the blatant attack against a specific element of curriculum—rather than quiet negligence—is a challenge to the gains made over the last forty years around inclusivity. One might even suggest that it is a threat to democracy.

NOTES

1. c.f. Steve Dempster et al., "What Has Harry Potter Done For Me? Children's Reflections on Their 'Potter' Experience," *Children's Literature in Education: An International Quarterly* 47, no. 3 (September 2016): 267–82; Ruth Nicola, "Returning to Reading with Potter," *Journal of Adolescent & Adult Literacy* 44, no. 8 (May 2001): 747–48; Beatty, "Natural Part of Us!"

2. c.f. Sharon Black, "Harry Potter: Enchantment for All Seasons," *Gifted Child Today* 26, no. 3 (Summer 2003): 46–54; Urvashi Sahni, "The Harry Potter Phenomenon," *Journal of Adolescent & Adult Literacy* 44, no. 8 (May 2001): 750–51.

3. Anthony Gierzynski and Katheryn Eddy, Harry Potter and the Millennials: Research Methods and the Politics of the Muggle Generation (Baltimore: Johns Hopkins University Press, 2013), 4–5.

4. Stephen King, "Review of *Harry Potter and the Order of the Phoenix*," *Entertainment Weekly*, July 11, 2003, quoted in John S. Nelson, *Defenses Against the Dark Arts: The Political Education of Harry Potter and His Friends* (Lanham: Lexington Books, 2021), 15.

5. *Cultivation theory*: the "repeated exposure to a media source [that] leads audiences to internalize the perspectives of that source and to see the world as similar to the world portrayed in that media," Gierzynski and Eddy, 29.

6. *SS*, 58.

7. *SS*, 32.

8. *SS*, 33–34.

9. *PoA*, 24.

10. Paul Hanstedt, *Creating Wicked Students: Designing Courses For a Complex World* (Sterling: Stylus, 2018), 3. Hanstedt defines wicked problems as "situations where the parameters of the problem and the means available for solving them [are] changing constantly."

11. Johan Huizinga, *Homo Ludens: A Study of the Play Element of Culture* (Boston: Beacon Press, 1950), 46–53.

12. One such commentator, Neil Postman supports play as entertainment, but not as a lifestyle. Postman echoes and quotes Hannah Arendt: "The dangers of mass education is precisely that it may become very entertaining indeed; there are many great authors of the past who have survived centuries of oblivion and neglect, but it is still an open question whether they will be able to survive an entertaining version of what they have to say." Postman, *Amusing Ourselves*, 124.

13. Erikson, 211–2.

14. Erikson, 212.

15. *CoS*, 149.

16. *CoS*, 150.

17. *FB:CoG*, 151–2.

18. Amy Berner and Joyce Millman, "The Case for Snape's Guilt: Is Snape Harry Potter's Foe?" in *The Great Snape Debate* (New York: Borders, Inc., 2007), 21.

19. Berner and Millman, 21.

20. Amy Berner, Orson Scott Card, and Joyce Millman, "The Case for Snape's Innocence: Is Snape Harry Potter's Friend?" in *The Great Snape Debate* (New York: Borders, Inc., 2007), 13–15.

21. *GoF*, 299–300.

22. *PoA*, 103.

23. The Gryffindors learn in their first lesson that Harry will die based on the tea leaves in his cup. In their next class, they share their collective anxiety with Professor McGonagall, whose first question is who Trelawney said would die this year. After assuring Harry that death omens are a common technique Trelawney uses (and no one has died yet), she reinforces that "Divination is one of the most imprecise branches of magic. I shall not conceal from you that I have very little patience with it. [. . .] You look in excellent health to me, Potter, so you will excuse me if I don't let you off homework today. I assure you that if you die, you need not hand it in." This is one of the many scenes that makes McGonagall my personal favorite, enhanced by the acerbic portrayal by Dame Maggie Smith in the films. *PoA*, 109.

24. *OotP*, 312–5.

25. *OotP*, 595.

26. Accio Quote, "Fry, Stephen, Interviewer: J.K. Rowling at the Royal Albert Hall, 26 June 2003," June 26, 2003, http://www.accio-quote.org/articles/2003/0626-alberthall-fry.htm.

27. *HBP*, 66–74.

28. *OotP*, 307.

29. *OotP*, 306–7.

30. *OotP*, 308.

31. *OotP*, 239.

32. *OotP*, 241.

33. *OotP*, 240.

34. Especially among Texas academics.

35. The Associated Press, "Texas Approves Disputed History Texts for Schools," *New York Times*, November 22, 2014, https://www.nytimes.com/2014/11/23/us/texas-approves-disputed-history-texts-for-schools.html; Zack Kopplin, "Was Moses a Founding Father?" *The Atlantic*, November 25, 2014, theatlantic.com/education/archive/2014/11/was-moses-a-founding-father/383153; Laura Isensee, "Texas Hits the Books," NPR, November 21, 2014, npr.org/sections/ed/2014/11/21/365686593/texas-hits-the-books.

36. Alexander Stille, "Textbook Publishers Learn: Avoid Messing with Texas: Textbook Publishers Learn: Better Avoid Messing With Texas," *New York Times*, June 29, 2002, ProQuest.

37. Stille, "Textbook Publishers Learn."

38. Daniel Czitrom, letter to the editor, *New York Times*, March 16, 2010, ProQuest.

39. "Controversial" is often presented as questioning Zinn's methodology, but he does nonetheless challenge the prominent American mythologies. Regardless of one's personal preferences regarding his work, his is an honorary member of Dumbledore's Army.

40. Howard Zinn, *A People's History of the United States* (New York: HarperCollins Publishers, 1980), 10.

41. Laura Isensee, "Why Calling Slaves 'Workers' Is More Than an Editing Error," NPR, October 23, 2015, npr.org/sections/ed/2015/10/23/450826208/why-calling-slaves-workers-is-more-than-an-editing-error.

42. Noam Chomsky, "'Containing' the Soviet Union in the Cold War," in *Understanding Power: The Indispensable Chomsky* (New York: The New Press, 2002), 37.

43. James Oliver Robertson, *American Myth, American Reality* (New York: Hill & Wang, 1980), 93–97.

44. *SS*, 298.

45. *GoF*, 212.

46. *OotP*, 551.

47. Henry Jenkins, "Unspreadable Media (Part Five): Back and Forth," Confessions of an Aca-Fan, June 21, 2017, henryjenkins.org/blog/2017/6/15/unspreadable-media-part-five-back-and-forth.

48. Marshall McLuhan, "The Gutenberg Galaxy," in *Essential McLuhan*, edited by Eric McLuhan and Frank Zingrone (New York: BasicBooks, 1995), 136.

49. Richard Delgado and Jean Stefancic, *Critical Race Theory: The Cutting Edge* (Philadelphia: Temple University Press, 2013), 2.

50. Sarah Hinger and Brian Hauss, "The Trump Administration Is Banning Talk About Race and Gender," ACLU, October 9, 2020, https://www.aclu.org/news/civil-liberties/the-trump-administration-is-banning-talk-about-race-and-gender/.

51. Donald Earl Collins, "Critical Race Theory and the Scam of the Ban," Aljazeera, June 27, 2021, https://www.aljazeera.com/opinions/2021/6/27/critical-race-theory-and-the-scam-of-the-ban; Adrian Florido, "Teachers Say Laws Banning Critical Race Theory Are Pulling a Chill on Their Lessons," NPR, May 28, 2021, npr.org/2021/05/28/1000537206/teachers-laws-banning-critical-race-theory-are-leading-to-self-censorship; Jane Coaston, "The Argument: What Are States Really Banning When They Ban Critical Race Theory in Classrooms? Transcript," *New York Times*, accessed August 18, 2021, nytimes.com/2021/08/18/opinion/critical-race-theory-us-schools.html?showtranscript=1.

52. Texas State Legislature, *An Act Relating to the Social Studies Curriculum in Public Schools*, Enrolled Version, 87th Leg., 3rd sess. (Austin: TLO, 2021); Texas State Legislature, *A Bill to Be Entitled an Act Relating to Civics Instruction Public School Students and Instruction Policies in Public Schools*, Introduced Version, 87th Leg., 3rd sess. (Austin: TLO, 2021). As a native Texan, I find the bill affirming my personal experience of the state's education policies. In preparing the draft of this bill, the writers note their founding documents: The Declaration of Independence; The United States Constitutions; The Federalist Papers, especially essays 10 and 51; excerpts from Alexis de Toqueville's *Democracy in America*; the first Lincoln-Douglas debate; the writings of the Founding Fathers of the United States. To the last item, do they include Moses? Without diving too deeply into the politics of these documents, it is noteworthy that all were written by white men. There is no representation of women or BIPOC. In fact, the inclusion of the first Lincoln-Douglas debate seems to appear to reinforce the racism latent to the American mythos.

53. The bill also excludes requiring an understanding of the *1619 Project*.

Chapter 6

Harry Potter and Social Activism

The wizarding world that Rowling has constructed thus far is rooted in Northern Europe and the United States and is built around the idea that the magical world needs to be hidden and kept secret from Muggles. The Statute of Secrecy exists as defined laws against public displays of magic and of wizarding communities.[1] Given the Muggle history of witch trials, this makes sense from a survival perspective. The biggest difficulty, however, is that the two worlds are constantly in a delicate dance, and one group is blind to the other. This places even more responsibility on the magical community to train novice wizards and witches how to control their magic. For example, once children enroll at Hogwarts at age eleven, suggesting that magical awakening and potency collides with adolescence, they are prohibited from doing magic outside of the school until they turn seventeen and "come of age." Adolescence is a developmental time when the body awakens to its potential, which is also going through unpleasant transition.[2] Harry's adolescence is fraught with the additional challenge of being a target for Voldemort, forcing him into a life-or-death struggle of defending himself, his friends, and his experiences from adults who, through their willful ignorance, would prefer that past should remain in the past, and ignore the generational trauma that affects their interactions with the students. It is natural for adults to fear confronting traumas when those traumas are resurrected in a newer generation; however, ignoring reality can have dire consequences. Voldemort was able to resurrect at the end of the *GoF*, because adults chose to ignore the warnings of both Harry and Dumbledore, and to stay blind to the signs and undercurrents of activity that hinted of his return. They chose to trust in the system of secrecy to shut down the conversation, creating an unspoken intergenerational "statute of secrecy." Rowling here suggests the privilege of education as a form of resistance, because the only adults who willingly believe Harry are those who are educated or are a part of the resistance movement—the Order of the Phoenix and its newer generation, Dumbledore's Army (both conveniently linked to Dumbledore).

DUMBLEDORE'S ARMY

The Order of the Phoenix is a grassroots group of witches and wizards founded by Dumbledore for the purpose of opposing Voldemort during his first rise to power. Many of the members identified throughout the books are the parents of Harry and his peers, along with Hogwarts professors, Ministry Aurors, and those who were victims of Death Eaters or close to someone who was. They worked with the Ministry to fight against Voldemort and the Death Eaters during the First Wizarding War.[3] Many of their number died, such as the Potters, and others, like the Longbottoms, were permanently injured. Those who lived reconvened the Order of the Phoenix after the return of Voldemort in *GoF*, setting up their headquarters in the familial home of Sirius Black. Unfortunately for the children, the adults choose to not allow them in to their meetings, claiming they are too young.[4] From this group, the kids are able to learn the value of building a resistance movement without having to carry the weight of their parents' experiences.

Their exposure to the Order of the Phoenix helped inspire Dumbledore's Army (DA), with the noteworthy difference that the DA was founded on the goal of teaching DADA to compensate for the lack of instruction Umbridge was giving. Hermione points out to Harry that he is the only one who has practical experience defending the Dark Arts, making him the best in the school to mentor those who want to learn the defenses.[5] Although Umbridge managed to break up the group before she left Hogwarts, DA members used the group during their seventh year to protect each other from the new Death Eater administration controlling the school, especially from the Carrows, who act as both professors and rule enforcement and are particularly aggressive toward any student who they deemed unworthy: Muggle-borns and Muggle-sympathizers. The DA establish a hideout in the Room of Requirement in Hogwarts. The entrance to the previous Room of Requirement DA hideout was destroyed by Umbridge. The new entrance is linked to a painting in the Hog's Head Pub run by Dumbledore's brother, Aberforth. This helps keep the DA ready and prepared to take up arms to support Harry and fight against Voldemort.

Canon says that the Order of the Phoenix was formed in 1970 and fought until 1981 when baby Harry defeated Voldemort.[6] Dumbledore's Army was able to achieve Voldemort's defeat within a few years thanks to their collective ingenuity and determination to protect Hogwarts. There is also an implied suggestion that Dumbledore's shadow loomed so heavily on these groups, that his death actually freed the DA to recognize what they needed to do and rally around their priorities. This unified the Hogwarts houses in solidarity against the Death Eaters. Harry, Hermione, and Ron had no idea that Neville had revived the DA while they were horcrux hunting. This new DA movement shows an initiative to not hide behind a single leader, as the Order did with Dumbledore, in whose absence the group folded. Here again is an example of the collective hero in action. When the trio reunite with the DA, this collective energy sparks the courage to defend the school. In the Final Battle, the Order's members play a support role relying on their ability to use advanced magic to support the younger DA, rather than to fight the battle for them.

This kind of bravery and collectivity winds its way through the fandom who recognizes the power that can happen when people work together for a common good motivated by love, compassion, and empathy for each other. Harry is a leader, but he is not the leader. His connection to Voldemort is a catalyst, not a purpose. When fandoms unite for social justice rather than under a single leader, they cast a wide net of support for multiple causes whether through meme-sharing or hard activism. They become the agents of change by simply changing the tone of the community and inspiring others to do the same. Understanding the activist's mindset is just as important as understanding their causes.

REPUBLICANS FOR VOLDEMORT

Political consciousness and Potter go hand in hand. DADA helps prepare young witches and wizards for the political world they are going to face. While Rowling connects the Dark Arts with dark witches and wizards, John Nelson suggests that they are actually a generational divide: "In Potter parlance, dark arts are crafts for inflicting effects on others. These are 'arts' in requiring advanced knowledge and practice to succeed at all, even as they repay refinement with reliability and experiment with discovery. They are 'dark' because they 'do unto others' without the others' initial awareness, or at least agreement, let alone direct benefit."[7] Additionally, for

> a young witch or wizard, the dark arts signal adult power and respect. The damage they can do and the skill they can require mark an ascension to mature responsibility as a mage. For student mages, the dark arts sound mysterious, dangerous, and sexy. For good or ill, their effects can reach beyond family and friends into the larger world: just like the headline politics of offices, elections, movements, or revolutions. To face these responsibilities is to come of age.[8]

Here, there is no implication of the Dark Arts being about the dark side of magic. Rather, knowledge of the Dark Arts is a benchmark for the degree of maturity that mandates authority and commands respect. DADA, in this metaphor, is the ability to learn enough about the Dark Arts to recognize them but resist their seductiveness, for lack of a better word.

During the election seasons of the 2000s, fans used *Harry Potter* imagery to create "campaign" slogans that linked their political bias with a particular party or ideology. This was a small act of taking a political stance that some fans bought into, while others questioned the validity of the message. One such example is "Republicans for Voldemort," which emerged ahead of the 2004 election and is credited to artist Jon Rosenberg.[9] This slogan was a response to the Bush Administration as a way to convey disagreement about the Republican Party's stance around domestic social issues, the approval of extreme war budgets, and treatment of suspected terrorists. Obviously, the bias in this statement is strong, suggesting that the Republican stance is akin to the kind of narcissistic power and Muggle cleansing of Voldemort. However, the message also conveys that Republicans are ambitious and ruthless, and willing to do whatever it takes to succeed. As such, "Republicans for Voldemort" becomes a message that can mean different things depending on one's political attitude of the Republican Party: it can be both a statement against the actions of a political party and it can become a motivator for those wanting to see Slytherin characteristics within their party.

The slogan lost steam during the Obama Administration and did not resurrect during the Trump election. However, fans have also been trying to get Hermione Granger elected president. In the 2020 election, one popular fan-driven campaign was "Granger / Lovegood 2020." This ticket would place Hermione Granger as president, with Luna Lovegood as her vice president. Hermione's leadership is recognized as canon; she is Minister of Magic in *CC*. This does make her a good metaphor for a president, but the other potent message of this ticket is that it positions two women in the seat of American power. Potter fans here acknowledge that it is time to see a woman attain these high positions, especially while witnessing what seems to be international success for countries that have women in powerful decision-making positions. The claim is that women in power will mean support for civic issues and social welfare. It is a win that Kamala Harris won the vice presidency in the 2020 election; perhaps other women will soon follow in her footsteps.

FAN ACTIVISM AND THE HARRY POTTER ALLIANCE

The distinguishing characteristic of the Harry Potter fandom is how it collectively uses the stories and the Internet to bring the world of Harry Potter into their real-life framework; in other words, turning the books into the foundational moral principles of community and social organization. Through the dominant themes of love and acceptance, Potter fans embark on social change through activism.

Henry Jenkins defines fan activism as, "Forms of civic engagement and political participation that emerge from within fan culture itself, often in response to the shared interests of fans, often conducted through the infrastructure of existing fan practices and relationships, and often framed through metaphors drawn from popular and participatory culture."[10] The common language of the fandom helps engage fans with each other and with local and global issues. Because of the composition of the Harry Potter fandom, many of the fan activists are millennials who unite under the auspices of using the Internet and social media as platforms for political discourse, mobilization that gets millennials to vote or attend protests, and to speak publicly about issues they find important.

One central organization behind Harry Potter fan activism is the Harry Potter Alliance (HPA), known as Fandom Forward as of 2021 to encompass other fandoms into the fold.[11] The HPA was established in 2005 on the belief in the unifying power of story, recognizing that "the Harry Potter universe is so rich and diverse that almost any real-world cause could be linked to it, allowing the organization to respond quickly to current events as well as to pressing issues raised by its members."[12] Central issues include global literacy, equality, and human rights.[13] An example of an early campaign for the organization was designed to "mobilize to help fans do their part to end the genocide in Darfur. HPA parties will consist of activities and activism geared around our love of *Harry Potter* and aimed toward helping fight the terrible injustice in the Sudan, the way Harry and the DA helped wake the world up to Voldemort's return."[14] The campaign successfully raised awareness for the cause and also for the Alliance itself. This was a new kind of activism, in particular a new kind of participatory politics, which refer to the intersection between participatory culture and civic engagement.[15] The participatory nature invites a play element that allows fans to try on and aim to establish "new" rules for social engagement. This allows the HPA to push beyond light-hearted charity into the realm of challenging the essential status quo at the heart of systemic inequities.[16]

In explaining the name change, Fandom Forward reinforces their belief in the "power of storytelling, but not from just one story. We believe that the stories we love can inspire and mobilize fans to create a better tomorrow for the world around us."[17] Two active campaigns in 2021 include Protego, named after the Harry Potter shield charm, to encourage action for trans rights; and #StopLine3, inspired by an episode of *Avatar: The Last Airbender*, to take action against an oil pipeline being constructed on Indigenous land that will impact water sources.[18] Similar to earlier campaigns, these new campaigns provide resources and toolkits for people who want to be involved. Also, like

Harry Potter, *Avatar* is a journey story aimed at children and young adults (not coincidentally the same millennials as Harry Potter) focusing on realigning the balance of power.

The name change is itself a form of activism. While not explicitly stated in their press release, dropping "Harry Potter" from the organization's name comes months after public outcry against J.K. Rowling's anti-trans tweets. Under the guise of fandom, Fandom Forward sends a clear message about inclusion in their divestiture from the author that inspired this journey. This will be discussed further in the next chapter.

RITA SKEETER AND THE 24-HOUR NEWS CYCLE

Compared to the Muggle world, media in the wizarding world seems archaic, relying on print media over all other forms. The primary source is the *Daily Prophet*, a daily newspaper that prints the news relevant to the British magical community. As the name implies, the newspaper suggests that it can deliver prophetic news, aiming to report news as close to real time as possible. Rowling's equation of journalism with prophecy—a form of magic she clearly dislikes—also implies an unreliability about the nature of the media. News stories tell a version of a story, but one that, like a prophecy, can be misunderstood, misinterpreted, or manipulated for the gain of a select audience. Although Hermione does take a subscription to the newspaper to stay informed of wizarding news, she also offers commentary about what is being reported, especially if she disagrees with it or recognizes its falseness. While journalists are not identified throughout the series, one is given a central role: Rita Skeeter.

Rita Skeeter is famous for her exposés and is the lead journalist covering the Tri-Wizard Tournament, showing special interest in Harry's story. She dictates her interviews to a quick quotes quill that fills in the narrative of the conversation (with embellishments), and her stories are widely read by *Prophet* readers. She also has a keen skill to uncover information that would otherwise not be known, including private conversations. Hermione later identifies her to be an illegal animagus, a witch or wizard who can transform into an animal at will. Skeeter's ability is to transform into a beetle who can spy unnoticed on Harry and his friends.[19]

Through her sensationalism, Rita Skeeter becomes a trusted journalistic voice in the community, demonstrating the role a journalist can take in shaping the outcomes and opinions of others. As an example, Skeeter writes a story about how Hermione's connection to Viktor Krum is causing Harry heartache, inspiring readers, including Mrs. Weasley, to treat Hermione less cordially.[20] While it seems obvious to Harry and Hermione that Skeeter's story is wrong, it, nonetheless, as with all of the stories she writes during the Tournament, has the power to sway opinions. Skeeter, however, is not trying to tell lies as much as she is chasing the story and giving the versions her readers want. This is similar to the power of American media, which is most commonly influenced by corporate bottom lines especially as revenue from print media decreases. With the rise of the Internet, chasing subscribers became chasing likes and trying to have the headline or the version of the story that goes viral.[21] As such, it is no longer a game of sensationalist journalism, as seen during the newspaper battles of William Randolph Hearst, but a matter of who is funding the story and the targeted audience.

Media imbalance was not a new phenomenon by the writing of *Harry Potter*, but the reliance on the Internet was. The flexibility of the Internet made it possible for webmasters to quickly get news out there. If an event was taking place, they could blog about it almost as a teaser for the later, "formal" publication in a newspaper, magazine, or radio show. The quickness of the spread of information accelerated the desire for speedy news, allowing the market for the 24-hour news channels and news on social media to rapidly expand.

With the rise of the 24-hour News Cycle and social media, pressure exists to keep the stories fresh as long as possible, even at the expense of newsworthy information related to global affairs. "Talking heads" such as MSNBC's Rachel Maddow or Fox's Tucker Carlson become the icons whose perspectives are respected, even taken as gospel, by their audience such that they have to continue to deliver, often repeating pithy soundbites to maintain audience attention. Jean Baudrillard recognizes this as a by-product and a catalyst in a consumer society that keeps the cycle revolving. "We have already seen how," he writes,

> through mass communications, the pathetic hypocrisy of the minor news item heightens with all the signs of catastrophe (deaths, murders, rapes, revolution) the tranquility of daily life. But the same pathetic redundancy of signs is visible everywhere: [. . .] everywhere we see the historical disintegration of certain structures celebrating, as it were, under the sign of consumption, both their real disappearance and their caricatural resurrection.[22]

In the intersection of disappearance and caricatural resurrection sits nostalgia and the longing for an idyllic culture, so the media fuels this hunger with simulacra, the artifice of signs manipulated to project a cultural narrative that needs reclaiming. The more saturated this narrative becomes, the harder it is to discern its meaning.[23] The more muddled the meaning, the easier it becomes for the media to evolve into propaganda.[24] It is this ability of the media writ large that has significantly transformed American culture as a whole.

S.P.E.W. AND WORKER'S RIGHTS

"Hermione—open your ears," said Ron loudly. "They. Like. It. They *like* being enslaved."[25]

When Hermione learns about house-elves and their roles within wizarding society, she decides to take up the cause of supporting their rights to equitable compensation. As a Muggle, she is not surrounded by house-elves and her perspective is based on two acquaintances: Dobby, the house elf who tried to help Harry in *CoS*, and Winky, Crouch's house-elf in *GoF*. House-elves are freed from their servitude through the presentation of clothes, usually as a punishment. Dobby is freed from an abusive life at the end of *CoS* when Harry tricks Lucius Malfoy into giving Dobby a sock. Harry, Hermione, and the Weasleys meet Winky at the Quidditch World Cup, where she is hold-ing a seat for her master even though she is terrified of heights. When, later that evening, she is found holding Harry's wand after it cast a Dark Mark, Mr. Crouch fires Winky with clothes. Both Dobby and Winky wind up at Hogwarts—Dobby as a paid employee, and Winky as a sheltered guest. She is not recognized by the other house-elves, however, as a co-worker; she is too distraught about losing her family and is frequently drunk on butterbeer. Her treatment, in particular, inspires Hermione to become an activist for house-elves.

To raise awareness of house-elf rights, Hermione creates S.P.E.W., or the Society for the Protection of Elvish Welfare.[26] The primary goals of the group are, in the short term, to "secure house-elves fair wages and working condi-tions," and, in the long term, to change "the law about non-wand use" and to "get an elf into the Department for the Regulation and Control of Magical Creatures, because they're shockingly underrepresented."[27] The plight of the house-elf reflects a common perception about the disenfranchised, that they must like the lifestyle they are living, based on the perception that they chose to live this way. Workers' rights has been central to the nation, especially when the rise of industrialization created jobs that were laborious and often staffed by women and children of the lower socio-economic classes, includ-ing immigrants. The bulwark of consumerism rests in the history of these factories: producing things produces money, money allows for consumption, consumption is key to happiness; however, these factories frequently oper-ated without regulation and oversight, requiring long hours of its employees in oppressive conditions reinforcing an image of these workers as disposable commodities.[28] Sometimes workers were provided housing constructed by the factory owners specifically to house workers nearby, but this was little compensation for the injuries these workers could endure as a result of their work. Once maimed, a worker was fired with no compensation.

The power dynamics are strong in this narrative, and the nature of the system kept the lower classes in a cycle of slavery, although not called such, encouraged by the hope of someday achieving upward mobility out of the grips of poverty. The 19th century established the capitalist construct of the poor living in urban areas in abysmal conditions while the rich fled to the outer edges.[29] The historical record is limited, but some evidence suggests that protests and demonstrations for better working conditions are a cornerstone of American society.[30] Unions brought workers together, and the organization was seen more as a disruption than as a recognition of the realities of the working class. When events such as the publication of Upton Sinclair's *The Jungle* in 1906 and the Triangle Shirtwaist fire of 1911 brought visualization to American consciousness, reform for safer working conditions was quick. Recognizing this shadow of capitalism contrasts the utopian illusion of "progress."

Even with safer working conditions, the line between economic status and job status has remained pervasively unyielding. In spite of the New Deal's establishment of a minimum wage in 1938 to help jump-start the Depression-era society,[31] the struggles of the poor persisted because such reforms avoid the root causes of capitalism and consumerism. If anything, the Great Depression was an equalizer between "high" and "low" culture, and the post-war reintegration of veterans into the workforce helped paint an illusion of an America so prosperous that poverty is seen as a life choice rather than a systemic barrier. As such, Hermione's frame for S.P.E.W. is less about the intrinsic value of the house-elves, and more about their access to bourgeois leisure, including vacation time. She is convinced that the house-elves are brainwashed into thinking their enslavement is acceptable and that it is the responsibility of those in the wizarding community to unravel this perception. While she is arguably coming from a place of privilege, and this affects the goals of her activism, her awakening eventually allows her to start to see other inequities against the Other throughout the wizarding world.

While 9/11 played a significant role in developing the mythos, the Great Recession in 2007 changed everything for the millennials. Coming into adulthood, still full of optimism in spite of student loans, the economic rug was pulled out from under the entire generation's feet dashing the American Dream. Under the heavy weight of debt from student loans and credit cards,[32] it was clear by the time Bush left office that the distribution of wealth was imbalanced and that the younger generations and the generationally impoverished would wind up bearing the brunt of the economic plunge.

The struggle is real for those who find themselves in a cycle of relatively low pay to high rent, especially in increasingly saturated markets experiencing skyrocketing housing values. Reports note that millennials, as a generation, are less likely to own property, less likely to have savings, and less likely to have children compared with previous generations.[33] In 2021, the birthrate in the United States was recorded as the lowest it has been for some time.[34] This simply boils down to the fact that the cost of living no longer has a positive return on investment (ROI). Government supports are continually cut, and the value of work is disproportionate especially between executive leadership and everyone else. Preferring autonomy over corporate drudgery, millennials in general favor self-employment and are attracted to the gig economy even at the expense of personal financial stability.[35]

As such, it should not come as a surprise that readers raised on Harry Potter would see the value in redistributing wealth. Rowling's economy paints wealth and affluence as bad (Malfoys) while those who are able to love, regardless of their financial stability, as good (Weasleys). Money for characters like Harry is a means to an end rather than as a definition of one's place in the social ecosystem. This is a challenge to the core values of capitalism by shifting the value from goods and services to the interactions and construct of community.

NOTES

1. Pottermore, "How Do Wizards Keep Themselves So Secret from Muggles?" January 24, 2018, https://www.wizardingworld.com/features/how-do-wizards-keep-themselves-so-secret-from-muggles.

2. Sexuality is consciously left out of the books, limited to snogging, hugging, and holding hands.

3. Harry Potter Wiki, s.v. "Order of the Phoenix," last modified August 6, 2021, https://harrypotter.fandom.com/wiki/Order_of_the_Phoenix.

4. *OotP*, 87–91. Molly Weasley is especially guilty, firmly believing that excluding the children is the best way to protect them. Her worry is reflected in a clock she owns with hands for each Weasley that point to the status of their degree of safety. She looks worriedly and often at the clock anytime a Weasley is not where she expects them to be.

5. *OotP*, 328.

6. Harry Potter Wiki, s.v. "Order of the Phoenix."

7. Nelson, 16.

8. Nelson, 16.

9. Emily Lauer, "Harry Potter and the Book Burners' Mistake: Suppression and its Unintended Consequences," in *The Harry Potter Generation: Essays on Growing Up*

with the Series, eds. Emily Lauer and Balaka Basu (Jefferson: McFarland & Company, 2019), 63.

10. Jenkins, "Cultural Acupuncture."

11. Katie Bowers and Janae Phillips, "We are Fandom Forward (The Harry Potter Alliance's New Name," YouTube, June 8, 2021, youtube.com/watch?v=VrPKF3H-Bvo.

12. Neta Kligler-Vilenchik, "'Decreasing World Suck': Harnessing Popular Culture for Fan Activism," in *By Any Media Necessary: The New Youth Activism*, ed. Henry Jenkins and et al. (New York: New York University Press, 2016), 108.

13. Harry Potter Fandom Wiki, s.v. "The Harry Potter Alliance," last modified July 16, 2017, https://harrypotter.fandom.com/wiki/The_Harry_Potter_Alliance.

14. NickTLC, "Harry Potter Alliance," The Leaky Cauldron, December 2, 2007, the-leaky-cauldron.org/2007/12/02/hpalliance.

15. Henry Jenkins, "Youth Voice, Media, and Political Engagement: Introducing the Core Concepts," in *By Any Media Necessary: The New Youth Activism*, ed. Henry Jenkins et al. (New York: New York University Press, 2016), 2. Jenkins defines participatory culture as "Culture in which fans and other consumers are invited to actively participate in the creation and circulation of new content." *Convergence Culture*, 290.

16. Kligler-Vilenchik, "Decreasing World Suck," 104.

17. Fandom Forward, "The Harry Potter Alliance Announces Rebrand Campaign," June 8, 2021, https://fandomforward.org/pr-6821-the-hpa-announces-rebranding-campaign.

18. Fandom Forward, "Take Action," accessed September 18, 2021, https://fandomforward.org/takeaction.

19. *GoF* describes her as a beetle, but her name implies mosquito.

20. *GoF*, 511–2.

21. It is noteworthy that the most centrist, neutral outlets identified on the Media Bias Chart published by Ad Fontes Media still chase subscribers and donations to maintain freedom from corporate influence.

22. Jean Baudrillard, *Consumer Society*, 119.

23. Baudrillard, *Simulacra*, 79.

24. A recommended definition of propaganda: "the deliberate, systemic attempt to shape perceptions, manipulate cognitions, and direct behavior to achieve a response that furthers the desired intent of the propagandist. Garth S. Jowett and Victoria O'Donnell, *Propaganda and Persuasion*, 3rd ed. (Thousand Oaks: Sage Publications, 1999), 6.

25. *GoF*, 224.

26. "I was going to put Stop the Outrageous Abuse of Our Fellow Magical Creatures and Campaign for a Change in Their Legal Status—but it wouldn't fit." *GoF*, 224.

27. *GoF*, 225.

28. Robertson, 187.

29. Zinn, *People's History*, 218.

30. Zinn, 221.

31. Zinn, 403.

32. Student loans became a necessity for millennials as tuitions rose and the cultural narrative spun the value of a college education into a societal requisite. Similarly, it was common for credit card companies to set up tables in main student areas, signing up students in exchange for swag. This "mysterious money" funded early millennial consumption as a means to a degree of comfort and mobility as they moved away from home.

33. Kristen Balik and Richard Fry, "Millennial Life: How Young Adulthood Today Compares with Prior Generations," Pew Research Center, February 14, 2019, pewresearch.org/social-trends/2019/02/14/millennial-life-how-young-adulthood-today-compares-with-prior-generations; Amanda Barroso, Kim Parker, and Jesse Bennett, "As Millennials Near 40, They're Approaching Family Life Differently than Previous Generations," Pew Research Center, May 27, 2020, https://www.pewresearch.org/social-trends/2020/05/27/as-millennials-near-40-theyre-approaching-family-life-differently-than-previous-generations/.

34. Brady E. Hamilton, Joyce A. Martin, and Michelle J.K. Osterman, "NUSS: Vital Statistics Rapid Release, Births: Provisional Data for 2020," CDC, May 12, 2021, cdc.gov/nchs/data/vsrr/vsrr012–508.pdf.

35. Kelly Monahan, Jeff Schwartz, and Tiffany Schleeter, "Decoding Millennials in the Gig Economy: Six Trends to Watch in Alternative Work," Deloitte, May 1, 2018, www2.deloitte.com/us/en/insights/focus/technology-and-the-future-of-work/millennials-in-the-gig-economy.

Chapter 7

The Problem of J.K. Rowling

While the *Harry Potter* series fostered a new era in fandoms and convergence culture, one constant factor remained stagnant: the role of J.K. Rowling as an author. In fact, her retention of creative control has done more to stifle the post-Potter fandom and its ability to fully embrace the wizarding mythos, such that it merits a brief analysis of the author's role in mythmaking *qua* popular culture and the limits of authorship.

The concept of "author" parallels the rise of the modern novel and "the privileged movement of *individualization* in the history of ideas, knowledge, literature, philosophy, and the sciences"[1] The period of the Enlightenment helps establish an ownership over knowledge and ideas that had not been seen in previous eras. One can surmise myriad reasons—the rise in print technology, being a crucial example—but it rests on the confluence of events that shaped the development of the modern world. With the ability to associate a creator to an idea comes the notion of capitalizing on it for the benefit of one's self-interests or the perception of a common good. The emergence of the Scientific Method helps illustrate this. As one scientist proposes an idea, others may pose counterarguments. The Scientific Method, however, is itself neutral. The scientists are writing social by-laws to establish the veracity of an idea. Because the idea has a defined author, they receive the laurels for its conception. Thus, Newton "discovered" gravity, or the "laws of planetary motion" are Kepler's.

This concept of authorship quickly seeps into the social sphere, and author's names are carved into the historical canon. Some are forgotten and their works appropriated to the extent that their position as Thought Owner is denied or claimed by someone else, as happened to many women and non-white creatives over the time. For the sake of the current argument, the focus is on the privileged few rather than those forgotten, because it is this branch that is relevant to discussion of J.K. Rowling. Not coincidentally, authorship coincides with the rise of modern democratic and capitalist governments. This is important for acknowledging the monetary gain and social prominence that comes with authorship, as well as the metaphorical influence those works can have in shaping society. Because it became possible under a capitalist society to become a successful, relatively wealthy career author, the counter-narrative of the struggling author manifests as a tragedy. Furthermore, because the values of grit and tenacity are deeply embedded in capitalist ideology, the ability to overcome economic struggles and become successful is romanticized. Rowling's own biography connects to this latter ideal. Described as a single mother receiving social welfare, she represents the pinnacle of the "rags to riches" figure archetypal to the American audience who considers social welfare a privilege rather than a right such that those who are able to break the mold and establish independent wealth are lauded, marking the dynamic connection between Harry's and Rowling's successes.

Unlike the authors of a pre-Internet era, Rowling is situated in a convergence of events when the act of becoming an author was placed into the hands of the masses. With digital technology, anyone can become an author, musician, or a scholar, simply with a website and tools native to their computer, phone, or tablet, and without the reliance on the established infrastructure that could be called the Business of Authorship. Rowling's success offered hope of self-success, and fan energies led to exciting ways to create and interact with the mythos. Under clarifications of copyright laws protecting fan creations, internet authorship was essentially given permission to thrive.[2]

As mentioned, Rowling retained creative control over Potter during its expansion. She was heavily involved in the casting and design of the film adaptation of the first book and was an active consultant throughout production to make sure the crew stayed faithful to the books. This is understandable given the fact that the series was not yet finished when the films began production, but also because the series had attracted a large number of children (and adult fans) who would notice if the films were not accurate to the books. Having creative control helped Rowling ensure the look and feel of the franchise, but it also unfortunately became arguably the biggest blunder in the franchise life cycle.

THE HARRY POTTER LEXICON

Rowling's gracious respect of the fandom endeared her to the fans. With the still youthful Internet, fandom and creative expression were still under assessment from corporations. While Warner Brothers (WB)—the corporate Potter copyright holder—did send cease and desist letters to children for their fan websites, Rowling advocated for their freedom to express their love for Harry. The relationship was built on an exchange of love: a love of children

(Rowling) and a love of Harry (fans). Because the series was still unfolding, any interview or web posting from Rowling became of clue of what was to come. She would also, in exchange, embrace the fandom by sharing acknowledgement of the websites, Wizard Wrock groups, crafts, and other fan creations.

One such fan creation was the website the Harry Potter Lexicon created by Steve Vander Ark. Vander Ark and his team would comb the Potterverse to create a definitive web resource for Potter details. If someone wanted to know the meaning of a spell, the Lexicon not only explained it, as many other "unauthorized" *Harry Potter* guides did, but used Rowling's own words from the books, films, and interviews (with citations) to do so. The Lexicon would also help maintain the distinction between *canon*, the officially sanctioned Rowling-isms, from *fanon*, the fan theories threading their way through fan sites and fictions prior to the release of *DH*. In 2007, Vander Ark announced plans to publish a print version of the website. Of all the fan activities, this one struck a nerve with Rowling who sued Vander Ark and the Lexicon to halt the project.

The crux of the lawsuit rested on the fact that the website would essentially be reproduced into print for profit. As Rowling explained on her website: "From what I understand, the proposed book is not criticism or review of Harry Potter's world, which would be entirely legitimate—neither I nor anyone connected with Harry Potter has ever tried to prevent such works from being published. It is, we believe, a print version of the website, except now the information that was freely available to everybody is to become a commercial enterprise."[3] The movement from freely available to commercial enterprise caused concern, especially how much of the site used her intellectual property. With this lawsuit, Rowling mentioned her own intentions to publish an encyclopedia she planned to write for charity.[4] In response to the lawsuit, Vander Ark, seemingly caught in the crossfire between Rowling and the intended publisher RDR Books, claimed that his intent was to share the content at the request of fans, and assumed he had Rowling's support given that she referenced the website herself to verify facts.[5]

What is significant about this case is that Rowling attacked the fan community after a decade of supporting their efforts, and this becomes a turning point in the fandom where the author (Rowling) wrestles with control of the canon. In a Q&A with a blog site, Vander Ark shares that a "victory for RDR Books will protect the rights of fans to create based on someone else's work. If RDR Books loses, copyright holders will be given a broad new control over fan activity, control which will allow them to shut down sites, stop authors from writing about their works, etc."[6] This statement and similar comments divided fandom and supporters for either side of the case. For example, the Leaky Cauldron cites the lawsuit as a catalyst for rethinking their connection to the Lexicon, stating, "we do not think a win for J.K. Rowling means tighter controls on fan creativity at all, and are concerned for the opposite, as well as the attempt to misportray the issues of the case as stated in sworn affidavits."[7] In contrast, in an opinion article for Slate, Tim Wu declares that Rowling should lose the lawsuit on the basis that the Lexicon is nonetheless *discussion* rather than *adaptation*. Wu ends the article raising a very important question: "In the end, this dispute is about the current meaning of authorship. Rowling is the initial author and deserves the bulk of the credit, respect, and financial reward. But she has all of that. What she wants is a level of control over the Potter world that just isn't healthy."[8] It is this that French philosopher Roland Barthes identifies as the place where the act of writing needs to become the act of reading for a text to gain any meaning. For this to happen, he advocates for the "death" of the author; in other words, a release from the cultural construct that situates an author as the wise ideation worthy of laurels rather than as the conveyor of quotations.[9] He concludes the essay "Death of the Author" stating, "We are now beginning to let ourselves be fooled no longer by the arrogant antiphrastical recriminations of good society in favor of the very thing it sets aside, ignores, smothers, or destroys; we know that to give writing its future, it is necessary to overthrow the myth: *the birth of the reader must be at the cost of the death of the author*."[10]

It is, perhaps not coincidental that shortly after this lawsuit, the Harry Potter fandom deflated, and the corporate narrative moved in to fill the void. It should be noted that corporate narratives do not always stifle the creativity of a fandom. In fact, in the right hands, the source content can continue to feed the fandom and encourage its iterating in support of new content, as seen with *Star Wars* or *Doctor Who*, for example. Warner Brothers has the power to determine the future of the Potter myth, especially in light of the post-Potter controversies.

THE TERF WARS

In June 2020, Rowling was on Twitter sharing children's drawings related to her newest project, *The Ickabog*. In the middle of the *Ickabog* tweets, Rowling shared an article titled, "Opinion: Creating a more equal post-COVID-19 world for people who menstruate," tweeting: "'People who menstruate.' I'm sure there used to be a word for those people. Someone help me out. Wumbed? Wimpund? Woomnd?"[11] It did not take long for the responses to roll in, prompting a response thread that simultaneously conveyed disappointment toward Rowling for the comment, but also a debate between sex and gender. Rowling responded with a thread:

If sex isn't real, there's no same-sex attraction. If sex isn't real, the lived reality of women globally is erased. I know and love trans people, but erasing the concept of sex removed the ability of many to meaningfully discuss their lives. It isn't hate to speak the truth.

The idea that women like me, who've been empathetic to trans people for decades, feeling kinship because they're vulnerable in the same way as women—ie, to male violence—"hate" trans people because they think sex is real and has lived consequences—is a nonsense.

I respect every trans person's right to love any way that feels authentic and comfortable to them. I'd march with you if you were discriminated against on the basis of being trans. At the same time, my life has been shaped by being female. I do not believe it's hateful to say so.[12]

Twitter called out the transphobic undertones of those tweets, and a number of different websites reporting on the tweets used this opportunity to raise awareness of TERFs, or trans-exclusionary radical feminists, who rose out of debates during Second Wave Feminism in the 1970s. Core to the TERF philosophy is the belief in biological determinism (i.e. that one's sex assigned at birth supersedes their gender identities and therefore their inclusion in selective spaces).[13] For instance, a trans woman who has not fully transitioned should be excluded on the basis that she still possesses male anatomy. In the reverse, trans men are welcomed because of their female anatomy. The key problem with this perspective is that it effectively diminishes the reality of women who embrace their gender regardless of their biology.

This was not the first time Rowling was called out for TERF comments. In 2017, she tweeted support for a British woman, Maya Forstater, who was fired for intentionally misgendering her coworkers, negatively affecting the work environment. She sued and lost her case.[14] One tweet Rowling shared regarding the case:

Dress however you please. Call yourself whatever you like. Sleep with any consenting adult who'll have you. Live your best life in peace and security. But force women out of their jobs for stating that sex is real? #IStandWithMaya #ThisIsNotADrill.[15]

The fundamental takeaway for most readers of *Harry Potter* is the importance of love: self-love, love of friends as family, love of family, and most of all, love and acceptance of the Other. Because of this previous stance, when Rowling posted her transphobic thread in June 2020, also celebrated as Pride Month, it landed in a potent cultural environment juggling the century's most controversial presidency against the backdrop of global protests in support of #BlackLivesMatter following the murder of George Floyd by a police officer.[16] The Internet quickly mobilized to "cancel" Rowling, questioning the dissonance between her views, her popularity, and the messages of acceptance sprinkled throughout the series.

Since 2016, movements such as Black Lives Matter, founded in 2012 around the acquittal of Treyvon Martin's murderer,[17] and the Women's March, founded in 2016, giving new energy to the Women's Movement in response to the misogynist comments of the then-newly-elected president Donald Trump, have compounded and expanded. People, many of whom are part of the initial Harry Potter demographic, are asking why change is not happening. The politicians who hold the highest seats of power turn blind eyes to the voices of constituents demanding change. These same followers exuded optimism when they saw vestiges of hope in the actions of the Obama presidency, only to observe the Trump administration unravelling the perceived social progress and threatening to revert the country to ideologies of anti-inclusivity—these same ideologies that were favored by Voldemort and similarly enacted upon by his Death Eaters.

Essentially, it is no longer okay to promote a society that excludes any marginalized group, and the response to Rowling's tweets divide among political affiliation as much as generation. Actors involved in the Potterverse tweeted support for trans women following Rowling's 2020 TERF storm. Harry Potter himself, Daniel Radcliffe, posted a statement on the website for the Trevor Project, an organization dedicated to the help and support of LGBTQ+ young people. In his statement, Radcliffe writes:

> To all the people who now feel that their experience of the books have been tarnished or diminished, I am deeply sorry for the pain these comments have caused you. [. . .] if these books taught you that love is the strongest force in the universe, capable of overcoming anything; if they taught you that strength is found in diversity, and that dogmatic ideas of pureness lead to the oppression of vulnerable groups; if you believe that a particular character is trans, non binary, or gender fluid, or that they are gay or bisexual; if you found anything in these stories that resonated with you and helped you at any time in your life—then that is between you and the book that you read, and it is sacred. And in my opinion nobody can touch that.[18]

As though channeling Barthes, Radcliffe demonstrates the power of the reader's experience over the ideology of the author, because to the fandom, Rowling's perspective about women feels like a betrayal. The mother who taught them to love outed herself under the guise of feminism as not wholly embracing inclusivity. Other Potter actors added their voices to Radcliffe's, including Emma Watson (Hermione), Bonnie Wright (Ginny Weasley), and Eddie Redmayne (Newt Scamander), in solidarity with trans fans.[19]

Melissa Anelli, who has long been a figurehead for the Potter fandom, summed up the feelings surrounding the tweets: "For somebody who stood so much for equality and tolerance for so many years to actively punch down on a marginalized group—like all 'Harry Potter' fans who feel this way, I'm just kind of devastated."[20]

It is worth noting that, as this TERF storm was unfolding, other events sat at the front of American consciousness, especially the deaths of George Floyd and Breonna Taylor, the protests they inspired, and the government's response to the protests. These tweets became just one more thing in a culture constantly throwing vitriol toward marginalized groups. The protests for BLM were part of an energetic push to make sure to speak up and speak out. While the cultural soup was focused on BLM, it shed renewed light on diversity and the need for awareness of our relationship to the Other. Rowling is Othering a specific population and subsection of fans in her tweet campaign, and this Othering comes from fear based on her own experiences and struggles as a woman,[21] but overlooks the struggles of those who are fundamentally different from the status quo of cis white people.

The storm continued when Rowling posted a statement on her website explaining her stance and interest in the subject: "It's been clear to me for awhile that the new trans activism is having (or is likely to have, if all its demands are met) a significant impact on many of the causes I support, because it's pushing to erode the legal definition of sex and replace it with gender."[22] She then continues to explain her concern with the Trans Rights Movement, followed by explanations of misogyny and the research around rapid onset gender dysphoria. In essence, she believes that young women are being persuaded to transition too young and struggle with regret and depression. She also voices a recognition of a fear from cisgender women, regarding their trans sisters, that allowing them into safe spaces like restrooms opens the door to allowing men into those spaces on the assumption that predators will take advantage of an opportunity.[23] It is a legitimate fear as women are frequently taught that men are predators and how to protect themselves if attacked, and the message is reinforced through media, especially within the popular true crime genre and in similar crime and forensic drama series. In the realm of comedy, stories where men dress as women to gain access to people and spaces create a narrative that becoming a woman is a means of escape rather than a legitimate life change.[24] Such perceptions create more challenges for the trans community, and when someone of Rowling's stature lends her voice to the cause in a way that harms her fans reveals an oversight on her part about the impact she has had on their identity development. Language matters, and who says the messages matters. Echoing Anelli's previous statement, it is difficult to reconcile such an exclusionary stance as demonstrated through her public postings from the one who designed a world so heavily committed to tearing down the barriers that divide us.[25]

THE GRINDELWALD PROBLEM

In an attempt to hopefully punctuate a PR fury, Warner Brothers issued their own statement of inclusivity, recognizing that Potter fans were calling for boycotts and for cancelling Rowling. In declaring their commitment to inclusivity and diversity, the studio notes that while they "deeply value the work of our storytellers," they also "recognize our responsibility to foster empathy and advocate understanding of all communities and all people, particularly those we work with and those we reach through our content."[26] The most immediate concern for Warner Brothers is that they were already swimming in controversy for the *Fantastic Beasts* films and the character of Gellert Grindelwald, in particular.

In the seven novels, little is revealed about Grindelwald. He is painted as Voldemort's predecessor in terms of a dark-wizard-unifying leader. We know he was Dumbledore's opponent, but also learn in Dumbledore's biography and at King's Cross that the two of them were once best friends who pursued the Deathly Hallows together, were interested in magical superiority over Muggles, and that an event occurred between them that culminated in the death of Dumbledore's sister, Arianna. Beyond that, Grindelwald's legacy becomes intertwined with that of Voldemort. In the publicity following *DH*, Rowling made an offhand comment that she considers Dumbledore to be gay. The fandom lit up with excitement at the outing of such an influential character, adding the belief in an unrequited love between Dumbledore and Grindelwald to the narrative.

The *Fantastic Beasts* films give Grindelwald a backstory written by Rowling: his pursuit of power, his willing embrace of Othered wizards, and his campaign for magical superiority. Given what we can surmise from other works regarding Rowling's views of leaders and politics, as well as the current cultural atmosphere, it is apparent that Grindelwald is a magical extremist whose charisma helps build a cult following. He has the perfect personality to draw in those who are in search of a leader who speaks the messages latent in their hearts and minds.

The films are notable additions to the *Harry Potter* canon because they help provide an alternative to the Voldemort plot of Harry's story and adding refreshing depth to the wizarding world. Grindelwald paves the way for Voldemort, and it is because of his involvement in the rise of Grindelwald that Dumbledore does what he can to intervene with Voldemort, which may, in a Greek-style tragic twist of fate, have actually set Voldemort on the path to become the wizard that he did. Grindelwald is charismatic and speaks a good game about the relationship between wizards and Muggles, while Voldemort is less interested in the wizarding world breaking down the barriers, and more in dominance and annihilation.

The controversy Warner Brothers faced primarily revolved around the casting of Johnny Depp as Grindelwald. At the time of his casting, and throughout the production of the first two films, Depp was involved in a highly publicized lawsuit related to his divorce from fellow actor Amber Heard and allegations of domestic abuse. Initially, both Rowling and Warner Brothers stood behind this casting decision stating that they respected the privacy of those involved, that this was a private matter, and that Depp is the right actor for the job.[27] This was seen by fans as an endorsement of abuse. In addition to the tweets and casting of Depp, lead actor Ezra Miller (Credence Barebone) stirred his own controversy when he was caught choking a woman, revealing that the people in this *Fantastic Beasts* era of Potter is "out of step" with the franchise's core values.[28]

With the production of the third film in the series paused by COVID-19, Warner Brothers had a chance to reflect on the franchise's future. In November 2020, as his contentious lawsuit hit a turning point, Johnny Depp was asked by Warner Brothers to resign from the role before the film went into production, which Depp shared in a brief letter on his Instagram feed,[29] seeming to put the future of the franchise in question. However, Warner Brothers chose to move ahead, recasting Grindelwald with actor Mads Mikkelsen and developing a story around Dumbledore and World War II.[30] In their blog, Rachel Leishman posts on *The Mary Sue* the observation that this seems to be an attempt to draw in fans who are leaving the franchise. She writes, "All of that leads us into an era of *Harry Potter* where most of us really don't want to support Rowling in any way, and that is clearly at the forefront of the minds of those in charge, and they're grasping at straws with the series. So now they want to give us the *secrets* of Dumbledore? Okay."[31]

BREAKING UP

The seemingly certain future of *Harry Potter* is now uncertain. With every tweet and public declaration of her beliefs, J.K. Rowling further alienates her fanbase. To many fans, Rowling and her characters came to represent and perhaps replace the family that would not accept them. The sheer volume of such souls who found each other through Potter speaks to a larger conversation around inclusion and community. Embraced as a millennial text, Potter helped lay a foundation for an America that embraces fluidity in concepts of race and gender, intersectionality, positive thinking, and self-love and self-respect. When anyone's intersections are leveraged as an excuse for subjugation and disenfranchisement, this is a call for Potter activism. This resurgence in utopian values capitalize on the millennial optimism that was shattered by events in the early 2000s: Growing into their collective identity, an entire generation became jaded overnight. Anti-Boomerism continues to rise, enhancing a generational divide at the heart of a decade of "culture wars" and the vehement clash between American fundamentalism and social justice reform, opening the doors that allow politicians to build political platforms around these issues and fuel the fires of discontent. However, when we see this through the eyes of Harry Potter and his friends, we see Fudge's extreme denial and the brewing of fascism right below his nose, so when Potter and his friends push for justice and change, they are ignored until it is too late to stop the political machine. While not all of the political players in the series are Death Eaters, they nonetheless share a common mindset, further teaching Potter's peers and Potter fans that evil is not black versus white, but grey, expansive, and attractive. It is hard to know who to trust, so one has to formulate their own opinions through careful consideration and critical thinking. As Mad-Eye Moody (Barty Crouch, Jr.) constantly reminds his students: CONSTANT VIGILANCE!

"The Establishment" is its own entity, maintaining the status quo and the thin veil of campaign promises. The 2016 election proved how powerful "The Establishment" had become. Both major parties put forth candidates thinking they would bring in the votes, completely ignoring the progressive values of millennial voters who are looking to the government to help fix the mess it caused: erasing the debt burden, providing healthcare and social services, addressing the realities of climate change. Millennials are frustrated when it seems the government, like Fudge, ignores what is happening, or spends more energy "proving" that the issues are the other party's fault and barring legislation. This is an America where the American Dream is an elusive fantasy of a past world. For a country so economically verdant, people should not have to choose between rent and health care or run into systemic barriers at every twist and turn through life. The generations following millennials experience their own trauma through active shooter drills and the reality of global pandemic.

What is fundamentally lacking is empathy and the ability to recognize the struggles of others. As Americans have seen, the culture is systemically unable to unravel its Othering of black and brown people and to recognize the deep abuse and trauma of social instability; it is difficult to undo the Othering of others unless one develops a willingness to embrace them. Millennials and post-millennials learned inclusiveness from a young age through school curricula and media. Harry's Hogwarts acceptance letter is a metaphor for moving from under the stairs to a place where love and acceptance are paramount, especially for those who cannot live up to the standards of their community's status quo. It is a utopian ideal, one imparted from boomers to millennials, but one that is pushed to new limits as a culture influenced by idealism and hyperreality continues to build and restructure around this idyllic paradigm. Digital technology and artificial intelligence help create environments and experiences that increasingly blur the lines between real and fake—the hyperreal is more real than reality. Additionally, digital algorithms allow for customization and personalization the user experience showing only the content that computer data calculates the user wants, creating their own utopian echo chamber.

However, this echo chamber has its own set of rules and parameters. Algorithms may believe that the user wants to connect with family and familiar friends, when in reality they may be harmful community and do not share the user's values, forcing the user to make the difficult decision that it is time to separate from these toxic connections. In July 2020, both major fan sites MuggleNet and the Leaky Cauldron posted a joint statement "breaking up" with J.K. Rowling, outlining new practices around Potter news coverage, and also redefining Potter fandom beyond its author: "We have seen countless people use the *Potter* books and fanfic to explore their own identities while spreading love and acceptance. We know that this is still possible, and we know that we want to continue to be part of that movement."[32]

A PERSONAL REFLECTION

I found out about the tweets during a scroll on my Facebook feed. Some of my friends shared an article and were clearly angry about it. My researcher's curiosity piqued, and I spent the better part of the day clicking through articles and tweets, watching the story unfold and feeling that a very important bubble burst.

J.K. Rowling changed how an entire generation of readers process the world; importantly, how they make meaning of it and identify themselves in that space. It does not take deep research and analysis to be able to see the impact Harry Potter has had across the world. Readers of all ages can find enjoyment in her fantasy world, while others find a nugget of themselves that they have been afraid to share and want to try on with other Potter fans. This latter aspect drove the Potter fandom to the Internet, where like-minded people put themselves out there to find other fans and commune. Because the Internet had just landed in the homes of many users, the value of the tool in community building was nascent, but not without precedent. Fandoms invariably find a way to come together, often leveraging existing tools like fanzines or newsgroups to build connections. It makes sense that a new generation of Internet users would also find ways to build social networks where fans can interact in "real time," redefine their identity through their avatars, and, especially, to realize that they are not alone in an otherwise lonely existence.

The Potter fandom was immediately successful for children and adults as a safe space for all ages and identities to interact. The fandom moderators were highly engaged in the groups in order to enforce group rules, and to quickly shut down trolls or other threats. When people met at Potter cons and meet-ups, it was like meeting the 3D version of their best friend, redefining the value of friendship and relationships as transcendent experiences demonstrating that connections built on social network platforms could be just as strong as those forged in "real" life. One of the legacies of the 21st century is simply that the Internet redefined community building and helped break down barriers between different groups. The Harry Potter fandom helped establish guidelines for acceptance and inclusivity that lie behind the social justice movements of the century's first quarter.

Around all this was awe for an author who seemed to build her craft from unexpected circumstances: a single mother living on state welfare writing Harry Potter's story in cafés and on trains until a fully developed novel and series outline manifested. Taking a chance, she submitted the first book for publication and found a publisher willing to take a risk on a new author in recognition of the unique spark of her story. Initial criticism was sharp. At the time, children's and young adult novels were comparatively slim volumes and stories were not overly complex. The reviews tore the book apart, convinced that the book would fail. The book, however, proved otherwise, and it quickly shot to the top of the charts. In the years and sequels that followed, the book industry made adjustments to accommodate Harry's popularity. The *New York Times* created a new young adult literature chart, on top of which Potter sat for weeks on end. Bloomsbury published "adult" covers, so adults reading *Harry Potter* would not have to hide the books in more "acceptable" covers on their train ride. Mainstream merchandizing began featuring book characters, not just those from visual media. And, importantly, intellectual property laws had to figure out how to allow for fan creations without seeing them as copyright violations.

The fever from 2000 until 2007, roughly from *GoF* through the *DH* book release, was invigorating. Everyone who wanted to know what would happen to Harry and his friends became personally invested in the trajectory of the story identifying with characters and places. Collectively, the fans felt righteous indignation when Lucius Malfoy taunted Arthur Wesley or when Mr. Crouch fired Winky for being in the wrong place at the wrong time. We celebrated when Mad-Eye Moody turned Draco Malfoy into a ferret and bounced him around, or when Harry and his friends escaped from Gringotts on a dragon. We cried when beloved characters died in the story and celebrated their memory.

Harry Potter was as real to us as the world around us, perhaps as a result of the overlay of the magical world over the Muggle, or perhaps just because it was the right escape at the right time as crazy complications started seeping into the cultural narrative. When *GoF* was new, we were still processing the Columbine shooting and the Y2K scare. We recognized in the aftermath of 9/11 the rebirth of Voldemort and connected the presence of Death Eaters in the Ministry to the new wave of American nationalism and fear of terrorism. Through the books and their film adaptations, the *Harry Potter* series continues to serve as a beacon of light in trying times. I reread the series as a way of coping with the Trump administration from 2016–2020, which led to finally writing this book. While the series brought me as much comfort and hope in this reread as it did the first time around, it is difficult to not interpret the series as a meta text reflecting the first part of this century given of all the events and turmoil.

So, after all of that, those tweets were soul-crushing. Did Rowling really mean to exclude a key part of the fandom who found their identity from her books? Rather than responding with love (and a degree of *mea culpa*) for the tweets, she instead posted a manifesto on her website supporting her opinions. It is depressing, but also pushes Harry Potter onto the precipice of change. One day, I walked into my favorite coffee shop and the barista was wearing a *DH* t-shirt. I asked them how they felt about the tweets and their response was simply, "I love Harry. The author is dead to me."

This is the critical moment when the series transcends from being the author's by-product and becomes a cultural epic. The series will always be "by J.K. Rowling" but that does not mean it will be Rowling's work. In order to remain prescient in the culture, we have to let go of Rowling and embrace Harry for what he is despite the faults we may read into the novel as a result of her alienating bias: a symbol of the heroic, giving us the courage to stand up against the evil that lurks in every corner of our culture, and to carry the love in our hearts for the betterment of our society.

NOTES

1. Michel Foucault, "What Is an Author?" in *The Foucault Reader*, ed. Paul Rabinow (New York: Vintage Books, 2010), 101, emphasis original.

2. Jenkins, *Convergence Culture*, 189.

3. J.K. Rowling, "Companion Books," J.K. Rowling Official Site, October 31, 2007, https://web.archive.org/web/20110504051826/www.jkrowling.co.uk/textonly/en/news_view.cfm?id=102.

4. Melissa Anelli, "J.K. Rowling and WB File Suit Over Unofficial Encyclopedia," The Leaky Cauldron, October 31, 2007, http://www.the-leaky-cauldron.org/2007/10/31/rowling-and-wb-file-suit-over-unofficial-encyclopedia/; Melissa Anelli, "J.K. Rowling Updates 'Companion Books' Article, RDR Books Responds," The Leaky Cauldron, November 01, 2007, the-leaky-cauldron.org/2007/11/1/j-k-rowling-updates-companion-books-article/.

5. Melissa Anelli, "Harry Potter Lexicon Makes Statement Regarding Suit," The Leaky Cauldron, November 5, 2007, the-leaky-cauldron.org/2007/11/05/harry-potter-lexicon-responds-to-suit.

6. Melissa Anelli, "Lexicon Trial Updates and Important Announcement About Floo Network," The Leaky Cauldron, March 24, 2008, the-leaky-cauldron.org/2008/03/24/lexicon-trial-updates-and-important-announcement-about-floo-network.

7. Anelli, "Lexicon Trial Updates."

8. Tim Wu, "J.K. Rowling's Dark Mark," Slate, January 10, 2008, slate.com/news-and-politics/2008/01/j-k-rowling-should-lose-her-copyright-lawsuit-against-the-harry-potter-lexicon.html.

9. Roland Barthes, "Death of the Author," in *Image - Music - Text*, ed. Stephen Heath (New York: Hill and Wang, 1977), 146.

10. Barthes, "Death," 148, emphasis added.

11. J.K. Rowling (@jk_rowling), "'People who menstruate,' I'm sure there used to be a word for those people. Someone help me out. Wumben? Wimpund? Woomud?" Twitter, June 6, 2020 5:35pm, twitter.com/jk_rowling/status/1269382518362509313.

12. J.K. Rowling (@jk_rowling), "If sex isn't real [thread]," Twitter, June 6, 2020 6:02pm, twitter.com/jk_rowling/status/1269389298664701952.

13. Urban Dictionary, s.v. "TERF, accessed June 12, 2020, urbandictionary.com/define.php?term=TERF; Evan Urquhart, "J.K. Rowling and the Echo Chamber of TERFs," Slate, June 12, 2020, https://slate.com/human-interest/2020/06/jk-rowling-trans-men-terf.html.

14. Evan Urquhart, "J.K. Rowling and the Echo Chamber of TERFS," Slate, June 12, 2020, https://slate.com/human-interest/2020/06/jk-rowling-trans-men-terf.html.

15. J.K. Rowling (@jk_rowling), "Dress however you please. Call yourself whatever you like. Sleep with any consenting adult who'll have you. Live your best life in peace and security. But force women out of their jobs for stating that sex is real? #IStandWithMaya #ThisIsNotADrill," Twitter, December 19, 2019, quoted in Urquhart, "J.K. Rowling."

16. Mr. Floyd was not the first such death, but his death resonated loudly in an enough is enough sort of way such that some have referred to his death as this generation's Emmitt Till, a victim of a senseless, racist-driven lynching in 1955.

17. Black Lives Matter, "About," accessed August 21, 2021, blacklivesmatter.com/about.

18. Daniel Radcliffe, "Daniel Radcliffe Responds to J.K. Rowling's Tweets on Gender Identity," The Trevor Project, June 8, 2020, https://www.thetrevorproject.org/blog/daniel-radcliffe-responds-to-j-k-rowlings-tweets-on-gender-identity/.

19. Emma Watson (@EmmaWatson), "I want my trans followers to know that I and so many other people around the world see you, respect you and love you for who you

are," Twitter, June 10, 2020, twitter.com/emmawatson/status/1270827488915214338; Bonnie Wright (@thisisbwright), "If Harry Potter was a source of love and belonging for you, that love is infinite and there to take without judgment or question. Trans-women are Women. I see and love you, Bonnie x," Twitter, June 10, 2020, twitter.com/thisisbwright/status/1270846127206588418; Brent Lang, "Eddie Redmayne Criticizes J.K. Rowling's Anti-Trans Tweets (Exclusive)," Variety, June 10, 2020, variety.com/2020/film/news/eddie-redmayne-jk-rowling-anti-trans-tweets-harry-potter-fantastic-beasts-1234630226. When the title for the third Fantastic Beasts film was announced in September 2021, one could question why Redmayne continues with this project after speaking out against Rowling. This is a valid question as there is a dissonance that will play out as the film releases.

20. Adam B. Vary, "What J.K. Rowling's Anti-Trans Views Could Mean for 'Fantastic Beasts' Franchise—and 'Harry Potter' Fans," Variety, June 10, 2020, variety.com/2020/film/news/jkrowling-anti-trans-fantastic-beasts-harry-potter-1234630008.

21. Rowling has been vocal about being a survivor of domestic violence, and critique of the tweets is not intended to diminish that reality.

22. J.K. Rowling, "J.K. Rowling Writes About Her Reasons for Speaking Out on Sex and Gender Issues," J.K.Rowling.com, June 10, 2020, jkrowling.com/opinions/j-k-rowling-writes-about-her-reasons-for-speaking-out-on-sex-and-gender-issues.

23. Rowling, "Sex and Gender Issues."

24. Famously, 1993's *Mrs. Doubtfire* starring Robin Williams, 1959's *Some Like It Hot* with Tony Curtis and Jack Lemmon, or 1982's *Tootsie* with Dustin Hoffman.

25. It is the opinion of this author that celebrities, imperfect and prone to gaffes, have responsibility to consider how their actions can impact the global community. Fame and public status make one more prone to scrutiny. For someone as colossal as J.K. Rowling, whose fan base scrutinized every last syllable of the books to predict the ending of the novels, those gaffes can deeply hurt her greatest supporters. I, for one, acknowledge fallacy as long as the perpetrator owns their impact. An analysis of Rowling's manifesto reveals the fear underlying her bias, the same kind of fear that kept Remus Lupin out of society, that allowed Fudge to ignore Harry's claims of encountering Voldemort, and that led the Dursleys to raise Harry from beneath the stairs rather than as a member of the family. It also reveals an unyielding perspective. Since June 2020, Rowling has continued to double-down on her stance, prompting WB to quietly place distance between the Potter franchise and author.

26. Adam B. Vary, "Warner Bros. Responds to J.K. Rowling Controversy: 'A Diverse and Inclusive Culture Has Never Been More Important," Variety, June 10, 2020, variety.com/2020/film/news/jk-rowling-warner-bros-1234631061.

27. J.K. Rowling, "Grindelwald Casting," J.K.Rowling.com, December 7, 2017, jkrowling.com/opinions/grindelwald-casting. For responses from director David Yates and producer David Heyman, see also: Stewart Clarke, "J.K. Rowling Defends Casting of Johnny Depp in 'Fantastic Beasts,'" Variety, December 7, 2017, variety.com/2017/film/news/j-k-rowling-warner-bros-defend-johnny-depp-grindelwald-fantastic-beasts-1202632964.

28. Vary, "J.K. Rowling's Anti-Trans Views."

29. Johnny Depp, "Resignation Letter," Instagram photo, November 6, 2020, https://www.instagram.com/p/CHQXHimJvAC/.

30. Rachel Leishman, "Fantastic Beasts: The Secrets of Dumbledore? Who Asked for This?" The Mary Sue, September 23, 2021, themarysue.com/fantastic-beasts-secrets-of-dumbledore-why.

31. Leishman, "Who Asked For This?"

32. Melissa Anelli, "Addressing J.K. Rowling's Recent Statements," The Leaky Cauldron, July 1, 2020, the-leaky-cauldron.org/2020/07/01/addressing-j-k-rowlings-recent-statements; MuggleNet, "Our Commitment," accessed September 25, 2021, mugglenet.com/site/our-commitment.

Conclusion

WHERE DO WE GO FROM HERE?

It is difficult to know what is going to come next given the steady stream of uncertainty plaguing American culture and global society. It is clear that change is needed, and it is overwhelming to consider where to begin. The same problems continue being problems: climate change is accelerating and is bringing more deadly storms and ecological catastrophes with it, while an entire segment of the American population thinks that it is either untrue or is being blown out of proportion; politicians continue to hold the American people hostage to their corruption, because they enjoy their power; corporations monetize popular culture and benefit from the consumerist machine; and wealth distributions are so unbalanced that the super wealthy can fly into outer space on private rocket ships while the working and middle classes struggle to pay for rent and healthcare.

Harry Potter helped inform the lens of perception towards social imbalance and helped inspire the language around change. Rowling did not coin terms like "woke" or "intersectionality," but her books did reinforce the importance of naming the issue to make it seem less scary. Similarly, Harry's journey inspired many people to be forthright with their identities and truths. This work gained traction through the sheer expansiveness of the Potter fandom and has seeded younger Americans with the tools and resources for change. However, change can only happen if, collectively, the core mythos of American society is rewritten.

The utopianism of the American Dream was never a reality, but it did give an image of hope that it might be possible. Pursuing the American Dream helped promote equality movements, suggesting that this dream needs to be accessible to all in deed not just in word. While the late 20th century offered the optimism that, perhaps, America had reached that point, the entry into the 21st century proved otherwise as wide-eyed, idealistic millennials grew into social consciousness. Their biggest aggravation is that utopian optimism persists at the highest levels of influence, clouding perceptions of reality's social struggles.

The cultural shift is noticeable from the Mindset Lists originally published by Beloit College and now published by Marist College that identify certain features of the incoming college freshman class. For example, from the list for the Class of 2002 who graduated from high school in 1998:

- "They have no meaningful recollection of the Reagan era, and did not know he had ever been shot.
- "They were prepubescent when the Persian Gulf War was waged.
- "There has only been one Pope. They can only remember one other president.
- "They were 11 when the Soviet Union broke apart, and do not remember the Cold War.

And:

- "Star Wars looks very fake to them, and the special effects are pathetic.[1]
- "Most have never seen a TV set with only 13 channels, nor have they seen a black & white TV.
- "They have always had cable.
- "There have always been VCRs, but they have no idea what Beta is.
- "They cannot fathom what it was like not having a remote control."[2]

Comparing this list with the Class of 2005, who graduated in 2001, a mere three years later:

- "The Social Security system has always been on the brink.
- "There have always been warnings about second-hand smoke.
- "They have never experienced a real recession.
- "They were born the same year as the PC and the Mac.
- "There has always been a hole in the ozone layer.
- "They do not know what the Selective Service is, but men routinely register for it on their financial aid forms.
- "Recording TV programs on VCRs became legal the year they were born."[3]

And finally, the Class of 2019 who graduated in 2014, the last list from this Beloit group of authors before handing the project to the Marist College group:

- "Google has always been there, in its founding words, 'to organize the world's information and make it universally accessible.'

- "They have grown up treating Wi-Fi as an entitlement.
- "The announcement of someone being the "first woman" to hold a position has only impressed their parents.
- "Cell phones have become so ubiquitous in class that teachers don't know which students are using them to take notes and which ones are planning a party.
- "Attempts at human cloning have never been federally funded but do require FDA approval.
- "They had no idea how fortunate they were to enjoy the final four years of Federal budget surpluses.

Finally,

- "They have avidly joined Harry Potter, Ron, and Hermione as they built their reading skills through all seven volumes."[4]

While these lists have the ability to make one feel "old," they are also generalized time capsules of America's changes. Popular culture changes dominate the list, especially around influential figures and new technologies. The political changes, however, though only a small part of the lengthy lists, hint at the downward change that shaped these Americans. The 2002 list, for instance, points out that those students only remember one other president and do not remember the Cold War. In contrast, the 2005 list notes that Social Security, once seen as a reliable source of retirement income, has always been under threat and they have never experienced a real recession—but would a couple years after graduation. The 2019 class demonstrates that the expectations of diverse environments is normal and that the federal budget is a constant problem. In a relatively short span of history, the popular culture changes have been exponential while the political changes have quietly grown more problematic as these adults face an economically uncertain future.

2020: THE YEAR OF CLARITY?

The year 2020 was a pivotal year that no one will forget. It represents the year of clarity, 20/20 vision, and what it revealed about America is scary. Half of the country supports a government that teeters on fascism just to avoid having to pay more in taxes or to pay into health care plans that benefit other people. Their racism and bigotry are not surprising, but the overtness of it is, since it is something younger Americans have not experienced first-hand. The other half of the country supports a government that is pretending to not be an oligarchy, because they are the politicians supporting the social issues that matter to them. *Harry Potter* helped understand the implications of the social divide bringing it into awareness and providing language to understand the events. It is a reasonable expectation of this constituency that change is needed. However, over the last two decades, it would seem that American history has replayed elements of the past century—and not necessarily the positives ones—to keep them prescient while the cultural and global paradigm shifts.

With paradigm shifts comes the shift in the cultural narrative that manifests through the mythology, highlighting what has been working and filtering what has not been working. The popular culture franchises at the heart of 21st Century mythology give us insight into where America is at right now. Disney acquired Marvel Studios and the *Star Wars* franchise and has expanded those universes beyond their original boundaries. Marvel has provided imagery for multiverses, a fictional trope rooted in quantum theory of multiple universes co-existing in parallel but rigidly separate until something rips the fabric of space and opens those barriers. When the multiverses collide, everything falls out of whack and it is up to the heroes to restore balance. Multiverse imagery also supports the collective hero as an emergent archetypal image: the heroes from each universe must collaborate or the entire construct will destruct and destroy time and existence. Similar collisions happen now and then within the on-going plot of the BBC's time-traveling epic, *Doctor Who*. The Doctor is Earth's guardian and works with other characters to protect the planet, her people, and the timeline. Much like Marvel's multiverse, the timeline is a linear construct in delicate balance that can have an impact in all versions of an event. Here, the mythos is about how even the smallest thing can have a big impact.

Star Wars, similarly, has expanded far beyond the Skywalker Saga of George Lucas's vision. Disney has used the acquisition to create new series that reflect on better understanding the essence of the Empire, even after Luke Skywalker and his friends worked with the Ewoks to destroy the second Death Star. Underneath every new *Star Wars* property is the subtext that the Empire is really the face of a shadow that is always hiding in the galaxy. Palpatine may be the Emperor, but he is just a face for the power and corruption that informs this galaxy long ago and far away. *Star Wars* is not just about the manifest plot that surrounds the Jedi versus Sith, but also about the real struggles that happen on individual planets (communities) in contrast with the actions of the government.

There have also been shows that have dealt with the supernatural and the darker side of fantasy. Shows like *Supernatural* and *The Walking Dead* have heroes collaborating to protect the community from invading evils. These evils become metaphors for those things that plague and upend a community.

Whether demons or zombies, these evils are unnamable and inspire fear, reflective of cultural anxieties afraid of invasion from the unknown. This genre offers two prospects: one is to battle these evils head-on, and the other is to embrace these characters as different but diverse turning them into sympathetic characters. The latter can be seen in the vampire romance genre, where humans and vampires work together to protect a community. The romance of the stories reflects the value of non-homogenous relationships, a normal element of contemporary society.[5]

While the century's myths have been filled so far with imagery of apocalypse and dystopia, they also introduce collective heroes who help bring change by tearing down the old, established infrastructure and rebuilding a new world from the ashes. Collective heroes like those in *Avatar: The Last Airbender* or *The Hunger Games* demonstrate that it is possible to tear down the establishment without destroying the world. *Avatar* also has a subtext about restoring balance between the four bending elements that the Fire Nation has knocked out of balance in pursuit of greed and power.

The diversity offered by the library of mythologies caters to the diversity of psychologies. Twenty-first century mythologies highlight that anyone can be a hero, that there are different ways to be a hero, and that authenticity to self is essential for healthy community. *Harry Potter* opened the doors for these franchises and continues to play its part as foundational toward this new heroic and the possibilities for the future of America.

COVID-19

For Americans, one unique feature of the first part of the 21st century is global pandemic. Other natural disasters, such as hurricanes, forest fires, colossal heat waves, are familiar even if the intensity and frequency is a newer by-product of global warming. Modern society knows what to do to prepare, fight, and rebuild. As these natural disasters continue to intensify, the biggest challenge for governments is to know what resources to allocate and to whom, especially if there are any other disasters at the same time. This can leave people without homes and other essential resources for longer than reasonable.

Until COVID-19, the American perception of diseases was that they were either under control through medication and vaccines or were some other country's problem. Disease scientists warned that a pandemic would affect America sooner rather than later—more virulent diseases have appeared across the planet as the climate has changed—but they were largely ignored by politicians. The Trump Administration went so far as to disband the National Security Council directorate that was in charge of pandemic preparation.[6] When COVID hit, it seemed like it came out of nowhere, and hit the country hard. In March 2020, schools and cities moved into lockdown to slow the spread of the disease, eventually prompting entire states to close. Hospitals were overflowing with patients who needed special respirators, and the death rate was so high that morgues were overflowing. Meanwhile, non-essential workers (primarily those not in healthcare) were either seeing their hours cut or were getting laid off as workplaces either shut down or limited staff to reduce exposure.

The bigger surprise should not have been the arrival of the pandemic, but that the entire country went into lockdown. The news from the Trump Administration was that COVID was just another flu-like disease, there was nothing to worry about, and that it was all a liberal plot to undermine Trump. The misinformation at the beginning of the pandemic planted the seeds for misunderstanding throughout its spread, making it difficult for the country to get it under control. As of the time of this writing, the pandemic is still out of control. Although vaccines are now available, many Americans refuse to get them claiming familiar anti-vaxx excuses and conspiratorial claims, especially given the rapidity of the medicine's development and release to the public. Additionally, the COVID virus rapidly mutates, and each new iteration has different symptoms and effects.

Going into the 2020 election, the pandemic prompted conversation around mail-in ballots, so those who needed to social distance could still vote. The press coverage made mail-in ballots sound like a new thing, and conservative media remarked that this was a way to cheat the election away from Trump, calling the ballots fraudulent. The pervasive voter fraud rhetoric especially fueled the January 6 coup attempt, and voter rights continue to divide along political party lines as the currency for social power.

The country's reaction to the pandemic revealed how far out of balance the country has become. The delicate balance between utopianism and consumerism has shifted such that they are no longer mutually supporting each other as the keystones of the American Dream. This is not a matter of Magic versus Dark Magic, young versus adult, Magical versus Muggle. COVID-19 showed the fractures in the social fabric between those with means and those without, turning them into fissures. While America prevailed through the first and second waves of the pandemic, those fissures continued to widen, and destabilization more apparent. Rowling's Potterverse illustrates how far things need to destabilize before it is possible to reset the balance. *Harry Potter* captures the hope that this hard work is possible. That change is possible with compassion, empathy, and love if everyone works together to be the collective hero America needs to usher into a new era.

Eventually, the scar on our foreheads will no longer hurt, and all will be well.[7]

NOTES

1. Fake or not, *Star Wars* was a cultural influence for some of us but had not achieved complete cultural saturation yet that came with the release of the prequel trilogy and the later acquisition of the franchise by Disney.

2. Tom McBride, Ron Nief, and Charles Westerberg, "2002 List," The Mindset List, accessed October 02, 2021, http://themindsetlist.com/lists/2002/.

3. Tom McBride, Ron Nief, and Charles Westerberg, "2005 List," The Mindset List, accessed October 02, 2021, http://themindsetlist.com/lists/2005-list/.

4. Tom McBride, Ron Nief, and Charles Westerberg, "The Mindset List For the Class of 2019," The Mindset List, accessed October 02, 2021, http://themindsetlist.com/lists/the-mindset-list-for-the-class-of-2019/.

5. They can also reflect unhealthy relationships, because vampires at the core of their characters are bloodsuckers who literally drain the life out of their victims. Even "vegetarian" vampires may slip from time to time. The undertone of abusive relationships was not widely explored until the *Twilight* saga, with older readers questioning Bella's constant clinginess toward Edward, which he returned with an abusive degree of over-protectiveness and possessiveness.

6. Deb Reichmann, "Trump Disbanded NSC Pandemic Unit That Experts Had Praised," AP News, March 14, 2020, https://apnews.com/article/donald-trump-ap-top-news-virus-outbreak-barack-obama-public-health-ce014d94b64e98b7203b873e56f80e9a.

7. *DH*, 759. Last line of the series: "The scar had not pained Harry for nineteen years. All was well."

Bibliography

Adams, Laurie. "The Sustaining Power of Imagination: Biography of J.K. Rowling." In *Critical Insights: The Harry Potter Series*, edited by Lana A. Whited and M. Katherine Grimes, 17–23. Ipswitch: Salem Press, 2015.

Anelli, Melissa. *Harry, a History: The True Story of a Boy Wizard, His Fans, and Life Inside the Harry Potter Phenomenon*. New York: Pocket Books, 2008.

Baker, Carissa Ann. "Universal's Wizarding World of Harry Potter: A Primer in Contemporary Media Concepts." In *Harry Potter and Convergence Culture: Essays on Fandom and the Expanding Potterverse*, edited by Amanda Firestone and Leisa A. Clark, 2018.

Balik, Kristen, and Richard Fry. "Millennial Life: How Young Adulthood Today Compares with Prior Generations." Pew Research Center, February 14, 2019. pewresearch.org/social-trends/2019/02/14/millennial-life-how-young-adulthood-today-compares-with-prior-generations.

Barratt, Bethany. *The Politics of Harry Potter.* New York: Palgrave MacMillan, 2012.

Barroso, Amanda, Kim Parker, and Jesse Bennett. "As Millennials Near 40, They're Approaching Family Life Differently than Previous Generations." Pew Research Center, May 27, 2020. https://www.pewresearch.org/social-trends/2020/05/27/as-millennials-near-40-theyre-approaching-family-life-differently-than-previous-generations/.

Barthes, Roland. "The Death of the Author." In *Image - Music - Text*, edited by Stephen Heath. New York: Hill and Wang, 1977.

Baudrillard, Jean. *The Consumer Society: Myths and Structures.* Rev. ed. Thousand Oaks: Sage Publications, 2017.

———. *Simulacra and Simulation*. Translated by Sheila Faria Glaser. Ann Arbor: University of Michigan Press, 1994.

Bausman, Cassandra. "'Elder' and Wiser: The Filmic Harry Potter and the Rejection of Power." In *Transforming Harry: The Adaptation of Harry Potter in the Transmedia Age*, edited by John Alberti and P. Andrew Miller, 38–70. Detroit: Wayne State University Press, 2018.

Beatty, Bronwyn E. "'It's a Natural Part of Us!' The Potter Generation Reflect on Their Ongoing Relationship With a Cultural Phenomenon." In *From Here to*

Hogwarts: Essays on Potter Fandom and Fiction, edited by Christopher E. Bell, 99–122. Jefferson: McFarland & Company, 2016.

Bell, Christopher E. "Heroes and Horcruxes: Dumbledore's Army as Metonym." In *Wizards vs. Muggles: Essays on Identity and the Harry Potter Universe*, edited by Christopher E. Bell, 72–88. Jefferson: McFarland & Company, 2016.

Berner, Amy, and Joyce Millman. "The Case for Snape's Guilt: Is Snape Harry Potter's Foe?" In *The Great Snape Debate*, 1–76. New York: Borders, Inc., 2007.

Berner, Amy, Orson Scott Card, and Joyce Millman. "The Case for Snape's Innocence: Is Snape Harry Potter's Friend?" In *The Great Snape Debate*, 1–109. New York: Borders, Inc., 2007.

Bettleheim, Bruno. *The Uses of Enchantment: The Meaning and Importance of Fairy Tales*. New York: Alfred A. Knopf, 1977.

Borojevic, Jelena. "Quenching the Quill: How Fan Art Builds Meaning, Creates Bonds and Triggers Imagination." In *Wizards vs. Muggles: Essays on Identity and the Harry Potter Universe*, edited by Christopher E. Bell, 133–148. Jefferson: McFarland & Company, 2016.

Butler, Michelle Markey. "*Harry Potter* and the Surprising Venue of Literary Critique." In *Transforming Harry: The Adaptation of Harry Potter in the Transmedia Age*, edited John Alberti and P. Andrew Miller, 129–154. Detroit: Wayne State University Press, 2018.

Bryman, Alan. *The Disneyization of Society.* Los Angeles: Sage Publications, 2004.

Campbell, Joseph. *The Flight of the Wild Gander: Explorations in the Mythological Dimension*. Novato: New World Library/Joseph Campbell Foundation, 2002.

———. *The Hero with a Thousand Faces*. Novato: New World Library/Joseph Campbell Foundation, 2008.

———. *The Masks of God: Creative Mythology*. New York: Penguin Compass, 1968.

———. *The Masks of God: Occidental Mythology*. Novato: New World Library/ Joseph Campbell Foundation, 2021.

———. *Pathways to Bliss: Mythology and Personal Transformation*. Novato: New World Library/Joseph Campbell Foundation, 2004.

———. *The Power of Myth With Bill Moyers*. Edited by Betty Sue Flowers. New York: Anchor, 1991.

———. *Thou Art That: Transforming Religious Metaphor*. Edited by Eugene Kennedy. Novato: New World Library/Joseph Campbell Foundation, 2001.

Chomsky, Noam. "'Containing' the Soviet Union in the Cold War." In *Understanding Power: The Indispensable Chomsky*, 37–41. New York: The New Press, 2002.

Cole, Kristen L. "Transcending Hogwarts: Pedagogical Practices Engendering Discourses of Aggression and Bullying." In *Wizards vs. Muggles: Essays on Identity and the Harry Potter Universe*, edited by Christopher E. Bell, 149–167. Jefferson: McFarland & Company, 2016.

Columbus, Chris, dir. *Harry Potter and the Chamber of Secrets*. 2002; Burbank: Warner Bros., 2003, DVD.

———. *Harry Potter and the Sorcerer's Stone*. 2001; Burbank: Warner Bros., 2002, DVD.

Cuarón, Alfonzo, dir. *Harry Potter and the Prisoner of Azkaban*. 2004; Burbank, Warner Bros., 2004, DVD.

Delgado, Richard, and Jean Stefancic. *Critical Race Theory: The Cutting Edge*. Philadelphia: Temple University Press, 2013.

Dicieanu, Maria. "*Harry Potter*, Henry Jenkins, and the Visionary J.K. Rowling." In *Transforming Harry: The Adaptation of Harry Potter in the Transmedia Age*, edited by John Alberti and P. Andrew Miller, 93–112. Detroit: Wayne State University Press, 2018.

Edinger, Edward F. *Anatomy of the Psyche: Alchemical Symbolism in Psychotherapy*. La Salle: Open Court, 1985.

Eliade, Mircea. *Patterns in Comparative Religion*. New York: NY World Publishing, 1963.

———. *The Sacred & The Profane: The Nature of Religion*. Translated by Willard R. Trask. San Diego: Harcourt Brace & Company, 1959.

Erikson, Erik H. *Childhood and Society.* New York: W. W. Norton & Company, 1950.

Fabricius, Johannes. *Alchemy: The Medieval Alchemists and Their Royal Art*. London: Diamond Books, 1994.

Foucault, Michel. "What Is an Author?" In *The Foucault Reader*, edited by Paul Rabinow, 101–120. New York: Vintage Books, 2010.

Frankel, Valerie, ed. *Fan Phenomena: Harry Potter*. Bristol: Intellect Books, 2019.

Gans, Herbert J. *Popular Culture and High Culture: An Analysis and Evaluation of Taste*. rev. ed. New York: Basic Books, 1999.

Gierzynski, Anthony, and Kathryn Eddy. *Harry Potter and the Millennials: Research Methods and the Politics of the Muggle Generation*. Baltimore: Johns Hopkins University Press, 2013.

Giroux, Henry A., and Grace Pollock. *The Mouse That Roared: Disney and the End of Innocence*. Rev. Ed. Lanham: Rowman & Littlefield, 2010.

Graebner, William. *The Age of Doubt: American Thought and Culture in the 1940s*. Long Grove: Waveland Press, 1991.

Granger, John. *Unlocking Harry Potter: Five Keys for the Serious Reader*. Wayne: Zossima Press, 2007.

Hanstedt, Paul. *Creating Wicked Students: Designing Courses For a Complex World*. Sterling: Stylus, 2018.

Hillman, James. *Alchemical Psychology*. Putnam: Spring Publications, 2014.

———, *Re-Visioning Psychology*. New York: HarperPerennial, 1975.

Howe, Andrew. *"Harry Potter and the Popular Culture of Tomorrow."* In *Transforming Harry: The Adaptation of Harry Potter in the Transmedia Age*, edited by John Alberti and P. Andrew Miller, 19–37. Detroit: Wayne State University Press, 2018.

Hughes, Brendan G.A. "The HIV Metaphor: J.K. Rowling's Werewolf and Its Transformative Potential." In *Wizards vs. Muggles: Essays on Identity and the Harry Potter Universe*, edited by Christopher E. Bell, 49–71. Jefferson: McFarland & Company, 2016.

Huizinga, Johan. *Homo Ludens: A Study of the Play Element of Culture*. Boston: Beacon Press, 1950.

Ide, Todd J. "The Dark Lord and the Prince: Machiaellian Elements in Harry Potter." In *Critical Insights: The Harry Potter Series*, edited by Lana A. Whited and M. Katherine Grimes, 180–207. Ipswich: Salem Press/Grey House Publishing, 2015.

Jarazo-Álvarez, Rubén. "Gender, Sexuality and the War on Terror in Harry Potter and *Fantastic Beasts and Where to Find Them*." In *Cultural Politics in Harry Potter: Life, Death and the Politics of Fear*, edited by Rubén Jarazo-Álvarez and Pilar Alderete-Diez, 178–192. New York: Routledge, 2020.

Jenkins, Henry, ed. "Acafandom and Beyond: Week Two, Part One (Henry Jenkins, Erica Rand, and Karen Hellekson)." Henryjenkins.org, June 20, 2011. h t t p : / / henryjenkins.org/blog/2011/06/acafandom_and_beyond_week_two.html.

———. *Convergence Culture: Where Old and New Media Collide*. New York: New York University Press, 2006.

———. "'Cultural Acupuncture': Fan Activism and the Harry Potter Alliance." *Transformative Works and Cultures* 10 (2012). https://doi.org/10.3983/twc.2012.0305.

———. "Unspreadable Media (Part Five): Back and Forth." Confessions of an Aca-Fan, June 21, 2017. henryjenkins.org/blog/2017/6/15/unspreadable-media-part-five-back-and-forth.

———. "Youth Voice, Media, and Political Engagement: Introducing the Core Concepts." In *By Any Media Necessary: The New Youth Activism*, edited by Henry Jenkins, et al., 1–60. New York: New York University Press, 2016.

Jowett, Garth S., and Victoria O'Donnell. *Propaganda and Persuasion*. 3rd ed. Thousand Oaks: Sage Publications, 1999.

Jung, C.G. *Aion: Researches into the Phenomenology of the Self*. Vol. 9, part 2. Translated by R.F.C. Hull. 2nd ed. New York: Bollingen Foundation, 1959.

———. *The Archetypes and the Collective Unconscious*. Vol. 9, part 1 of *The Collected Works of C.G. Jung*. Translated by R.F.C. Hull. 2nd ed. New York: Bollingen Foundation, 1969.

———. *Memories, Dreams, Reflections*. Edited by Aniela Jaffé. Translated by Richard Winston and Clara Winston. rev. ed. New York: Vintage Books, 1989.

———. *Mysterium Coniunctionis: An Inquiry into the Separation and Synthesis of Psychic Opposites in Alchemy*. Vol. 14 of *The Collected Works of C.G. Jung*. Translated by R.F.C. Hull. 2nd ed. New York: Bollingen Foundation, 1970.

———. *The Practice of Psychotherapy: Essays on the Psychology of the Transference and Other Subjects*. Vol. 16 of *The Collected Works of C.G. Jung*. Translated by R.F.C. Hull. 2nd ed. New York: Bollingen Foundation, 1966.

———. *Psychology and Alchemy*. Vol. 12 of *The Collected Works of C.G. Jung*. Translated by R.F.C. Hull. 2nd ed. New York: Bollingen, 1968.

Kligler-Vilenchik, Neta. "'Decreasing World Suck': Harnessing Popular Culture for Fan Activism." In *By Any Media Necessary: The New Youth Activism*, edited by Henry Jenkins and et al. New York: New York University Press, 2016.

Lauer, Emily. "Harry Potter and the Book Burners' Mistake: Suppression and Its Unintended Consequences." In *The Harry Potter Generation: Essays on Growing Up with the Series*, edited by Emily Lauer and Balaka Basu, 53–68. Jefferson: McFarland & Company, 2019.

Lee, Chin-Ting. "Keeping the Magic Alive: The Fandom and 'Harry Potter Experience' After the Franchise." In *From Here to Hogwarts: Essays on Potter Fandom and Fiction*, edited by Christopher E. Bell, 54–77. Jefferson: McFarland & Company, 2016.

McCain, Katharine. "*Epoximise!* The Renegotiation of Film and Literature through *Harry Potter* GIF Sets." In *Transforming Harry: The Adaptation of Harry Potter in the Transmedia Age*, edited by John Alberti and P. Andrew Miller, 113–130. Detroit: Wayne State University Press, 2018.

McLuhan, Marshall. "The Gutenberg Galaxy." In *Essential McLuhan*, edited by Eric McLuhan and Frank Zingrone, 97–148. New York: BasicBooks, 1995.

McLuhan, Marshall and Quentin Fiore *The Medium is the Massage: An Inventory of Effects*. Berkeley, Gingko Press, 1967.

Newell, Mike, dir. *Harry Potter and the Goblet of Fire*. 2005; Burbank: Warner Bros., 2006. DVD.

Nelson, John S. *Defenses Against the Dark Arts: The Political Education of Harry Potter and His Friends*. Lanham: Lexington Books, 2021.

Noxon, Christopher. *Rejuvenile: Kickball, Cartoons, Cupcakes, and the Reinvention of the American Grown-Up*. New York: Three Rivers Press, 2006.

Plato. *Symposium*. Translated by Alexander Nehamas and Paul Woodruff. Indianapolis: Hackett Publishing Company, 1989.

Postman, Neil. *Amusing Ourselves to Death: Public Discourse in the Age of Show Business*. New York: Penguin Books, 1985.

———. *The Disappearance of Childhood*. New York: Vintage Books, 1994.

Ritzer, George. *Enchanting a Disenchanted World*: *Revolutionizing the Means of Consumption*. 2nd ed. Thousand Oaks: Pine Forge Press, 2005.

———. *The McDonaldization of Society: Into the Digital Age*. 9th ed. Los Angeles: Sage Publications, 2019.

Robertson, James Oliver. *American Myth, American Reality*. New York: Hill & Wang, 1980.

Rowling, J.K. *Fantastic Beasts: The Crimes of Grindelwald, The Original Screenplay*. New York: Arthur A. Levine Books, 2018.

———. *Fantastic Beasts and Where to Find Them, The Original Screenplay*. New York: Arthur A. Levine Books, 2016.

———. *Harry Potter and the Chamber of Secrets*. New York: Scholastic, 1999.

———. *Harry Potter and the Deathly Hallows*. New York: Scholastic, 2007.

———. *Harry Potter and the Goblet of Fire*. New York: Scholastic, 2000.

———. *Harry Potter and the Half-Blood Prince*. New York: Scholastic, 2005.

———. *Harry Potter and the Order of the Phoenix*. New York: Scholastic, 2003.

———. *Harry Potter and the Prisoner of Azkaban*. New York: Scholastic, 1999.

———. *Harry Potter and the Sorcerer's Stone*. New York: Scholastic, 1997.

———. *The Tales of Beedle the Bard*. London: Children's High Level Group, 2008.

Rowling, J.K., John Tiffany, and Jack Thorne. *Harry Potter and the Cursed Child*. London: Scholastic/Arthur A. Levine Books, 2016.

Sammond, Nicholas. *Babes in Tomorrowland: Walt Disney and the Making of the American Child, 1930–1960*. Durham: Duke University Press, 2005.

Samuel, Lawrence R. *The American Dream: A Cultural History.* Syracuse: Syracuse University Press, 201.

Saraco, Maureen. "Squibsm Disability and Having a Place at Hogwarts School of Witchcraft and Wizardry." In *Cultural Politics in Harry Potter: Life, Death and the Politics of Fear*, edited by Rubén Jarazo-Álvarez and Pilar Alderete-Diez. New York: Routledge, 2020.

Saxena, Vandana. *The Subversive Harry Potter: Adolescent Rebellion and Containment in the J.K. Rowling Novels.* Jefferson: McFarland & Company, 2012.

Scamander, Newt. *Fantastic Beasts and Where to Find Them.* London: Arthur A. Levine Books/Obscurus Books, 2001.

Schlosser, Eric. *Fast Food Nation: The Dark Side of the All-American Meal.* New York: Perennial, 2002.

Schuck, Raymond I. "'The Anti-Racist-White-Hero-Premise': Whiteness and the *Harry Potter* Series." In *Wizards vs. Muggles: Essays on Identity and the Harry Potter Universe*, edited by Christopher E. Bell, 9–26. Jefferson: McFarland & Company, 2016.

Tatar, Maria. *The Heroine with 1,001 Faces.* New York: Liveright Publishing Corporation, 2021.

Tolkien, J.R.R. "On Fairy-Stores." In *The Tolkien Reader*, 3–84. New York: Ballantine, 1986.

Turner, Victor. *The Ritual Process: Structure and Anti-Structure.* New York: Aldine de Gruyter, 1969.

Van Gannep, Arnold. *The Rites of Passage,* Translated by Monika B. Vizedom and Gabrielle L. Caffee. Chicago: University of Chicago Press, 1960.

Von Franz, Marie-Louise. *Alchemy: An Introduction to the Symbolism and the Psychology.* Toronto: Inner City Books, 1980.

———. *Interpretation of Fairy Tales.* rev. ed. Boston: Shambhala, 1996.

Whited, Lana A. "A Survey of the Critical Reception of the Harry Potter Series." In *Critical Insights: The Harry Potter Series*, edited by Lana A. Whited and M. Katherine Grimes, 49–81. Ipswich: Salem Press, 2015.

Yates, David, dir. *Fantastic Beasts and Where to Find Them.* 2016; Burbank: Warner Bros., 2017, Blu-ray.

———. *Fantastic Beasts: The Crimes of Grindelwald.* 2018; Burbank: Warner Bros., 2019, Blu-ray.

———. *Harry Potter and the Deathly Hallows, Part 1.* 2010; Burbank: Warner Bros., 2011, Blu-ray.

———. *Harry Potter and the Deathly Hallows, Part 2.* 2011; Burbank: Warner Bros., 2011, Blu-ray.

———. *Harry Potter and the Half-Blood Prince.* 2009; Burbank: Warner Bros., 2009, Blu-ray.

———. *Harry Potter and the Order of the Phoenix.* 2007; Burbank: Warner Bros., 2007, DVD.

Zinn, Howard. *A People's History of the United States.* New York: HarperCollins Publishers, 1980.

Index

About the Author

Priscilla Hobbs, PhD, is senior associate dean at Southern New Hampshire University. She earned her doctorate in mythological studies from Pacifica Graduate Institute. Her research focus emerged in response to reading *Harry Potter* and wanting a new language to understand a post-9/11 America. Her key subject areas are American popular culture, consumerism, and utopianism. She is the author of the book *Walt's Utopia: Disneyland and American Mythmaking* (2015) about Disneyland and the Cold War, and editor of *Interpreting and Experiencing Disney: Mediating the Mouse* (2022) about the impact and significance of Disney culture. Additionally, Dr. Hobbs is series editor for Lexington Books' Studies in Disney and Culture series.